.

"...Nicholas has really captured not only the importance of knowing who we really are and facing up to that, but how... to be aware of our weaknesses and how to use these to our advantage... Read this book and be enlightened!

- Lesley Everett - International Speaker and Best Selling Author of Drop Dead Brilliant

"M.H. has given people at all levels the final exam answer key for the school of hard-knocks."

– Roxanne Emmerich, Wall Street Journal Best Selling Author of Thank God It's Monday

"This is a book that makes you look at yourself, your colleagues, and the world of work with fresh eyes. It'll make you laugh out loud while you shake your head--but mostly it'll make you think."

- Alan M. Webber, Founder of Fast Company Magazine and Best Selling Author of Rules of Thumb: 52 Truths For Winning at Business Without Losing Your Self

"Even in a world of rapid change, some things are unchanging. Read this book and let Nicholas show you those unchanging realities in the business world. It will take a decade off your learning curve."

–Matthew Kelly, New York Times Best Selling Author of The Dream Manager...

"M.H.'s It's (Not) Just Business is a colorful look at the business of business. A light book about a serious matter, it's a highly entertaining read!"

– Marshall Goldsmith - Million Selling Author of What Got You Here...

"This should be required reading for all business majors and anyone else who has not yet figured out corporate navigation."

– John Simmers, CEO

"This is a VERY powerful book. It should be required reading for anyone in the workplace. I've been with Fortune 500s and startups dealing at all ends with the points in this book. *It's (Not) Just Business* nailed it! My 18 year old son gets it next!"

– Jeff Evans, Entrepreneur

IT'S (NOT) JUST BUSINESS

Your Guide to Politics, Ego and Negotiating in the Workplace

An In-The-Trenches Business Survival Guide

By

M.H. NICHOLAS

Barely Lit Spaces Publications

Cover design by Eat.Sleep.Work., Inc. (www.eatsleepwork.com)
Cover vector art © iStockPhoto / Contributor Michael Monu (Mikey_Man) [edited]
Editing by Alan Perlman (www.alanperlman.com)
Indexing by Jeff Evans / Updating by Thu-Thuy Tran (artoftttran@gmail.com)
"Ego" definition by Merriam-Webster

Printed in the UNITED STATES OF AMERICA

Hard Cover: ISBN: 978-0-9826888-3-0 / 0-9826888-3-0
Soft Cover: ISBN: 978-0-9826888-6-1 / 0982688865
Electronic Book ISBN: 978-0-9826888-5-4 / 0-9826888-5-7
Published by: Barely Lit Spaces Publications
For contact information, visit: www.thebusinesspersona.com

THANK YOU

To my father, Dr. Marvin Nicholas

This book is dedicated to my father, who passed away during the completion of the final draft of this book. My father was an amazing businessman and enthusiastically embraced the subject matter of this book. He identified many of the quotes you see scattered throughout the text. I miss him dearly and think of him daily.

To my wife, Kahla

...who so patiently tolerates her sleepless and opinionated husband. It is a better book because of her and is dedicated to her with my gratitude and love.

And to my daughter, Gabrielle

...who sleeps next to me as I craft her dedication. "They" say that authors offer their advice with themselves in mind. So may this book continue to give me the perspective and balance to dedicate my life to those things that are the most important. Sleep well my angel.

E-GO

—NOUN, PLURAL E-GOS.

1. THE "I" OR SELF OF ANY PERSON; A PERSON AS
   THINKING, FEELING, AND WILLING, AND DISTIN-
   GUISHING ITSELF FROM THE SELVES OF OTHERS AND
   FROM OBJECTS OF ITS THOUGHT.

2. PSYCHOANALYSIS. THE PART OF THE PSYCHIC
   APPARATUS THAT EXPERIENCES AND REACTS TO THE
   OUTSIDE WORLD AND THUS MEDIATES BETWEEN THE
   PRIMITIVE DRIVES OF THE ID AND THE DEMANDS OF
   THE SOCIAL AND PHYSICAL ENVIRONMENT.

3. EGOTISM; CONCEIT; SELF-IMPORTANCE: HER
   EGO BECOMES MORE UNBEARABLE EACH DAY.

4. SELF-ESTEEM OR SELF-IMAGE; FEELINGS: *YOUR*
   CRITICISM WOUNDED HIS EGO.

TABLE OF CONTENTS

FOREWORD

by Roxanne Emmerich

EVERYBODY REMEMBERS THE first day of your first real job. Your shoes were shined, your teeth were flossed, and the crease in your slacks could have diced celery. You were aiming high and had every intention of getting there.

We entered that world with the solemn hope that we were good enough to be a part of it—and some serious doubts about that. We knew our own faults all too well, and all these other people seemed so... perfect.

They weren't, of course. Within a few weeks, it became all too clear that we were surrounded by seriously imperfect people—complainers, liars, gossips, getters-by, people shooting wildly for mediocrity. We had brought our better selves to the workplace, only to discover that everyone else was a lot more like—well, our real selves. Within weeks, we were demoralized enough to begin shooting for mediocrity as well. Each passing year seems to confirm your assessment, and you reach the end of each week saying, "Thank God it's Friday."

It's (Not) Just Business provides the antidote for this vicious cycle, but not in the usual Stuart Smalley, ego-stroking way, promising that you are "good enough and smart enough" to join those around you on Olympus. Instead, M.H. Nicholas confirms your suspicions that you ARE a bit of a mess. But, he continues, so is everyone around you. And the journey to real success begins by forgiving ourselves and each other for what we are—human.

All of us, much of the time, are selfish, and afraid, lazy and uncertain. You aren't far below or far above the rest. Everyone from the custodian to the CEO has experienced the same failings and is filled with the same self-doubt.

M.H. Nicholas starts with this bracingly honest opinion, but he doesn't end there. Written in a style that is accessible and funny, *"It's (Not) Just Business"* is a book about how you can survive and thrive in the mess of human nature and conflicting interests that is the business world by seeing that world for what it is and managing the perceptions of those around you.

The book is filled with advice and observations that are somehow both common sense and not in the least common. You will learn what skills really matter in business, including showing up, listening, silence, patience, balance, and concision. You'll see why every job is a sales job, that you are the only one who can be counted on to care what you want, that we are all expendable, that most people who say they are busy are lying, that most leaders are faking confidence most of the time, and that a good handshake and office plants (that's right, office plants) can make all the difference.

By offering these powerful, unexpected, and simple ideas, M.H. Nicholas has given people at all levels the final exam answer key for the school of hard knocks. Those of us who spent years in that school can only envy readers who get that all-important answer key right up front. Not only will these ideas allow you to advance your career, but they'll also allow you to feel genuine fulfillment at work.

When I wrote *Thank God It's Monday*, my hope was to encourage a conversation of great ideas designed to revolutionize modern workplace culture. Now, with the publication of *It's (Not) Just Business*, it's wonderful to hear another voice adding a unique and invaluable contribution to that important conversation.

Roxanne Emmerich
CEO, The Emmerich Group, Inc.
Author, *Thank God It's Monday:
How to Create a Workplace You and Your Customers Love*

INTRODUCTION

IN BUSINESS WE ENCOUNTER AN ENVIRONMENT very much out of our control. We find managers and colleagues of all types, each with individual aspirations, issues and priorities. Some are very smart and competent; others, difficult, bossy and incompetent. We find geniuses, wise leaders and fools; we find people who are savvier than we are and others who are less savvy.

We might even find ourselves surrounded by inefficiency and indecision. As a matter of fact, we probably will.

No matter how hard we work, or how powerful we become, the business world is as it always has been: a bit unpredictable, subject to strong personalities and aspiring politicians, and in that sense is more than a little personal. It is, after all, a world filled with real people and all the humanity and personal baggage that follows dutifully along.

BUSINESS = ADULT PLAYGROUND

Business is the adult version of the neighborhood playground. And this book is, at its core, a discussion about how we interact in the business sandbox with all of these colorful characters (you and I, by the way, are equally colorful). I ask you to take the business world as it is, perhaps a bit less seriously, with all of its differences, neuroses, quirks, faults and foibles.

That's because the playground is undeniably and overwhelmingly human— and none of us can change the underlying nature of human beings. The playground is filled with its share of bullies and bullied. There are those who are popular and those who aren't. There are people of every possible kind.

My overarching goal is to remind you of the nature of your surroundings and to offer a discussion of the rules of the game. I couldn't tell you how to change the playground or the underlying nature of others; we have more than our share of work just taking care of ourselves.

Not cynical - but honest

Although a bit irreverent at times, *It's (Not) Just Business* aspires not to cynicism but acceptance. I hope to offer a broad discussion of business and workplace concepts and ideas, and I hope to push a few of your buttons and get you thinking. Disagree if you like, but engage. It's the same in business itself: In business, you may participate willingly or grudgingly. Willingly is more fun.

The book seeks to achieve the following goals:

First, it will help you to play in the sandbox. It will not offer you a *formula* for success. There isn't one. Not everyone is *suited* for senior management positions or has the personality, charisma or intellect to lead others. And furthermore, since everyone has his own idea of success, I ask you to define your own values and aspirations and to recognize the tools that are available to you. With these tools in your arsenal, along with careful consideration and contemplation, you can rest assured that you'll find yourself better equipped to play.

Second, while the discussion of many of these issues is by its design a bit abbreviated at times (many simple sections are entire fields of science on their own), I hope at least to *expose you to subjects you've often never considered (or considered too late).* For instance, *It's (Not) Just*

Business discusses scientific concepts regarding the way people in the workplace make decisions, offers a short course in negotiating, and explains perception issues and political tactics used every day and in practically every workplace interaction. If you read only one book, I hope that this one will give you the broadest education on a wide variety of essential, rarely taught subjects.

Third, It's (Not) Just Business is not psychological or therapeutic; *it is personal.* It takes the point of view of people who live in the trenches: aspiring, hiring, firing, scrapping, fighting, negotiating and maneuvering every day in some very complex environments.

Fourth, unlike books that direct their attention to people aspiring to the highest levels of the business world, *this one is designed for the daily struggle to get along, get by, and perchance, get ahead.* Whether you're at the beginning of your career— or anywhere in the ascent of the career ladder, I hope that you find this book an effective tool, particularly as your perspective and position change over time.

Fifth, you will not be asked to change the nearly unchangeable fabric that defines who you are, but hopefully you will get better at seeing your world more objectively and understanding the various tools available to you (and recognizing the ones that may be used against you). Specifically, I want to help you recognize the essential humanity of business and the people in it and to accept the haphazardness of people's emotions and personalities, aspirations, hopes, ambitions, attitudes, problems, and good days and bad. In doing so you will be more able to control your own presentation and to protect yourself in business and the world in general, and you will be prepared, if you so choose, to take better advantage of the countless opportunities that surround you.

It's essential to cultivate this external point of view. *Each person sees the world from his or her own vantage point. As you'll see, people perceive success and failure, rewards, and even simple fairness from the seat in which they sit.* More than anything else there is one point which I hope to drive home; *it's not about you. It's about them.* Even if whatever it is appears directed toward you, try to remember this one basic principle: Although the business world is highly personal, try not to take it personally—because it isn't.

HUMILITY AND FAILURE -- BRING IT ON!

No one is perfect. Certainly not me. This book is written from a place of tremendous humility. We are each striving for more victories, all while keeping our losses to a minimum—and in perspective. Failing and frustration are unavoidable in business and life in general. No set of skills, no matter how perfect, will change that.

But by the end of this book I want you to stand up and tell the world to bring it on. I want to convince you that even though you will win some battles and lose others you must cling to your values with all of your might—and still be willing to play in that sandbox. I hope you acquire the pragmatism that comes with understanding how people really are—and not be offended but prepared. It really is okay to play the game.

Business is really very simple.

Yet while this is all very serious stuff, I am not a very serious person. My tone walks a bit of this serious/comedic tightrope. While there is a bit of a tongue-in-cheek, lighthearted style to several of these sections, I do not mean to offend—but rather hope for an educated discourse. Business is very simple; it is, viewed objectively, a bunch of people, each trying to accomplish personal goals and maybe even get something collective and meaningful done along the way. If you can't accept this truth, then the business world may choose not to accept you.

ORGANIZATIONS, PRONOUNS AND QUOTES

One of the most challenging questions was how to organize the book. We (my focus groups, editors, advisors and I) all struggled with the best way to dish this stuff out. You'll notice that the 'chapters' are short and direct, oftentimes grouped with similar subjects—but sometimes not.

While the major topic categories and structure were carefully chosen, the underlying order resembles the reality of business: nothing comes in a perfectly logical order. So I decided to offer ideas and advice that at first might seem random but when viewed as a whole would make every reader better at something—and ultimately better at everything.

I struggled with gender pronouns (such as "he" and "she") quite a bit. Everything I tried in an attempt to offer a gender-neutral book looked obvious and contrived. The word "he," where used, is intended to be gender neutral. I mean no offense in this regard.

Lastly, I've included quotes throughout this material. These are intended to be humorous or entertaining sound bites. Some may not be perfectly consistent with the point I'm making, and the people I'm quoting have not endorsed the material. I tried on many occasions to use quotes from the past, if for no other reason than to show that business is today as it always has been.

We (my wife, my father, and I) looked at thousands of quotes, and we picked the ones we felt were the most appropriate for the context. Every quote was identified in multiple sources, and we did everything we could to try to ensure each is as accurate as possible. But if you discover an error, please let us know. We sincerely hope that you find the quotes as interesting and entertaining as we have.

And now, without further delay...

Let's be honest. There's not a business anywhere that is without problems. Business is complicated and imperfect. Every business everywhere is staffed with imperfect human beings and exists by providing a product or service to other imperfect human beings.

—Bob Parsons, Founder/Executive Chairman/Founder, GoDaddy

LET'S GET STARTED...

IF I HAD MY WAY, I'd make this a better world, one with less lying, manipulation, and self-serving behavior, and one with more sharing, compassion, respect, and decency. Unfortunately, ambition, aggression, jealousy, selfishness, and materialism are basic human traits—and it is unrealistic to think that in the workplace they can somehow be separated from the humans displaying them.

When it comes to changing the world, in particular the business world, it is clear that I will not have my way.

Understanding, Surviving -- and Succeeding

The solution to surviving and succeeding within business lies in knowing how to see, understand, and take advantage of (not fix) the behavior that surrounds you, all the while knowing how to utilize the best and most effective characteristics of your own humanity, along with your talents, skills, and resources, in a manner that allows you to get where you want to go.

It can be exceedingly complicated to draw fine lines to establish moral, ethical or decency guidelines for behavior within the business world. We are not talking about the obvious stuff, but rather the day-to-day manner in which a business is run and the people in that business act. It seems that a natural default position for many of our colleagues is to be constantly offended. Instead, our ongoing challenge is the acceptance of many of the realities of business.

In fact, **the negative qualities of business exist because business is run by people**, the same people who have problems with friends and lovers, who have affairs, who experience depression and temper tantrums, who lose control of their emotions, who take advantage of situations, who bully or who are bullied, who get tired, sick, disillusioned and bored, and who don't know how to deal with their own parents or children.

Business is just one more place where humans coexist. It is only in light of this fact that we can understand how to survive business and even life in general. It's all people, and similarly, *It's (Not) Just Business* is about… people.

It's (Not) Just Business is a collection of rules and ideas, maxims and mantras, offered for your consumption and consideration. The ideas come not only from my own experience in the business world (including the multitude of mistakes that I myself have made), but also from the experience (and mistakes) of my colleagues, mentors, and executives at all levels of the corporate ladder.

In the end, this book is not about changing the world. It's about helping you to recognize and use the available tools to influence the circumstances that surround you.

Business doesn't want to be changed

In my own way, I've tried and failed to change the world, although I have learned to maneuver very effectively within it. As a CEO of a company designed to provide important family protections at an affordable price, I continue to struggle to make a difference. In past years I have climbed the corporate ladder, started a very successful business, and managed countless employees and projects.

All along the way, I've seen again and again that *the business world, like the world entire, simply doesn't want to be changed.* There are countless examples of human beings trying (and failing) to change. Call it inertia or stubbornness or any other word you prefer to rationalize this core attribute of human nature. What motivates us is often beyond us. Conscious change is typically overcome by unconscious reversion. True change is localized and generally unreliable. This book is about participating in the business world, a world of extremes, where a lot of very good and very bad behaviors co-exist. Like everything else in this world, either you will conquer what surrounds you *as it is* or it will conquer you.

INHERENT CONFLICTS OF INTEREST

The public be damned! I'm working for my stockholders.
—*William Henry Vanderbilt*

Business exists for only one reason: *to make money.*

This is not a cynical but a rather realistic doctrine—that a business' first duty is to stay in business. While that generally requires a fine product and satisfied customers, no one can benefit from a business that cannot stay in business. And no goal of any business, no matter how virtuous, can be achieved by a business that lacks the money or resources to accomplish its purpose.

Most businesses fail or go out of business within their first four years, and there is no sympathy for the failed.* Society accepts the fact that any business that cannot sustain itself doesn't deserve to be in business. We all drive past failing businesses and going-out-of-business signs every day without any inclination to offer a helping hand. In the rare event someone does offer some financial assistance, it invariably comes in return for a piece

---

* According to Census Bureau data, one half of the businesses employing other people and a larger percentage of non-employing firms are no longer in business within four years of commencing operations. Note, however, that being out of business does not necessarily mean that the business has failed financially.

of the ownership of the business or an interest-bearing loan in exchange for the *generosity*.

People generally work for one reason: *to make a living*.

That's not to say that people don't seek great fulfillment in things other than money, but in the end we all need to eat and afford shelter. From the entry-level person to the high-ranking officer, employees want paychecks, advancement, stability, prestige, and benefits. Most people want to help their company succeed—but if the business decides not to pay you, regardless of its virtues, you will at some point (most often immediately) choose to work someplace else. In a sense we are all mercenaries, subject not to one master but two, serving the best interests of the business as well as the best interests of ourselves, though usually not in that order.

Individual perspective is the fundamental conflict

This is where we find the root of the conflict of interest that is so much a part of the fabric of corporate life; it is summarized by the simple phrase: "I come first." Despite the frequently articulated, collective goals of the company or the business unit, despite all the effort invested in strategy-setting and mission statements, *it is the fact that each person sees the world from his or her own perspective, applying the circumstances of that perception to evaluate what is perceived as fair, kind, decent, mean-spirited, and so forth.* This means that conscious or otherwise, most people in the workplace assume the role of defending their own positions, departments, projects, employees, goals, needs and best interests. Individuals seek to make more money not for the benefit of the business but for the opposite reason—for the benefit of him/herself and his/her family and lifestyle. While many of these factors can result in parody and workplace balance, the core behavior will often appear selfish and offensive. *Ultimately it is this collection of unique vantage points, not outright selfishness or a desire to unfairly benefit, that drives the apparent self-interest (including self-preservation and self-promotion) that can be the driver of most of the behaviors in the workplace.*

Ignore this principle at your peril. Accept it, and you will understand the game and play it better. Even if you are one of those rare people who do not think they come first, most other people around you will not share your generosity of spirit.

Here are some ways in which the principle is manifest every day:

- Managers want to be promoted, take vacations, and find personal enhancement just like you and practically every other person in the business environment.

- Executives and managers want to work on the things that help them succeed at their own jobs, not on the things that don't. Thus, your manager prefers anything that makes managing you and other people easier. If you do not help your manager succeed at his or her job, or if you place your manager at risk, then your manager will attempt to distance him/herself from you.

- Businesses leverage the "I come first" principle by establishing monetary goals with limited bonus pools, and personal goals are judged subjectively. Supervisors, bosses, and executives might intentionally pit team against team and employee against employee to enhance individual and team productivity. They want their people to compete among themselves to determine who will earn the biggest bonuses and who will rise and fall within the corporate ranks.

- The "I come first" principle is at work when people naturally, whether consciously or subconsciously, treat those they personally like better than others they don't like, regardless of the other person's skills or value. Subordinates and peers who are otherwise equal are not treated equally. It does happen that some people are treated favorably as a result of competence, but being liked will offer tremendous advantages, particularly over those who aren't.

- Because the power of vantage point and perception is such a powerful driver of behavior, many corporate managers and executives, even at the highest levels, feel free to indulge in verbal abuse—yelling at and humiliating employees—and even libel, slander, and defamation, treating these as accepted parts of the corporate process, with no concern for the feelings of the person on the receiving end of the abuse.

- Theft is legitimized, often as a replacement for an unrewarded perk (or a suitable punishment for unfair treatment). It ranges from pocketing supplies such as pens and paper, to overstated and/or fraudulent expense reports, to the large-scale, obscenely self-indulgent and self-serving behaviors of so many notable and newsworthy executives.

- Objective truth is another casualty of "I come first." It is not that intentional lying is rampant as much as it is that facts evolve based on the perspectives of the person reporting those facts. Nevertheless, misinformation and outright lying are expected and even integral at times (e.g., keeping trade secrets, managing teams of employees, and negotiating prices).

- Bad employees, for a wide variety of reasons related to "I come first" (maybe they're better liked; or they are a litigation threat to the business; or they condone an exceedingly aggressive take-no-prisoners business strategy), rarely get fired. Despite their incompetence, they often remain employed occasionally placed into a position of greater protection, further corrupting others as well as the workplace.

- Finally, it's "I come first" for people who find themselves out of their league but still fight tooth and nail to keep their positions instead of stepping down. It's up or out, rarely down.

It's not just business.

Self-interest rules the day, every day. We are each wired to see the world from our own perspective. We judge everything—our importance and responsibilities, the value and competence of others, and our sense of fairness and entitlement—from that isolated vantage point.

We may think we have empathy and that we can understand the plight of everyone around us. Yet we are limited to our own narrow perspective. What we are observing can be deeply colored by our personal interests, responsibilities, loyalties and experiences.

I don't mean to rationalize self-serving or substandard behavior, nor do I mean to suggest that the corporate world consists only of bad deeds and backs stabbed. There is enthusiasm, stability, excitement, money, creativity, and even love in the corporate world. But if you really see the "bad" stuff for what it is—integral, even natural—you'll see it's not dramatically terrible. It's just... there.

So we deal with it.

ACCEPTING OUR HUMANITY

We are mostly selfish.

Studies have shown that people will take longer to pull out of a parking space if someone else is waiting to pull in. Holding onto a parking space for those extra few seconds is selfish and territorial for its own sake, an often subconscious behavior, without logic, existing for no apparent reason other than to deprive another person of something that is about to be voluntarily surrendered anyway. It is evidence of our natural predisposition to protect our territory, in the end inflicting on someone else a loss of time, as a punishment for our unnecessary actions.

This is obvious as well on any roadway when one person refuses to let another person pull ahead, oftentimes opting to play a dangerous game of chicken when a bit of generosity would offer safety and cost nothing.

Selfishness and martyrdom

Even in cases of otherwise pure generosity, many people expect something of equal value in return. For instance, instead of just asking us to write a check to a worthy cause, charities organize lavish fund-raisers. Donations give us tax deductions, personal satisfaction and sometimes big parties, political advantage and business opportunities.

Even martyrdom brings with it pride and principle. Religious fanatics who blow themselves up expect that they will automatically go to heaven (and their enemies to hell). As far as reasons go, a person may do practically anything if he or she believes it will be of some corresponding personal benefit. Unfortunately in this world, depriving others of something seems to constitute a personal benefit.

Fear and other motivators; the great equalizer

Also, we are mostly *afraid*.

Perhaps we fear the loss of our jobs, but we also fear not making progress, being embarrassed, getting punished, being saddled with too much work, having too little work (thus being perceived as dispensable), missing out on something, losing the people and things that we love, coming up short, and (admittedly less likely) watching the world end.

We are driven by emotions, intellect/logic, risk tolerance, animalistic urges, sex, desires to be wanted and loved, attempts to hide our own deficiencies, and by our complex subconscious pushing and pulling us where it will.

I'll leave the psychology to the psychologists. For the purposes of this book, there are two kinds of emotions: those that help us (and should therefore be nurtured) and those that hinder us (but should be de-mystified, recognized, acknowledged, and quietly left at home, not bottled up, ignored, or "fixed").

While businesspeople can embrace limited amounts of compassion, emotion, and sensitivity, *business' primary nature is driven by healthy amounts of self-interest, jealousy, aggression, territorialism, controlled vindictiveness, and the drive for power and prestige.*

But take heart: These traits, among others, have the power to help us; recognizing them in others also helps us. Conversely, traits like neediness or being overly emotional or sensitive, although natural, can be crippling in the business world.

In the end, our humanity is the great equalizer. The executive with the fancy title and the houses and cars is every bit as human, and just as fallible, as the entry-level employee. In that way, we are all peers.

THE FOUNDATION OF POLITICS: THE PRISONER'S DILEMMA

Much of our humanity, as well as the root of the corporate dynamic, is laid out in the classic negotiating exercise called "The Prisoner's Dilemma."*

The exercise tells us, over and over, that even among groups of good friends people generally have a very hard time trusting each other when their own personal welfare is at risk. When one person distrusts others, that person is much more likely to look out for his or her own interests and is more willing to sacrifice others'.

---

* Originally created by Merrill Flood and Melvin Dresher at RAND in 1950. Formally named by mathematician Albert W. Tucker.

The dilemma is this: Two people are detained for a major crime and interviewed separately by detectives. The detectives do not have enough evidence to convict the two men of the crime, but do have enough to charge each of them on a minor offense. The detectives offer each suspect the same deal:

1. if one person testifies against the other, and the other remains silent, the betrayer goes free, and the silent suspect goes to prison for ten years;

2. if both suspects stay silent, they both go to prison for six months on the minor charge; or

3. if each suspect betrays the other, they each end up with a five-year sentence.

Each prisoner must make the choice to either betray or remain silent. Of course, neither prisoner knows for sure what the other is going to do.

So imagine that you and a close friend or co-worker find yourselves in the dilemma.

The two of you benefit most if no one talks. This requires total trust and a personal sacrifice, since you are agreeing to spend six months each in jail. Your dilemma is that if your friend decides to talk and you don't, he'll go free and you'll find yourself in jail for ten years. So as you begin to get nervous, you consider talking, then persuading and even lying to your friend to convince him not to speak. You consider talking because you don't want to go to jail. But even if your friend speaks, five years in the clink is better than ten. By the end of the exercise, you learn that *looking out for the group is very difficult to do when you aren't sure if the entire group is looking out for you.*

The Prisoner's Dilemma and corporate life

Corporate existence is very much the same. If we all do our part, work hard, and achieve our goals, we all benefit. As we do, the business earns the greatest amount of money, and more money, in total, is paid to the employees in salaries and bonuses. Society as a whole benefits.

However, if too many people do well, the best performers might end up with less, as more people share in the profits than if more people did poorly. Too many good performers make it harder to stand out and get the highest rating. Even a few top performers make it harder to be promoted.

On the other hand, if one or more others do not do their jobs, we don't want them to bring us down, and we are therefore more likely to sell that person out to protect ourselves rather than risk having that person take some of our money or make us look bad.

Just as the prisoner likes his freedom, the typical person likes money and stability and aspires to promotion. Some strive for power and responsibility, although many strive to avoid responsibility. The dynamics of the Dilemma explain why it is easy for us to want to look out for ourselves right now rather than for the whole group later. There are fewer things left to chance.

The "Manager's Dilemma"

Managers are required to act as the prison warden in the Dilemma every day—even while participating in their own Dilemma. They have employees who exist not to be productive but to cover their butts, as well as those who pretend to be very busy in order to avoid additional work, and those who cause others to look bad so that they can look good.

The Dilemma finds its way into the company's relationship with us as well.

We want to believe that in return for our caring about the business, the business will look out for us. But time and time again, we are shown that the common corporation (and its executives) will look out for itself (*e.g.*, golden parachutes and executive salaries while a business loses revenues and lays people off), so the employees feel further justified in making personal long distance calls, surfing the Internet, wasting corporate time, taking company supplies home, and so on. The formerly loyal employees decide that minimizing corporate expenses at their own risk and inconvenience is no longer worth the effort.

Everyone's dilemma

The Prisoner's Dilemma is replayed constantly, in every situation in which employees interact with one another; the more that is at stake, the more likely one employee or team may end up acting in their own interests, at the expense of (or even sabotaging) the others. This trade-off exists prominently in every situation of blame, every "cover-your-ass" memo, and every case in which one person speaks negatively of another.

In fact, it is the basis for practically everything that follows.

PERCEPTION ISSUES

The personal success story in business is actually made up of three parts: getting hired, ensuring that you are perceived as a superior performer, and engaging in whatever process is necessary to continue to be valued, retained, and moved to the next level.

You may be wondering where "fulfilling your job requirements" or "performing excellently" fit into this equation. Well, they don't. Not necessarily. Fulfilling your requirements and performing excellently are good, but are only helpful from a career perspective if you are known and recognized for your achievements. Since this book is not about how to do your job, but about how to survive, achieve and succeed, let's assume you are already satisfying your job requirements. Quite honestly, if you are not capable, even if you are perceived as brilliant, you might eventually be discovered to be a fraud (although I know of people who have feigned competence for decades).

Actual and perceived performance

How can businesses ignore actual performance in favor of perceived performance? There are several answers:

1. we don't know what we don't see (if no one knows what great things you've done, you won't be rewarded for them);

2. we trust and retain the people we like;

3. while many activities maintain objective criteria to be judged against, there are typically subjective "factors" which are used to impact that judgment, producing a largely subjective and even predetermined result;

4. there are almost always fuzzy variables in success that must be weighed right along with the rest of the performance criteria, such as the ability to build and inspire teams, sell ideas, and build relationships.

Accordingly, managers rely not on absolutes but on patterns and generalizations. Everyone is busy and finds it much more convenient to draw conclusions based on patterns and past experience rather than actual facts and outcomes.

Despite the problems inherent in relying on generalizations, including some inaccuracies, patterns do tend to provide consistent results.

For instance, it is reasonable to presume that people who show up on time and dress well are good and desirable employees. It is more likely that people with past criminal convictions will commit theft or violence again. History tells us that those who use drugs might not show up on time or work as hard as those who don't. A newly married woman in her twenties or thirties is more likely to become pregnant in the near future and may take extended time away from work, or perhaps not come back at all. Single employees in their mid-twenties are far more likely to be distracted by the lures of social exploits and other vices. And married people of all ages are far more stable, particularly those with children.

Like so many other managers, I have hired and fired enough people to know that these presumptions are generally quite accurate.

THE IMPORTANCE OF PERCEPTION

Except for those jobs that judge performance solely on objective/quantitative criteria, how you are perceived is more important than who you are or what you do.

If you are perceived as smart, a hard worker, or an asset to the corporation, then you are. Once you become trusted by your superiors, it becomes much harder to be perceived negatively, and positive reviews become more automatic. Bad work is excused because it is inconsistent with the general pattern.

If, on the other hand, you are perceived to be looking out solely for yourself, then it doesn't matter whether you are or are not in fact acting in the best interests of the corporation. If you are perceived to lack trustworthiness, then your expense reports will be more closely reviewed. And you might as well be a lying thief.

Perceptions resist change

It can be difficult or even impossible to convince people that their perceptions are not true. If it can be done at all, it can take months or years, particularly if someone is trying to overcome negative experiences. Once trust is damaged, repair can be nearly impossible. Just look at how long it takes one spouse to begin to trust another after an affair.

Everything counts

How you dress, act, speak, walk, move, react, answer the phone, show up at meetings, decorate your office, arrive and leave every day, handle stress—and every other action, no matter how inconsequential—it all matters, in every possible way, contributing to other people's perception of your trustworthiness, seriousness, competence, and connection to other people and to the business.

Corporate politics plays off these perceptions. It accepts the difference between perception and reality; it can cause great people to fail and bad people to appear trustworthy.

So "success," in this context, equals satisfactory work. Manage others' perceptions of you by behaving in a more conscious and self-aware manner, and focus on developing a sixth sense about striving to see who other people really are.

PLAYING KEEP-AWAY

Play "keep-away"— draw firm boundaries between your work life and your personal life. You have a closet for a reason. Keep your skeletons and personal life away from the spying eyes. Show only what you want them to see. Keep your work colleagues out of your personal space and, except for special occasions, out of your home. *Never* let your personal problems or sexual interests enter the workplace. And never lose control of your temper or emotions.

But on those occasions when you do allow your personal essence, emotions, and instinctive reactions to manifest themselves in your behavior, which will (and should) happen naturally from time to time, find a way to do it in a mindful manner, and in a way that exerts a positive rather than negative impact.

This game of "keep-away" can be a challenge, but consider it in light of the fact that you are protecting the way you are perceived—your most important asset. Protect it with your corporate life.

IN DEFENSE OF POLITICS

At its purest level, the word *politics* relates simply to the manner in which people, often with different degrees of power, interact with one another to get things done. The most common political process simply involves getting the *right* ideas adopted. Effective politics starts with building friends and relationships, because people tend to listen to their friends and with those who are loyal and whom they trust. This process helps our ideas find a receptive audience.

Politics is the art of the sale

We sell our ideas and value to the company and to the client, and we survive in business by getting people to invest in us, hire us, trust us, and listen to us. In this sense, politics is pure and virtuous, merely a good discussion with knowledgeable people that leads to decisions that benefit the business and perhaps all of society.

Understanding "playing politics"

However, that's not what the phrase "playing politics" has come to signify. It implies something far worse—a persuasive and manipulative, sometimes unethical tactic that presumes people might seek to undermine, injure, lie and lobby, not publicly, but privately.

But reality compels us to take a broader view.

Politics starts with convincing your friends and allies of the worth of your idea (or convincing them that they should adopt or support you as a person offering an idea). Promotion of one idea might implicitly involve attacking other ideas or people.

Politics can involve the use of leverage or other tactics to suggest consequences or otherwise motivate others to support your idea or cause at their own personal and/or professional risk. Or it can involve forming coalitions and crushing counter-ideas that might otherwise be considered and adopted.

"Politics" (according to *www.thefreedictionary.com*) also refers to dealing with internal conflicts and with "maneuvering within a political unit or group in order to gain control or power." As defined by Merriam-Webster's Dictionary, to "play politics" means:

"a. to engage in political intrigue, take advantage of a political situation or issue, resort to partisan politics, etc.; exploit a political system or political relationships; and

"b. to deal with people in an opportunistic, manipulative, or devious way, as for job advancement."

The behavior of politicians shows the inherent conflicts we have already discussed. Politicians are often more concerned about their own re-election than their constituencies. The most effective politicians align with people who can help them accomplish their objectives, all the while protecting their livelihoods and perceptions.

Corporate politics in action

Politics in action is, albeit natural, often not purely benign (particularly when viewed from the vantage point of the non-politically savvy), particularly in larger, higher paying or more bureaucratic settings. It can appear as a game of power and self-interest, finding its strength in controlling and manipulating perceptions. We all have experienced circumstances in which power politics has worked against us. While it's a natural process, it sure can be an ugly, dirty game.

In my own career, after several years of practicing law in a major firm and enjoying considerable success as an entrepreneur and in the corporate world (see *About the Author*), I took an upper-level position in a highly political environment working for a person who was broadly despised (both in the company and throughout the industry).

It was impossible for me to succeed, because the other executives were interested in sabotaging my boss. Since I had no direct representation within the executive team, my advice could be discounted or refused outright because of the person I worked for.

I decided that I would rise above the political game by displaying very high standards for truth and integrity, hoping to survive with flying moral colors.

I took a "the-buck-stops-here" approach. My clients were senior executives who had their own agendas, and the people who worked with me took full advantage of my naïve approach. They soon learned that my butt was always available to cover theirs. Eventually, this became a very real problem for me, and there is nothing harder to overcome than a problem you allow to continue for too long.

The inevitability of politics: play or lose

One thing is absolutely clear: *it is not possible to stay above, or outside, the political fray.* Whether you have extremely high personal values or are entirely devoid of any moral or ethical scruples, you must engage yourself in the process.

If you fail to build relationships, you will have no political base to draw from. If you fail to make a case for your ideas in a way that forces them to be noticed, they will not be heard or adopted. If you fail to defend yourself, you will be trampled. The buck can only stop with you if you have the clout and power to rise *above* the buck.

If you don't—and most don't—a buck that stops with you will eventually be the cause for all kinds of problems sure to follow.

We do not get to hide from politics. Hiding from politics is akin to avoiding the entire decision making process. And while it is quite possible to engage in the game without sacrificing your values, it ultimately is play or lose.

Becoming familiar with the way in which the corporate political game is played in your company (and industry) should be a priority. Getting to know and connect with the people who matter to you should be one of the first things you do.

Success in business is, and always has been, largely related to who you know (including who will teach you, help you and inform you) and how well you're liked.

Getting things done with political savvy

When you have something to achieve, you should think through how you want to get that idea or project accomplished. Plan as if you are going into battle. *Your value and the value you bring are not enough. Quite simply, one rarely finds true karma in the workplace; good people and ideas are not au-tomatically rewarded but instead must be sold.*

Instead, the politically savvy among us *demand* to be accepted and not embarrassed; we take advantage of the way other people act and react so that we can get things done. Some are expert at taking advantage of others' flaws. Some players sit back and watch other people create their own problems without throwing a lifeline—and sometimes even encourage a problem or two here and there. Ultimately, the savvy almost always seem to find a way to rise to the top.

Be a realist

Until you are running the business or are in a profession in which you are somehow immunized, be a realist. See the world objectively, fully expecting, anticipating, recognizing, and appreciating its humanity.

Many people who succeed in business seem to harbor a constant cynicism and acceptance caused by their awareness of corporate self-interest, conflicts, corruptness, manipulation, and interpersonal disrespect; they accept these negative traits as part of human nature and the twisted reality of the world.

While you may (and should) adhere to those values that matter to you, your career is a type of game with no time-outs and no slip-ups, and if you hope to get things done and to reach higher places in the business world, you must embrace politics: *you must find a way to become more influential, more respected, and less manipulated.*

THE EVOLVING WORKPLACE

Just like almost everything else in the world, the workplace is constantly evolving. Just as the last generation was the first to be born into a world of computers, today's new employees are the first to be born into a world of cell phones, text messages, e-mail, social media, and the Internet.

They (if you're like me, you) don't (or have forgotten) a world without ubiquitous smartphones, instant messaging, and constant interactivity, and they/we are master multitaskers, researchers, and resource-mongers. They/we know how to use online tools to gather or convey instant information, and they/we use text and free web-based social networks and e-mail systems to become highly social, and to take on alter-egos and multiple personalities.

Members of this generation play video games against competitors located anywhere around the planet. They have been exposed to violence, sex, porn, and dirty jokes at a far younger age than anyone in past generations. And they know that location matters less than it ever has before.

Youth, diversity, and loyalty

The youngest participants in business have always set the tone, and there is a great deal of writing and media attention about this new world. Today's workplace is diverse in every sense; employees are working from home and are demanding perks previously unavailable—at least until the recent economic downturn.

On the productivity side, employees are accessing information and multitasking at levels never before possible.

Furthermore, statistics show that this generation is loyal more to itself, not only because of the transient aspects of the technology, but also perhaps because it's the first generation to refuse to be loyal to the modern business that has lost its ability to be truly loyal to its employees.

Business has evolved to the point where it does not offer (nor do its employees take) jobs with the expectation that the employee will stay for more than a few years. Employees are expected to leave when they find a better deal elsewhere. Then again, this was, until recently, the only generation never to have seen a failed economy. That has changed.

Navigating cyberspace

While few are born ready for the competitive world of business, vying for attention in the Internet world is a magnificent education.

Cyberspace is a hard, cold place built on anonymity and bluntness, where only the strongest survive in terms of prominence or fortune. Branding now begins in youth. Information is disseminated and manipulated (including biographical information) to an extent never before seen.

Navigating this landscape requires advanced political and marketing skills. Messages are tailored, images created, and people are transformed into legends—or diminished overnight. Networking, previously avoided by many, is now built into the fabric of communication, as we see with blogs and popular social networking websites such as LinkedIn, Facebook and photo and social sharing websites.

While these can be valuable strengths, they can raise complications (lost transparency, for one) for the exceedingly politically correct business world.

The unchanging human condition

Years ago I watched comedian George Carlin give a performance in which he launched insults at practically every group of people, eventually targeting the baby boomer generation. He reminded us that these are the same people whose slogan changed from "peace and love" to "just say no," a natural hypocrisy, perhaps based on acquired wisdom or conservatism, that sought to deprive the youth of those things that the boomers once deeply enjoyed and cherished.

The point is that we all keep changing along with our age, perspective and circumstances. Sometimes people end up wiser and other times parental, stubborn, cynical or disconnected, just as they did forty or even one hundred years ago.

This book presumes that as human beings we are and always will be very similar. Each of us must be able to adapt to any situation that might arise— and with the right skills and tools, we can. Each must develop personal and working relationships with people of all ages, regardless of the fact that as a species, we haven't changed much in thousands of years. Our music, fads and styles have changed, business has evolved, and technology has improved. But while our sensibilities change, we, as human beings, are still cut from the same cloth as we always have been—young and old, fat and thin, sharing the same emotions and stresses that human beings always have.

The lessons here do work. Just apply to taste.

REST OF THE BOOK: THOUGHTS, GUIDELINES AND PEARLS OF WISDOM

Here's an actual rule of my current company (paraphrased only slightly for dramatic effect): "In case of fire, leave the sick, old, and infirm behind in the stairwells. And be sure to remember to tell the fire department where you left them."

Now, this rule accomplishes its intended purpose—getting the greatest number of employees out of the building in case of an emergency—and it helps to ensure that other employees are not injured, while it allows the fire department to do what they have been trained to do and minimizes potential legal liability.

But this is exactly the kind of rule that illustrates our twisted corporate existence! We used to reward traits such as generosity, courage (particularly in the face of danger), and the idea that the sick or old deserve our special attention. We don't anymore.

"Save yourself" is literal corporate policy.

"Politically correct" vs. "correct politically"

This book aspires to be straightforward. Instead of focusing on being politically *correct*, we will focus on what it means to be correct *politically*.

To be clear, it is usually correct politically to be politically correct. There is great virtue and decency in seeking to avoid offensive statements and acts. However, in our case, we are following established rules of political correctness and etiquette not for the betterment or benefit of society, and not to make other people feel less offended, but for our own interest—to become a master at navigating our own corporate waters.

Our humanity is our primary obstacle. The irony in business is that smart business decisions can so easily be undermined by our human frailties.

Obvious examples are emotional outbursts, workplace hostility, and sexual misconduct. Why do some people lash out at others even at risk of being terminated? And why are some people who hold public office, or act as teachers, baby sitters, police officers or priests, unable to find a way to control their sexual desires and behaviors? Or tempers? Or greed?

Many politicians can't even find a way to restrain their damaging behaviors for the shorter length of time they are running for in office. Some even commit the same behaviors that they're already under investigation for!

While not condoning any bad behavior, I'd imagine that bad acts continue to occur because we are human beings first. Our emotions, urges, and tempers *always* get in our way.

The politically savvy employee

The concept of civility requires that many of our uncivilized, early-human traits, notions, functions, and reactions be unnaturally suppressed. And while the corporate world is a tug-of-war between incivility and humanity, and each is awarded its share of victories, politically savvy employees are almost always those that appear at all times to be the most calm and civil, correct politically, and able to act in a manner that is understanding and embracing of the treacherous environment that surrounds them.

Let's take the rest of our time together to offer some thoughts, ideas, guidelines, and pearls of wisdom for success in the modern business environment. These are for your consideration and contemplation. Perhaps you will find some insight here into how you should relate to your job and career, and perhaps you will become better aware of the behavior of others. Maybe you will be entertained. And of course it is fine if you disagree.

As an attorney, I hope that my clients listen to my advice and the advice of my team. I hope that they appreciate our knowledge, experience, research skills, and background.

Then, I hope that they will use their own intellect and intuition (which is usually quite outstanding) to consider the advice, develop an understanding of the issues that are being raised, and make their own decisions. When choosing a course of action, there is rarely an absolutely right or wrong answer.

Patterned behavior and human emotions

But in general, our advice, when judged in retrospect, is usually correct, because problems, when viewed objectively, tend to be simple and obvious and to follow the same patterns they have followed countless times before.

Yet, regardless of these objective patterns, once we add emotions and desires and the rest of human nature to the equation—including our constant desire to perceive ourselves as competent, moral and ethical—we become blinded to the obvious, and things always seem to end up a bit screwy.

Learning the rules

In the end, the business environment is a game of role-play; being savvy means respecting the rules of this strange and deceptive world. This advice is offered by lots of very smart and successful people.

How do we learn the rules? For most of us, these rules are learned and tested over time, over the course of thousands of mistakes big and small, from being around thousands of others, and having fired or been involved in decisions regarding the firing of others.

Whether you agree or disagree with the ideas presented here, the most important thing you can do is to weigh these thoughts against your own situation and values. In doing so, I hope that you end up more capable and better suited to the complex world you're in.

> *Disclaimer: I do not claim complete originality for some of this advice, but here it is—in one place—along with lots of stuff that you may not have heard and that is entirely original. These rules carry the weight of gospel (whose, I don't presume to know), and all bear repeating. No one rule can work for every person in any given situation. Worse, the ideas are offered to you by a fairly opinionated author.*

With that said...

BALANCE

I am often asked to describe this book. Is it a book about succeeding in business? Well... sure. A general survival guide? Of course. Are there tidbits on how to best crush your opponent? Definitely!

This book still sits on my own shelf—and its words resonate with me during all of my most challenging situations. While I hope that this book succeeds in all of these categories, it is my greatest hope that this book succeeds in one sense more than any other—as a reminder to find levity, humor, and balance throughout our jobs and our lives in general.

The core message of *It's (Not) Just Business* is that with power and money and territory comes, well... nothing else much. A bigger house, perhaps. And I do want a bigger house. A ticket directly to heaven—perhaps not. I am the same person regardless of my own success, and so I would imagine is everyone else. A person's success is personal to that person alone. While my profession and personal success is serious stuff to me, itself it means remarkably little to anyone else.

Is this all a fair bit of common sense? Sure. All reminders about behavior and perception involve a fair bit of common sense. Thus, many of these lessons are not things you must learn as much as things of which we must be reminded—particularly in difficult situations. For instance, when I find myself angry or frustrated in my work, which happens from time-to-time, I do appreciate the reminder to talk less, and even more importantly, to calm down, since emotion (and talking) is my enemy. I keep a copy of this book in sight first and foremost as a visual guardian angel reminding me to keep perspective.

I find balance when I am reminded that the world does not rotate around me, that apart from my work-product (which does matter) no one else is preoccupied with me and that whether I perform well or poorly in a situation will have little bearing on anything, including my job and family.

Part of our perspective recognizes each of our individual space in this world and that your primary job relates to things related to your and your circumstances. You don't fall in love with my perfect daughter, no matter how much I talk about her. When my parents passed away, I wanted the world to feel my loss. It didn't. It, like each person in it, had its own concerns. With this simple recognition that each person has their own issues to deal with, we can better relate to them and the world in general.

My profession is important (to me) for so many reasons not to mention that it pays my mortgage and will pay by child's college education. While I do find interest and challenge in my work, on its worst day it still ensures that I fulfill my financial responsibilities as a husband and father and helps me to be a person who is able to live life to the fullest. When the little things add up, I try to remember to let them go, since obsessing over them will only take away from the things that matter most to me.

The idea of perspective, allows me to worry less about my individual interactions, negotiation outcomes and petty details. Life is, after all, the product of more than its fair share of petty details.

So jump right in. Best of luck to you in your journey.

The difference between a job and a career is the difference between forty and sixty hours a week. —Robert Frost

THE ESSENCE OF EMPLOYMENT

A "JOB" IS AN ENDEAVOR undertaken for the purpose of earning money. A "career," on the other hand, is related to chosen life goals or a chosen field of expertise.

A job is typically performed over a fixed time period (*e.g.*, 8 hours) and/or on an hourly or project basis. People with jobs tend to go home at the end of their day, often without regard to whether or not the work is complete.

We speak of careers, on the other hand, as an extension of the person. People who recognize their job as a part of their career or trade often regard their work as function oriented and time insensitive (you work till you get the job done). While a career may not be lifelong, it is more likely tied to a person's identity; a person's life accomplishments may be tied to career achievement.

Managers work very hard to figure out which employees are just showing up to collect a paycheck and which ones care enough to give their best to the work product. The manager is on a constant search to find people who deserve the best that the manager and business have to offer. Consequently, *the employee has two choices: either commit to the job as a career or do a great job of faking it.*

SURVIVAL MEANS ADAPTATION

Adapt yourself to the things among which your lot has been cast and love sincerely the fellow creatures with whom destiny has ordained that you shall live. — *Marcus Aurelius*

We don't get to dictate the course of human events. Businesses and markets change, like laws. People live but die suddenly. And opportunity, like challenge, shows itself when it is least expected.

Embracing opportunity means taking risks—perhaps you might not be capable of doing the job or achieving goals that are set out for you (or by you). Survival, like opportunity, always means giving up something comfortable for an unknown result. Like asking that perfect person out on a date, life is intimidating, of course, but even a little bit of good can make all of the bad worthwhile.

DOES ANYONE REALLY CARE WHAT YOU WANT?

Pack your own parachute. —*T.I. Hakala*

Yes. You do. That's pretty much it.

Your manager and the business care about you only as long as you are performing as desired, and they might even care about you as a person. But when it comes to your place in business, you really are the only one who cares.

The impermanence of all things comes to mind as we watch the fading of once-shining stars in the workplace. People formerly thought of as indispensable become less than merely expendable; they become terminable when years or circumstances dictate time for a change.

As leadership changes, many who were previously top performers are let go. This is the natural evolution of things—the new people must ensure not only that they are backed with their own loyal team, but also that the older preferences and management styles are replaced with fresh ones. It is personal and entirely normal as well as beneficial to the new leaders.

As your only true advocate in the workplace, do *you* even know what you want? If you are that rare person who *does* know, are you taking steps toward achieving your goal? Most people do not know what they want. And the rest are reluctant to place themselves at risk in hopes of achieving their goal.

Know what you want to get out of your life. Set up your achievement and expect that your circumstances will change. Are you well positioned? You can always change. But if you don't know what you want, someone else will be forced to decide it for you.

SO IF YOU WANT TO CONTROL YOUR OWN DESTINY...

None of us will ever accomplish anything excellent or commanding except when he listens to this whisper which is heard by him alone. —Ralph Waldo Emerson

...perhaps suicide may be in order. It is, if successful, the only way for you to totally take control of your life's path (however, the afterlife may throw a wrench into your plans). If you fail (or get cold feet), rejoin the rest of us who operate in a world in which we really don't have control over anything.

We're all afraid.

Everyone is scared, from the entry-level employee to the accomplished executive. This bears repeating and deserves constant reminding. Being scared is the default human condition. It does not distinguish according to age or stature.

We all face our challenges with some degree of anxiety and trepidation. One key difference is that *people who consistently achieve their goals recognize their anxiety as natural, rarely if ever considering any other course of action. Achievers are not fearless people, but normal people who overcome their fears.*

I often hear people who dream of taking extended time off or early retirement, and I know from conversations with them that they never will. These stories are classic examples of the dream that buckles under the weight of the fear of living without a steady income.

Success at anything means overcoming your personal and professional challenges; how you choose to play the game depends on what you want out of it and whether you are willing to face your fears. For instance, if you want to become an executive or end up as big boss, then mastering skills such as public speaking, no matter how anxiety provoking, is essential.

If you hope to achieve your goals, then your natural fears must not cause you to waver. Most people fail merely because of fear of something that couldn't really hurt them in the first place.

Stay flexible in the face of uncertainty.

We don't know what will happen in the next few minutes, never mind what will happen tomorrow. But although you may not control the outcome of your life, a fair bit of it is in your hands. Stay flexible. Your greatest opportunities may not be those you recognized, expected, or hoped for just five minutes ago. And every day, you make decisions that may appear to be short-term—but actually have very long-term implications.

GETTING HIRED

> *The closest to perfection a person ever comes is when he fills out a job application form. —Stanley J. Randall*

Most managers hate to take time to interview candidates for open positions, even though hiring is one of the most important parts of any manager's job. The open position is likely hurting the business, especially if the position has been open for any length of time. Finding the right candidates and interviewing them is hard work and a terrible distraction, particularly when a manager is forced to *entertain* a candidate that he or she knows will never get the job. That's why the manager is dying for *you* to be the *right* candidate.

It's true: We, as managers and interviewers, want you to succeed. And we want the agonizing interview process to finally come to an end.

Companies rarely get to "try out" their people. Instead, your interviewer has your resume (some studies have reported that more than 50 percent of resumes include untruths, *a.k.a. lies*).

Moreover, some references will not be helpful or even used at all (many companies are too busy or lazy to check them, and the ones that do often receive only a mere confirmation of your past employment)—because even your former employers are afraid of saying something that might get them into trouble).

So the hiring manager is left with your interview(s) and a great deal of faith. On the basis of these few scraps, the interviewer has to make a decision that can either work out, sometimes spectacularly, or be a disaster for everyone involved.

In the end, the interview (call it an audition) is really all we have to rely on. Put on a really good show, get the job. Know somebody (and be liked by that person), get the job. Look and act like the person that the manager can see in the open position.

Help us to make the connection. Be prepared to take some control. Connect with us. We're only human—and if we know you, and particularly if we like you, your chances are infinitely better.*

THE MEANINGLESS VALUE OF EDUCATION

It is all one to me if a man comes from Sing Sing Prison or Harvard. We hire a man, not his history. —Malcolm Forbes

Apart from fulfilling basic job requirements, once you have the job, the school you went to or the amount of education you have typically no longer matter.** Unless my colleagues are college sports fans, I often have no idea of the schools they attended. I never know what people's majors were. I certainly don't know or care about their grades. We deal with people as they are, not how their resume tells us they should be.

---

* It is, however, a very small world, so don't underestimate informal communication channels. Everyone knows everyone, and oftentimes the hire decision is made upon recommendations made through these informal channels.

** Of course some businesses only hire people with certain degrees or require their employees to have degrees from only the most elite universities. While appearing elitist, this is often validly tied to these business' reputations or the desire to narrow down an overly broad pool of candidates.

Employers know that no amount of education will ever prepare you for a job you have never held. All real-life education happens in the process of performing a function. All your resume does is to tell us whether you *might* have the *potential*.

Once you have the job, your skill and talent will generally allow you to keep it, presuming that you have the interpersonal skills to make the company and your manager like you (most people are terminated not for lack of skills but for other reasons, such as not being liked by their coworkers or being unable to get along in the workplace).

While your resume will help you get the job, it will very rarely help you get anything beyond that. *You must be good and you must be liked. Your education got you through the door, but it's your skills and ability to navigate the politics of life that will get you where you want to go.*

EVERY JOB IS A SALES JOB (EVEN YOURS)

Pretend that every single person you meet has a sign around his or her neck that says, "Make me feel important." Not only will you succeed in sales, you will succeed in life. —Mary Kay Ash

Getting hired is a sales presentation. Even if you are not selling products or services to customers, every project, opinion, idea, and task must be sold, and you must constantly sell your value to the business.

Not realizing (or forgetting) that you are in sales may mean forgetting to pay attention to refining certain critical skills. Read a book on sales from time to time, and you will be reminded that the tools used to sell products are often the same tools that are used to convince other people that you are worthy of their respect.

Selling does not (necessarily) mean an intense, high-pressure sales pitch. It's more subtle. "Being in sales" refers to the general notion that adding value and benefit and reducing risk to an acceptable degree are good things. If you or your opinions or your project can help do that, you'll sell yourself and your projects right into a place of real success.

YOU'RE NOT THE CENTER OF THE WORLD

A man's interest in the world is only the overflow from his interest in himself. —George Bernard Shaw

Recall the degree to which self-interest drives almost everything that happens between people in business. Unless you are very bad at what you do, your manager isn't thinking about you.

When managers talk in private with other managers, they are probably not talking about you.

ARE OUR FLAWS BUILT IN?

How much of our personalities are within our control? Does nature tell each of us how we will react to different circumstances? Do we *learn* when to feel angry, jealous and lonely? Are we products of our environment or of our genes? Are our flaws built in or learned? How much can we change?

While we are miracles as living creatures we are (arguably) flawed in our anatomical design (among many examples: the off-balance, high stress, design of our single-axis spinal core; the proximity of our esophagus and trachea which makes it easy to choke to death). We laugh at funerals and forget where we put our keys. We forget what television show we are watching, even while the program continues. We are designed to lack a fluent ability to change our minds. We make questionable decisions like spending money on trivial items versus saving for an early retirement, and we eat one last cookie at the beginning of a diet.

Are greed, aspiration and cheating inherent? Addiction and mental illness can be genetic—why not the rest of our of thinking?

These questions relate to how we deal with our colleagues. If you are limited in your own ability to change, your colleagues who are less sensitive to these issues certainly cannot be expected to change. That being the case, there is no need to become preoccupied with the hope of changing—or changing them. It really doesn't matter where the "flaws" come from. We are just loaded with them. For a terrific read, check out *Kluge, The Haphazard Construction of the Human Mind* by Gary Marcus. Also, *Predictably Irrational* by Dan Ariely.

Managers and executives are not preoccupied with who you are or what you have done—and that includes the mistakes you've made. Everyone has a job to do. *The only person spending most of the time thinking about you is you,* just like the person who spends the most time thinking about me is me.

We fight our demons and battles alone. If you are paranoid, find a way to stop being paranoid. Get your job done—or we all might just start spending more time thinking about *you.*

YOU'RE SHY. ADMIT IT!

> *Shyness has a strange element of narcissism, a belief that how we look, how we perform, is truly important to other people. —André Dubus*

You might not know this, but you're probably shy. Maybe not in the same way as the child who stands in the corner of the playground afraid to speak to anyone, but you are probably clinically shy.

According to Dr. Bernardo Carducci, Ph.D., professor of psychology at the Indiana University Southeast and head of the Shyness Research Institute, shyness is a form of "excessive self-focus, a preoccupation with your thoughts, feelings, and physical reactions," and it becomes most evident in feelings of "self-consciousness, excessive negative self-evaluation, and excessive negative self-preoccupation."

Your question, of course, is: Why are you telling me this?

According to the good doctor, over 45 percent of the adult population considers themselves shy, and lots of others may not admit to being shy but suffer from similar symptoms.

The problem with being shy

Shy people feel as if all eyes are upon them. They suffer, from mild social awkwardness to total social phobia—or anything in between. They may have trouble finding and advancing in jobs. They may have trouble building and keeping strong relationships. They have trouble speaking in front of other people, maintaining conversations, and being assertive and authoritative.

Unlike introverted people, who have no fear of social situations but are quite comfortable on their own, shy people often want very much to be among others and part of the team. Shy people want to become leaders but trip over their own fears. And shy people want to ask for promotions and career advancement, but they just don't; many settle for jobs that require less skill or training.

Getting beyond shyness.

If you see these symptoms in yourself, recognize that you are among the majority of adults in society. Free yourself from the idea that people are watching you or care especially about you. Join public speaking support groups like Toastmasters. If you want, read Dr. Carducci's books on shyness and find a way to get out there and make contact with strangers. Rehearse your opening lines, conversations, and speaking engagements.

And remember that no one is really thinking all that much about you.

While we are exploring the essence of employment, let us not forget one fundamental fact:

ALL JOBS STINK

Nothing is really work unless you would rather be doing something else.
—*James Matthew Barrie*

While money does not ensure happiness, many of those in occupations considered most successful—such as attorneys, accountants, and doctors (particularly dentists, as it turns out)—are notoriously unhappy people, and the suicide rates for people in these professions have traditionally far exceeded others (excluding war veterans).* The bottom line is that *people are*

---

*   Some studies indicate that dentists are more likely to commit suicide. Researcher Stephen Stack of Wayne State University notes that dentists are more than six times more likely to commit suicide than the national average. Other studies have confirmed this, particularly with regard to female dentists, while still others have questioned these findings. For our purposes, I don't really care. The message is not contingent on the accuracy of these studies, and furthermore I find studies like this entertaining.

more likely to be unhappy in their lives if they are unsatisfied in their jobs, no matter the salary.

Reality check: Work as an end in itself

Our work, contrary to all of our ideals and desires, rarely constitutes the means to an end, but more often *is* the end. We work because that's what we do, whether we like it or not. Unless you are among the luckiest few, you would probably rather be doing something other than your job at least some of the time—yet many of us end up losing a bit of our vacation time every year because when it comes down to it, our jobs are our top priority.

It seems that most people do not know what they want to do when they grow up until they have already long since grown up and become tied to life's obligations. People with the *chutzpah* to change careers, even with a significant cut in pay, often find much greater happiness in what follows.

In fact, most people, including the highest paid executives, feel that work stinks.* In any event, not liking your job or enjoying your day is no excuse for apathy or poor performance, because even on your worst day you are still in the same boat as everybody else.

WE ARE ALL EXPENDABLE

> *One of the symptoms of an approaching nervous breakdown is the belief that one's work is terribly important.* —Bertrand Russell

In the grand scheme, almost no one person is essential—no one that I know of, anyway.

Although certain *positions* may be essential to a business (such as accountants in an accounting firm), businesses tend to survive and prosper regard-

---

*   Job satisfaction surveys do not try to determine if people are happy or if they would rather be somewhere else. In a study conducted by Harris Interactive Inc. (2004/2005), only 12% of people reported being extremely satisfied with their jobs, Thirty-three percent were satisfied and the reminder were dissatisfied. Only 15% reported being strongly energized by their work. The more recent The Conference Board survey demonstrated similar numbers.

less of who inhabits those positions, and they survive regardless of who chooses to leave, whether it be a person in the mail room or the founder/CEO. Life always goes on.

EXPENDABLE EXAMPLES

The world is littered with companies that have survived the departure of their key people, and then there are those arrogant folks who remain baffled when their former business continues on without them. Could Apple survive without Steve Jobs? Yes. It did—although that might be a bad example given its success after his return. Walmart without Walton? Sure. Martha Stewart departed for a bit, but her company survived. Bill Gates left Microsoft. It survives. My college roommate thought that Jerry Garcia, the lead singer for the Grateful Dead, was essential in keeping the world spinning on axis. Jerry died and the world still spins.

I tend to enjoy comments made by certain of our more egotistical brethren who believe that when they are no longer with the company, that company is sure to collapse. Of course, these comments are more often than not made by people in the process of being fired. (I had a boss who felt this way when she was terminated; that company is still alive and prospering many years later.)

Good management technique teaches us to make each person *feel* essential to the function of the business, thus elevating loyalty and morale by elevating self-esteem. But if the CEO is not essential, neither are you. No matter your role, perceived value, or self-image, someone else can always do your job. Your shoes can always be filled. And you can fill others' shoes as well.

That is not to suggest that you should not do everything in your power to convince the company that you are absolutely essential. But companies don't fail because even the most important people take vacations, or have babies, or leave. I find myself guilty of this delusion as well, losing vacation time and working when sick under the belief that I am absolutely needed. I am not. No one is.

SHOULD I STAY OR GO?

Two thirds of promotion is motion. —*Anonymous*

Companies prefer to offer open positions to existing employees before looking to hire from the outside (except for the most senior level positions).

Accordingly, employees seeking a change might find an opportunity for an internal position that helps bring them where they want to go. Instead of leaving, the employee enjoys continued health insurance, retirement plan vesting, and other benefits dating back to the time of his hiring.

While this can be a significant perk to existing employees, it is also a great benefit to the company, primarily because the company has first-hand knowledge about its internal candidate and no incentive to offer big salary adjustments or other inducements.

Problems with internal job change

One problem with internal transfers is that while they offer all of these wonderful opportunities, they come with a curse: everyone knows your baggage. The transferring employee is already liked or despised by others and, in the latter case, finds it nearly impossible to start afresh.

In additiona person is almost always viewed in the capacity in which he or she is first known. For instance, a good friend of mine was a paralegal. He attended law school after work every night and eventually became licensed as an attorney. The corporation was kind enough to give him a bump in pay—not too much, just enough to recognize that he had earned his degree—but they still viewed his advice as coming from a paralegal. And they paid him like one.

Result: He had to leave.

Remarkably few companies will take junior people and make them into senior employees, even over very long periods of time. This is not because people aren't ready or haven't earned the new role, but because the once junior person will continue to be perceived as being a junior and less sophisticated person.

While some businesses are terrific at helping people climb the corporate ladder, the perception issues remain an ever-present obstacle. Since my friend wanted to be a lawyer, he had to leave the place that viewed him only as a paralegal and find a place that knows him only as a lawyer. He left to follow his destiny. He has since become quite an accomplished attorney.

Stay or go?

Some companies are better than others at moving people up, but the real promotions happen when new pay rates and titles can be reset from scratch. While it stinks to have to abandon benefits, vesting periods, and options, leaving is often the only way to get where we want to go.

Always be prepared to follow your path. While staying for more than a few years earns you points for your dedication and stick-to-itiveness, qualities expected and prayed for by all employers (they show loyalty), your perseverance can be equally on display at the next job. The reluctant employee always claims that it is worth staying for "the great people," but really, there are great people everywhere else as well. Have your resume always on the ready (never stored on your office computer or sent via your office email, however), and if at all possible, be willing to consider unlikely opportunities.

JOBS DO GROW ON TREES

The unemployment rate is 100 percent if it is you who is unemployed. — Unknown

There are a lot of things that don't grow on trees, such as money. Money does not grow on trees. Jobs, however, do.

How can that be, especially in a lousy job market?

There's no doubt that being unemployed can be one of the most stressful experiences anyone can have. Likewise, even the risk of unemployment, perhaps even voluntary unemployment such as exploring career changes, can cause tremendous stress.

And yet, at any one time, thousands of businesses are looking to hire someone like you, even in the worst of times—if not today than tomorrow. And while it can take time to find the right match, once you do, you will once again feel as if you are the luckiest person in the world, with the greatest job ever.

When you think that your life depends on your having a particular job, or that your company is the best, or that you work with the greatest people that have ever lived, or that your life would end if you lost your job, you are lacking perspective and are disconnected from reality. There is always a job that pays more. There are great and smart people everywhere. And your life will not end if you don't get a job right away or if your job goes away.

There are options.

Avoid falling for the trap of thinking that there are no other options.

If your industry has dried up, change industries. When geographical areas dry up, look to the horizon. True, finding and changing jobs can be frustrating and scary. This advice is not offered blindly but with a true understanding of the dire circumstances in many geographic areas and industries and the complexity of reinventing oneself. But at any given time there are literally thousands of options, from small mom-and-pop businesses to international conglomerates—looking for someone exactly like you. One thing is for sure: the opportunities will be found only if your eyes are open to them and your feet are walking distance from them.

THE ART OF BEING FIRED

> *Most people work just hard enough not to get fired and get paid just enough money not to quit.* —George Carlin

Any person can be fired for any reason or for no reason at all. (There are exceptions, for instance, if you have an employment contract the employer must follow the terms of the contract. Also, you cannot be hired or fired for a reason such as your sex or race, although there are exceptions here as well.) This is what is known as "at-will employment:" you work at the *will* of your employer.

The challenge of getting fired

However, in many businesses it can be a real challenge to get fired. Many incompetent people—not you, of course—keep their jobs for a very long time.

Business is deathly scared of either (i) having an unfilled position (something is better than nothing), and (ii) getting sued. Companies would much rather find a way to encourage bad employees to leave without having to fire them. Fearing a lawsuit, many companies will engage in expensive and time-consuming reorganizations merely as a ruse, an excuse to get rid of people, rather than risk individual firings.

When it comes to firing an individual, managers are often required to follow strict procedures, including extensive documentation, probation periods, and so forth (absent clear and documented cause and, of course, depending on your industry and company policies). Consequently, an individual about to be fired generally has a fair bit of warning.

Furthermore, a business, as ruthless as it can be, often tries to take a moral stand, offering bad employees a chance to use probationary periods—not expecting improvement, but rather to allow plenty of warning, as well as time to permit the soon-to-be-fired employee to find an alternative position elsewhere.

It is worth noting that unless there is a contract, there is generally no requirement for severance pay or a period of notice. Typically these are intended as nice gestures on the part of the business or are provided in exchange for the terminated employee's agreement not to sue.

Sometimes people are physically escorted from the building. This is common in more sensitive positions; for other, less sensitive positions it is often an advisable tactic, although out of consideration for human dignity it is rarely employed. An escort is really just another way to find the door.

THERE IS NO SUCH THING AS BEING UNEMPLOYED

"I'm Not Unemployed - I'm a Consultant" — T-Shirt Quote

Apart from legal status issues such as workers' compensation and unemployment compensation rules, you do not benefit when you are known to be "unemployed," which clearly implies that someone is down on his luck--or worse, unemployable.

The "self-employed" option

If you ever find yourself without a job, go to the print shop and have business cards printed up that tell the world that you are self-employed, perhaps as a consultant/contractor. [Note: Try to avoid the home printer look. Professionally printed full color business cards can be manufactured by online providers for less than $10 for 500 cards.] After all, no one is ever so unemployed that he can't hire himself.

Similarly, for a very small investment, you can build and launch a website that displays your talents and experience in vivid color, with pull-down menus and keywords that help prospective clients find you.

I am not suggesting that you lie. Self-employment is real and recognized.* Fill in those resume blanks and you become automatically qualified to go pick up some of those temporary jobs (some consulting/freelance jobs pay much more than any similarly salaried employee could earn) while you look for a job—or even in lieu of a formal job.

Risks of stretching the truth

As I mentioned earlier, some studies show that more than 50 percent of job applicants submit resumes with discrepancies, lies, or claims that cannot be verified. While employers are working harder to verify each applicant's information, stretch-the-truth applicants understand that the worst

---

* People who are self-employed often use a title such as President or Owner on their business cards. This could be an instant tip-off that the person is self-employed and lacking real credibility. Perhaps downgrade yourself with a title such as Vice President or something that suggests that your business is legitimate with more than one employee so that you have earned a title with meaning rather than merely handed yourself a super title with no real value. If you need a title, pick one that people will believe.

that can happen is to not receive a job that would not have been offered to them anyway. It seems a safe risk for many.

The downside, however, is that if your discrepancy is discovered, even years later (a slim but real risk), you can be fired on the spot at that time. As a lawyer, I have been involved in several of these cases, and the liar who is caught always ends up out on the street.

But becoming self-employed is not a lie. It can be quite real, whether or not you bring in any work. And even without the work, with self-employment comes dignity and opportunity. Everyone understands that.

PLAYGROUNDS AND SANDBOXES

First, we were children—immature, irresponsible and sloppy.

On the playground we were all things: bullies and victims, athletic and nerdy, good looking folks and others not so. We had a pecking order: some children beloved by all and others resented or feared.

Although we grew up, we still are children—immature, emotional and built from the fibers of our youth.

That is not to say, of course, that we are not saddled with greater responsibility. The lessons of our childhood and lifetime traumas have affected us. We are older, and in many ways, wiser. And in many ways, not.

I still remember being told as a student in elementary school that we needed to become very serious, because otherwise high school would just eat us alive. It didn't. The high school teachers warned us about college. And yet my time in college was a blur of sports and booze. My college professors warned of the challenges of law school, with a life revolving around sleepless study. Some of that happened, but so did tons of hours watching sports games and boozing in the local bar.

My belief was that there would be a point when the fun would be over.

My arrival into a white-hair conservative law firm brought with it the same expectation. And while the hours were intense, the firm itself sponsored huge events, bought dinners and provided an all-you-could-drink (and eat) happy hour—which inevitably resulted in debauchery and all-you-could-suffer hangovers.

Now, many years later, the parties continue. We get business by networking and enjoying each others' company, oftentimes rather than by doing great work. Many of the most successful businesses (and people) allocate huge sums of money to those most social aspects of life.

Now I watch my twenty-two month old daughter play with other little children at her day care. The strong take the toys from the weak. They are scolded for it, but they do it anyway. And sometimes they get to keep the product of their thievery. One of my clients is the President of a major corporation. He takes things (including his job) from the weak as well. Sometimes he is scolded for it, but mostly he gets to keep his spoils. He has found great success in the doctrine of acting first and begging forgiveness later.

The TV is filled with images of adults behaving like children, with temper, lies and self-destructive conduct abound.

I recently returned to my high school reunion and it seemed as if the order of our youth returned. Despite years of growth, the groups reformed, pecking orders resumed and we became our former selves once again.

The point is this. Human beings are basic creatures, driven fairly predictably by emotions and desires. The frequency of adultery and divorce proves that a large percentage of people are certainly not driven by commitment or responsibility. While the playground may be a place despised by many, the lesson here is that human nature cannot be avoided.

This life of ours is just a playground and the same story lines are rewritten over and over again.

If at first you don't succeed, try, try again. Then quit. No use being a damn fool about it. —W. C. Fields

BEING EFFECTIVE

BEING EFFECTIVE at what you do is often much simpler than we make it out to be. The best people are the ones who seem to care (but not to a fault) and who are engaged in their work and show up, work hard, and use their heads. They take on challenges and they don't quit. Failure is rarely due to lack of trying.

While this might seem obvious at first glance, it turns out that managers observe that most of the people who don't perform well are failing at one of these very simple requirements. Often it is a question not of capability but of commitment, attitude, or concentration.

Being effective *and* successful

It is important to note that being effective does not *necessarily* equate to being successful (how you define success is a personal choice). Doing good work does not mean that your company will ever have an available position to promote you into, that your industry will not suffer from a financial downturn, or that your company will not go out of business. Success demands good work, tenacity, and choices, but it also involves circumstances and timing.

Nevertheless, doing good work is an important start.

IT'S [NOT] JUST BUSINESS

I'll keep it short and sweet - Family. Religion. Friendship. These are the three demons you must slay if you wish to succeed in business. —Montgomery Burns, The Simpsons

This phrase "it's only business" is not merely the cold rationalization of aggressive practices and betraying friends, but a doctrine that should provide you some honest advice in the business world. In theory, business should be straightforward, efficient, and dispassionate: every person's job is to do his part to benefit the business. If the job is an affront to your values, leave. It should not be personal.

Don't be fooled, however. *There is very little in business that is "just business".* We hire people we like and fire those we don't. Those people who crush their enemies do so not only because it furthers their business (sometimes it does, sometimes it doesn't) but often because they take simple pride in the ruthless glory of victory. The phase "it's only business" is the slogan that helps us all sleep better at night—dehumanizing the difficult, selfish or unfair decisions that are made.

Yet many business people will embrace competition and conflict even if the best interests of the business suggest that direct competition and confrontation be avoided. In fact, the most ruthless people I know can be found in the bars at the end of the night boasting about their crushing victories. Winning and making the most money is as much emotion as it is business. We all like to win—and winning is personal.

SELFISHNESS VERSUS RIGHTEOUS INDIGNATION

Could it be that many of our most successful leaders are not selfish but actually demanding something akin to fair play? Instead of being money hungry businesspeople, could they share a sense of entitlement that accompanies the belief that they are entitled to a larger slice of the pie? It would be unfair not to give them more money and vacation days!

There are studies that have demonstrated that a person will turn down free money if that person perceives that the allocation to be unfair. Why do we get offended by a lowball offer when there are no other opportunities?

The tendency to refuse benefits considered unfair, considered irrational and illogical by economic theory, is demonstrated time and time again in what psychologists call "The Ultimate Game", an economic exercise in the human relationship with fairness. We see the same thing in the animal kingdom: primates will actually refuse to participate in activities to acquire food (and will go hungry) if past experience has told them that they have been previously allocated an unfairly small amount of food. See studies by Frans de Waal and Sarah Brosnan.

Would we trade it all for a mere sense of justice? I have met countless homeless people who have.

Michael Shermer, author of *Mind of the Market*, writes that our sense of fairness is hardwired into our psyche and argues that human nature, often confused with selfishness, is actually exceedingly fair. Shermer states that true greed is really the exception. So: are our selfish leaders really not selfish at all, but really vigilantes demanding justice?

It is much easier to function with the mindset that everything is fair; a byproduct of circumstances, leverage and so forth. The way in which an outcome is judged is as much a question of perception as it is in the equality of the outcome. In that case, fairness is entirely relative—and therefore everything is by definition completely fair (at least to someone).

Instead of becoming corrupted by the concept of fairness, it is better to focus on the desired result you seek. In the end, if you perform well, you may actually have a result that you consider "fair" (and that others might not).

"DEDICATION", "COMMITMENT," AND "PASSION" ARE STUPID WORDS

Let me tell you the secret that has led me to my goal: my strength lies solely in my tenacity. —Louis Pasteur

Characteristics such as dedication, commitment, and passion are required elements of success in any business. Unfortunately, if your greatest qualities comprise merely these traits, then you are not yet ready for success. Yes, these are considered when it's time for reviews, salary increases, and bonuses. But it is tenacity, that special thing that fights every battle all the way through to the end that sets those few special individuals apart from the rest.

Almost everyone is passionate and dedicated. I speak at entertainment conferences, where I meet thousands of aspiring musicians and writers. All are dedicated and many are remarkably talented. But few are willing to do those extra things—the knocking on doors—that it takes to finish the job. I don't care if you're dedicated. Everyone is dedicated.

The elements of success

Some would argue that tenacity is the only trait of true success. While a tenacious employee might have a tendency to alienate him- or herself from others, this drive, combined with *interpersonal skills*, characterizes both the productive, effective employee and the classic executive.

Loyalty, to a particular boss or to the company as a whole, is another key ingredient. It can offer fantastic opportunities to otherwise ordinary people, and it explains how so many incompetent people end up leading us in our business and political worlds (most notably in governmental positions and agencies where our leaders are appointed).

Another aspect of success, perhaps with little relation to work quality, is *ambition*. Ambition, when tied to tenacity, can become a true force.

Yes, it's nice to be able to work well with others, but recent studies continue to confirm another obvious characteristic of the successful businessperson: selfishness. Many of our most successful people consider themselves to be maniacally selfish, expecting and demanding that benefits and opportunities be directed toward them and not anyone else. I have discussed this finding with executives from many different industries, and somewhat to my surprise, the vast majority believed it to be accurate without question or doubt.

YOU ARE JUDGED ONLY BY WHAT YOU FINISH (AND WHEN)

It is the job that is never started that takes longest to finish. —J.R.R. Tolkien

Your effectiveness is judged in large part by what you finish and when you finish it. (Are things delivered as promised? When promised?)

Since these bottom-line achievements are so important in how we are evaluated, be sure to keep track of your accomplishments, right down to the smallest stuff, and provide the information to your manager when helpful or requested.

More importantly, if your project is coming in behind schedule, be sure to advise your clients, managers, and other people interested in the project,. A single missed deadline can easily be the only thing that is remembered, despite an otherwise successful career.

EARNING TRUST AND RESPECT

I long to accomplish great and noble tasks, but it is my chief duty to accomplish humble tasks as though they were great and noble. The world is moved along, not only by the mighty shoves of its heroes, but also by the aggregate of the tiny pushes of each honest worker. —Helen Keller

Your opinions carry no value unless you are respected. Absent trust in your judgment, nothing you do will be good enough, and everything you do will be second-guessed.

Trust and respect start with great work, but like so many things that we do every day, *true trust and respect are not built merely on the quality of our work product; they are developed in connection with our relationships with the people who evaluate our work.* Again: It's not just business.

Stay involved—but not too involved

Getting work completed in a timely manner and engaging in regular dialogue about the project indicates that you care about what you are working on and how it turns out. That's why it's important that you stay involved in your projects until they are accepted, considered, and finalized.

However, you must watch your level of involvement carefully, because too much dialogue and interaction makes you look needy, self-doubting, untrustworthy, and, ironically, not ready for respect. The capable are not needy.

On the other hand, despite how hard you work to build trust, be aware that *most trust is lost behind a person's back*. If you can be present to explain problems, redo tasks or confirm issues that may be raised, you can minimize this risk. Even if you are not at those meetings, you should set expectations and manage problems by thoroughly communicating and following up. But once you are no longer included, you have lost the ability to defend yourself and your work. Fight tactfully, but bitterly, to be included.

Cultivate trust and respect

Other ways to lose trust: getting caught lying; being found (or feared to be) disloyal; and not being perceived to listen to or follow instructions. Managers commonly check and reconfirm their employees' work without the employees' awareness; being trusted depends on your surviving those secret tests.

Find ways to stand out

If you hope to achieve legitimate prominence, you *must* find a way to stand out in your field (apart from your day job) if you really want to be trusted and respected. Instant respect is offered to those who can get the world to look their way—even if they're otherwise full of baloney.

Perception, as we will see, is often far from reality, and the larger-than-life people who speak on television and at conferences and who are interviewed in the press are often not the smartest people, but they are almost always the most respected.

Try to be like them. Write a book; today, with companies that print on demand and market your book online, it's easy and inexpensive to self-publish. Submit a paper or article to a conference or journal or give a talk in your field of expertise. Run for public office (it doesn't much matter if you win). Perhaps there are ways, specific to your field, for you to cultivate respect.

It is perfectly reasonable—and easier than most people think—to manage perceptions to help solidify respect amongst your peers, bosses, subordinates, and your industry colleagues.

If you can enhance your status and respect within your industry, you can go a long way towards ensuring job opportunities, as well as great reviews year after year. Managers' hands are tied when it comes to downgrading (or not promoting) a person who is otherwise respected by his or her peers. And it is nearly impossible not to promote folks who are able to acquire this kind of respect.

THE IMPORTANCE OF JUST SHOWING UP

Eighty percent of success is showing up. —Woody Allen

Many of the achievements in your job, like most opportunities in life, are accomplished by merely showing up.

On your worst day, your job is to just get to the office. Once you are in the office, things always manage to get done. If you show up, you will get paid and (probably) keep your job. If you don't, you won't.

OPEN YOUR EYES TO LISTEN

The ear tends to be lazy, craves the familiar and is shocked by the unexpected; the eye, on the other hand, tends to be impatient, craves the novel and is bored by repetition. —W. H. Auden

The average person does not listen.

There are fascinating studies that explain that most of the time when people appear to be listening, they are really thinking about how to respond to what is being said, or they are deciding what questions to ask, or perhaps even thinking about something entirely unrelated.

Furthermore, if you are not speaking face to face, for all you know, the person you are speaking to might be surfing the web or tapping on his iPhone. Emotional reactions and psychological issues, such as having conflicting agendas and being defensive, also get in the way of actually hearing what is said.

The speaker's statements are being constantly filtered, evaluated and judged and are oftentimes lost in the message being heard.

(Not) saying what you mean

The irony is that while people don't often listen, they also rarely say what they mean.

While a dog that wishes to be walked will run over to the leash to tell the owner that it is time to go out, humans are neither literal nor open. Our words are often colored by our emotions, and our own and others' sensitivities tend to get in the way of clear communication. In addition, the very nature of the negotiating process means that our words are chosen not to convey truth but to accomplish goals and manage the listener's reactions.

Communication experts explain that more than 80 percent of communication is visual. How we stand and move, as well as such subtleties as the placement or movement of our hands and eyes, tells others quite a bit about what we are thinking.

Body language body gives you away

Body language is highly revealing. Some experts explain that although we can't *see* people's facial expressions when they stand 100 meters away, we can *sense* whether they are furrowing their brow, grimacing, or providing some other indication of their thoughts. Body language gives us away and can change or undermine a speaker's intended message.

You gain a great deal when you refine your listening skills, particularly if you can learn to *hear* (rather: *sense*) people's visual signals. Paying attention to the speaker and taking notes are helpful. Try not to become lost in your note-taking (excessive note taking is almost as bad a habit as not taking notes at all). Ask for clarification and offer confirming questions such as, "Do I understand you to be saying that...?"

All of this is essential to understanding the task at hand. I know it is hard, but try not to start working on an idea or project in your mind until the instructions are provided and discussed to their conclusion.

How to read other people

Perhaps you might decide to learn to read others' signs by studying the literature on visual communication and body language. (Reading books on poker playing can help.)

Police interrogators attempt to identify a wide range of behavioral traits. They look to see if the person's eyes are looking up and to the left (signifying that he or she is trying to remember something or thinking it through logically), if his eyes are looking up and to the right (lying/coming up with something creative), if he is sitting forward or reclining, and so forth.

Mostly though, "visual listeners" can see patterns of behavior that can reveal as well as conceal. Poker players look for what they call "tells"—little mannerisms that reveal a person's thoughts.

Many of these *tells* and body language tip-offs do not accurately represent what they are supposed to, though the observant person can often figure out what they do in fact mean. For instance, fear causes people to suppress their normal movements; while the average person may begin biting his nails when nervous, a person who naturally bites his nails may stop when he becomes nervous. *Understanding what a person is trying to say means listening with your eyes and finding the helpful clues for that specific person.*

Interrogators and poker players alike are looking not for untruths but for signs of fear and discomfort. If someone is comfortable, he or she will be more patient and can more easily hold a conversation. If a person is fearful, he or she will display some discomfort and the response can be evaluated.

You can easily detect uncomfortable shifting. If you see *tells*, start thinking about what might be underlying this awkwardness.

True listening; know thyself

Although there are no absolutes, true listening happens only when you are aware of what is unspoken. The words mean little unless the body backs it up. And don't forget to study yourself, apply what you know, and begin to recognize your own tells. While they may come from your subconscious and be difficult to stop, they may be easy to cover. Keeping a poker face, a steady rhythm, your hands on the table, and your feet on the floor all the time might be one place to start.

HOW TO STAND, MOVE AND PAY ATTENTION

The influence of the genuine educator lies in what he is rather than in what he says. —Oswald Spengler

Communicating well requires a good visual presentation. It is hard to look comfortable and feel grounded—particularly when you are excited or defensive—and even harder when you don't know what you look like. *Be present.* Eyes forward—but don't stare—and don't forget to blink. When you stand, plant your feet. When you sit, don't shift. Set your feet or cross one leg over the other.

Television anchors freeze from the shoulders down and tuck their jackets down tightly underneath them. People who are being interviewed on television freeze with their eyes forward. Always know what your hands are doing.

In a face-to-face, one-on-one situation, settle down and assume a position of comfort and stability. Visually, your goal is to communicate that you are exactly where you want to be. Don't look past the person or people you are talking to. Don't look at your watch or smartphone. Don't move your feet. Relax your hands.

And slow down. Hurried speech, like all things reckless, is a sign of weakness. It says you're afraid to take too much time or try the other person's patience.

Instead, be patient and present in the moment. Forget that there are other things you'd rather be doing and other people you'd rather be talking to. Undivided attention and comfort signify understanding and confidence— which mean a lot to the person with whom you are speaking and ultimately reflect very positively on you.

FOLLOWING INSTRUCTIONS, ASKING QUESTIONS AND CHECKING IN

In Japan, employees occasionally work themselves to death. It's called karoshi. I don't want that to happen to anybody in my department. The trick is to take a break as soon as you see a bright light and hear dead relatives beckon. —Scott Adams, Dilbert

Practically every job description, when boiled down to its essentials, is nothing more than following the instructions you are given. There is nothing worse for an employee than not following instructions, just as there is nothing worse than your employee not following yours. If our workplaces treated people as they should, people who fail to follow instructions would be fired on the spot for incompetence or insubordination.

There are four typical reasons why people don't follow instructions. For one, as we just discussed, they don't *listen*. For another, they can't *remember* what is asked of them. Maybe they don't *understand* what is being asked of them or they are afraid of embarking on the unknown. Finally, perhaps they don't *want* or care to do the work. (There may be political games going on as well—we'll get to that later.)

Getting manager feedback

There is no shame in not understanding what is being asked of you—but there is shame in failing to ask for clarification. Many managers are poor at explaining themselves. Also, in many cases, your manager knows something that can help you do your job. In other cases, the manager can provide some insights into what he or she hopes you will or won't produce. And in all cases, the manager has a specific time frame and way in which the product or information is expected to be delivered.

If a delegator starts to show frustration with your questioning, either postpone the remainder of them or explain that you really want to do the job right and need a few extra minutes of his or her time. If you can turn your superior into a mentor for a bit, your task will be much easier.

You might say something like, "I'm sorry that I don't understand exactly what you want, but if you could take just a couple of more minutes with me to help me understand…" It is important that you check back in, particularly if you are not certain of what is being asked. Delegators hate (really, really hate) when a task is assigned and then they don't hear anything until the project is turned in late or wrong.

When YOU are giving instructions…

On the other hand, if you are the one issuing the instructions, begin testing your instructions on the spot. Don't wait for the mistake. Get the other person to repeat the instruction back to you and ask what he or she intends to do.

The improvement should be nearly instantaneous.

WHAT DO YOU KNOW AND WHAT DO YOU THINK?

Every man has a right to his opinion, but no man has a right to be wrong in his facts. —Bernard M. Baruch

"What do you know, and what do you think?" This is the slogan that I have become known for. When people walk into my office with something that they are interested in discussing, I expect that they have already gone through this process, particularly because they can expect that I will ask these exact questions. But I don't want opinions first. I want facts. We will get to the opinions in time.

It is a real and far too common problem for people to base decisions on isolated facts or rumors. Politicians do it all the time, even live on the television. Of course, we don't always know the facts right up front, but I, like most managers, despise the mistakes and wasted time that come from inattention to detail and unverified information that's believed to be true.

And yet, when I ask about facts, most people can't tell me that they are accurate. *Before you even think about thinking, think about learning. In the end, knowing what is really true is the key to doing things right the first time. That's the key to real effectiveness.*

THE FREE-TRIAL-PERIOD EXCUSE

The mistakes we aren't allowed to make in our youth, we make later on in life—at greater cost and with less benefit. —Unknown

You actually have a free pass for your first six to twelve months of employment—not only to make mistakes, but also to test recommendations and, with a sense of humility, to solicit real change. While this novelty must be handled gingerly so as to not overly upset the existing corporate applecart, your creativity and even slightly overzealous ideas can be defended with the simple argument that you are new and didn't know any better.

This new-employee gloss fades, so use this time wisely, and you might accomplish great things.

BEING AT THE RIGHT PLACE AT THE RIGHT TIME

In the real world, nothing happens at the right place at the right time. It is the job of journalists and historians to correct that. —Mark Twain

A great mentor of mine once commented to me that the key to success is being at the right place at the right time. He explained that it is not so much something achieved by luck, but rather by striving to *be all places all of the time.*

What he means, quite accurately, is that opportunities will *never* find you when you are at home in front of the television, nor when you are at the movies or alone in your own thoughts. The right place involves people and dialogue, and if you decide to go out and be in the right place, eventually you might just find yourself there.

SCARY PROJECTS, PHOTOGRAPHING MODELS AND OUTER SPACE

I would sort out all the arguments and see which belonged to fear and which to creativeness. Other things being equal, I would make the decision which had the larger number of creative reasons on its side. — *Katharine Butler Hathaway*

It can be downright intimidating to do things that are unfamiliar. Many people would rather put off the unknown, so much so that they would rather get in trouble by delaying and perhaps deception than face their fears. To alleviate those fears, I'll offer a secret: *few things in business are so complicated that they can't be easily learned and accomplished.* And here's another secret: *to overcome your fears, the best thing to do is just get started.*

I remember the first time I was asked to call a powerful district attorney to negotiate on behalf of a well-known client. I was scared to death. But, after a week of delay, I finally realized that I could not hide any longer. So I picked up the phone and found that the powerful person was actually a nice fellow. We had a good talk, and although I did not get everything I wanted, my client received more than I could have expected—and I got a great life lesson.

Here's a third secret: *many of us never stop being afraid of those complex things that might arise from time to time. If there is any one master skill, it is that the professional does his or her job regardless.* It might sound trite, but it is the overcoming of fear and challenge that ultimately makes the achievements great.

Point and shoot

I am a photography fanatic. I travel with my camera and love taking pictures of people and nature. It's pretty easy; with a little bit of knowledge and experience, it's just point-and-shoot.

When I think of facing the unknown, there has probably never been anything that has intimidated me more than the first time I was asked to photograph a model with fancy lights in a big studio. How would I talk to

---

BUSINESS: MAKING IT UP AS IT GOES ALONG

Have you heard that the majority of colds clear up within three days of treatment? Turns out, most colds that go without treatment clear up in three days as well.

How is it that some businesses continue to succeed in hitting revenue targets even when their sales are down? Some businesses are more discriminating, hitting those targets that relate to paying out bonuses—even while missing revenue targets in every other way possible. As for resources, it is worth noting that there is rarely a time in which a business cannot find the money to pay for something it wants. That includes finding funds for salaries, promotions, stock options and job offers. It's a miracle! Sometimes, it's magic—and sometimes just make believe. In any case, it is business' greatest pastime.

All numbers can be stretched, picked and adjusted. Factor can be re-weighted to make the good stuff even better and to make the bad things matter less. If you want to see this in all of its gross reality, be sure to check out *Conspiracy of Fools*, Kurt Eichenwald's fantastic book on the Enron implosion.

If you want to be impressed, Google "manipulate numbers" and you'll find 4,720,000 positive hits (that's almost 10,000,000 when you add that to a search for "numbers manipulate" and round up). That's a lot of manipulation! Enron chief manipulator and felon Andrew Fastow would be proud. See also *How to Lie With Statistics* by Darrell Huff.

---

the model? What if I messed up? I was nervous, feeling unprepared and apprehensive, and I read lots of books and web pages on the subject.

Turned out, the camera still worked as it always had. Apart from a few differences that could have been learned with a fraction of the research, all I had to do, essentially, (apart from showing up and setting up properly) was point and shoot.

These days I have begun learning how to photograph outer space, among the most technical of all photographic endeavors. So again, I've studied and read tons of books. At the end of the day, I have realized once again that after making a few adjustments and learning a few more techniques, the camera still works as it always has. You point and shoot.

New = scary

It's all scary before we start something new. *We are intimidated only when we don't recognize our potential or the simplicity of the subject with which we deal.* This intimidation goes away the moment we decide to accomplish the task. As with my experience with the camera, our brains always manage to figure it out. It works the same way it always has.

When you don't know where to start, begin at the beginning. Just get started. The scary stuff is overcome when we settle down, dig in, and decide to just point and shoot.

TAKING RISKS AND STEPPING ON LIMBS

> *I've found that luck is quite predictable. If you want more luck, take more chances.* —Brian Tracy

The typical entrepreneur is a risk-taker, willing to risk reputation and personal finances in order to reach for goals. Like most things in life, the greater the risk, the greater the possible reward.

That, however, is not how it operates when you work for someone else. It doesn't matter whether you personally are a risk-taker or are risk-adverse. *What matters is that your risk profile matches your manager's, and that your manager's matches that of the business overall.* If you step out on a limb when your business doesn't want you to, then, when the limb breaks, as some inevitably do, you will fall all by yourself.

Are you in a risk-taking environment?

Practically every company says that it prizes risk-taking, but in reality, few of them do. The amount of risk a company is willing to take varies greatly from one organization to another but is integral to the company's overall personality.

If you are more aggressive than your manager, your manager will be cautious with you. If you take fewer risks than your manager, your manager will feel that you are not ready for the big leagues. Quite simply, your level of aggressiveness will be neither effective nor helpful unless it matches that of your environment.

Matching a risk level not naturally your own can be difficult. Pushing back can appear to indicate disloyalty. Working against your superior—in this case, having a different level of aggression or risk tolerance—means that you do not fit where you are, and it is time to look for another job. Perhaps one day you will find a way to influence the risks that are taken. Until that day, adapt and adhere.

MOVING AT THE SPEED OF BUSINESS

Business is like a bicycle. Either you keep moving or you fall down. — *John David Wright*

Business actually does not move that quickly. It is laden with inefficiency, false deadlines, and scarce resources. Most tasks end up being done more than once. Deadlines are extended. People take vacations. The average business environment is aptly known as "hurry up and wait." Business moves both fast and slow, depending on your vantage point and the speed at which things are currently happening.

The more efficient you become, the more time you will have to yourself. But you might appear to be less deserving... or to lack a sufficient workload—or possibly even to be undisciplined or lazy. On the other hand, the busier we are, or pretend to be, the more we hope we will be rewarded for our undying commitment to the business and work we manage to complete.

For any given task, remember: It's not supposed to be this hard. We decided it should be, and we fake it until it is. Sensitivity to your environment will help you decide how hard you should appear to be working.

WORK SMARTER, NOT HARDER

In guessing the direction of technology, it is wise to ask who is in the best position to profit most. —Ben H. Bagdikian

In many ways, we were more efficient before faxes, emails, and voicemails. In the days of Rolodexes (those things that sat on our desk and kept all of our phone numbers and addresses on rotating business cards), when assistants would receive and process the letters and calls and help us schedule our meetings and lunches, there was rarely a call or letter that went unreturned.

These days, however, the impersonal nature of communication means that there is less of a need to meet in person and therefore less opportunity for the benefit of real interaction. It's so easy to send a lengthy email that it's no wonder that our email sits unreturned and piled up with hundreds of others, and our voice-mailbox overflows.

Work smarter, not harder. This doctrine should be plastered to our walls and ingrained into our minds. Technology and efficient methodology can save hours or days of our lives. I emphasize the word "can": endless deliberation by email, with every reply dispatched to "Send All," does nothing for efficiency.

Leveraging technology

There are few obstacles in the workplace that technology cannot help us overcome, whether it be some aspect of organization, analysis, or communication. Just a little bit of extra creative thought, and many common problems can be solved with online sites and applications.

One aspect of working smarter requires not merely working more efficiently but of prioritizing and eliminating things not worth doing at all. Doing more stuff does not mean that you are doing all things better. Ironically, some business cultures are quite adept at focusing on the wrong stuff. Existing within that environment does not necessarily mean fighting to have your view of the correct priorities inserted into the business, an oftentimes impossible task, but rather the acceptance that doing the wrong stuff well may be the only *right* strategy for survival.

THE MULTI-TASKING CURSE

Anyone can do any amount of work provided it isn't the work he's supposed to be doing at the moment. —Robert Benchley

No discussion of modern technology and convenience is complete without consideration of the multitasking curse. Technology provides us all of the resources and tools we need to perform practically any job from any location. Computers allow countless web pages, documents, and programs to be open at the same time (made even more convenient with the advent of tabbed browsing).

Unfortunately, all of these high efficiency tools used in combination are slowing us down, as has been demonstrated scientifically.* *Multitasking makes us less efficient, and it severely hinders our listening skills.*

It is common sense that when a person is trying to concentrate on several things at once, no thought or focused attention can be dedicated to any one thing. The result is an overall longer time to completion for projects and a lower quality of work.

Scientists (see, for instance, see "Multi-Tasking: Efficient or a Waste of Time?", *Psychology Today*, September 26, 2008) identify other inefficiencies, including the amount of time it takes to subconsciously decide to switch tasks (known by some researchers as "rule shifting") and the time lost as the mind releases one task and begins another (known as "rule activation").

---

* "Executive Control of Cognitive Processes in Task Switching," *Journal of Experimental Psychology - Human Perception and Performance*, Vol. 27. No. 4.

Work avoidance and other distractions

Of course, as a great yet inefficient multitasker, I think that the scientists forgot one major element in the lost time: the time spent not really working (known as "work avoidance").

To see this in action, walk around the halls in any office and look at people's computer screens. Sometimes employees will switch their screen quickly to make it look as if they have been working. In other cases just glance at how many programs are open (you'll see this in the taskbar) and check out how many of those have nothing to do with work.

And look at the seemingly incessant office parties and celebrations, the gossip sessions and the side conversations, the personal phone calls and on-line shopping and the vacation days and early departures. Looking busy is for most people unrelated to actual workload. Most people are quite literally more "pretend busy" than "real busy."

Multitasking, even If all the tasks are legitimate business projects, undermines efficiency (and others' perception of you—we'll return to that issue shortly). The solution is ridiculously easy: when you need to be efficient, turn the distractions off.

THE RESOURCE GAME: ASKING FOR MORE THAN YOU NEED

I have no money, no resources, no hopes. I am the happiest man alive. —
Henry Miller

The subject of getting more resources (*e.g.*, money, space, full-time employees, part-time employees, temps) is as political as anything else that happens in the workplace. It's not that the business world suffers from limited resources, but rather that every available resource is gobbled up by politically savvy managers and employees, whether they need it or not.

While a business' profit targets are often arbitrary, they serve to justify the withholding of otherwise available resources. When a business' resources are allocated for a given year, there will typically be no more for that year. But if all the allocated resources are not used, then next year, less will be provided, and the extra resources allocated elsewhere. Ironically, groups and individuals are punished if they do their jobs too well.

But if you don't ask, you don't get. Get it and spend it.

Once you decide to ask for resources, you enter the political resource arena. The business is accustomed to allocating limited resources among

---

BUZZWORDS, CS (CORPORATE SPEAK) AND CODE

I'm sure that you've heard such corporate classics as "call out", "tasking", "taking temperature", "seamless", "out of the loop" and "outside the box". We "parachute in" and "talk at 30,000 feet" and then "drill down". We'll "move the goalposts" to "leverage" things that are "mission critical". We "push the envelope", "level set" and "put out fires" all before we'll "pull the trigger". And then we use acronyms—we need to discuss the POS and put together a RFP with our SMEs and get an NDA by COB.

Once you've got the speak mastered, you're ready to be introduced to the buzzwords of your industry. Perhaps you might have heard the joke comedian Steve Martin told to an audience he (facetiously) believed was comprised in part of plumbers from a plumbing convention: *...so he went and got Volume 14 of the Kinsley manual, and he reads to him and says, "'The Langstrom wrench can be used with the Findlay sprocket.'" Just then, the little apprentice leaned over and said, "It says 'sprocket,' not 'socket!'"*

Language is the vehicle for all business interactions and it is essential to understand the language others are using around you. Buzzwords are like corporate speak on steroids. While corporate speak is often designed to illustrate complex concepts with coded shorthand, buzzwords are also designed to define a group (and exclude others). Buzzwords, while used to cut to the chase, are also used to confuse or embarrass others or to display superiority of knowledge.

Code words or the use of complexity could be used to form a position of dominence or to convey some kind of covert point. They are politically comfortable euphemisms, sounding great to all but having a unique meaning to certain audiences who are in the know. Inside your business, listen carefully for codes. Perhaps it is something like "expand the service base" to mean "move production overseas and fire all domestic employees". The code is designed to replace an unpopular thing with a neutral or positive statement. Examples are routinely found in politics, e.g., President Nixon's "law and order" to mean "crack down on minority crime."

---

many greedy hands, and senior managers are familiar with all of the posturing that comes along with requests.

Political moves

Savvy managers have been known to let projects falter and fail just to prove that the business needs to do a better job supporting the projects.

Some managers reserve offices, cubicles, and filing space—even when space is at a premium and even when they don't need to fill the offices or files just yet—recognizing that once the space is given to someone else, it may never be recovered. Others hoard supplies. And managers spend as much money as they are allocated, even if they don't need to, to demonstrate that the money is needed to preserve the budget allocation in future years.

The allocation decision

The request for resources is typically evaluated according to two questions: What can you offer? And what do you need?

In terms of what you can give back to the business, you must be prepared to answer the question of why the business should *invest* its resources with you. How much (or what) will it get in return?

When it comes to the actual request, consider asking for more than you need. The request is a first offer in a negotiation in which the business can be expected to provide a counteroffer. If you need one person, ask for two. If you need $25,000, ask for $40,000. It's the way the game is played.

And if you don't get it when the budget is being created, you might have to wait until next year or the year after. Anticipate what you'll need as far in advance as possible, and try not to take no for an answer.

ON SPEAKING WELL

> *Lucidity of speech is unquestionably one of the surest tests of mental precision... In my experience a confused talker is never a clear thinker.* — *David Lloyd George*

Not surprisingly, your speaking skills are closely related to your effectiveness.

SEEING WITH HALF YOUR BRAIN

Why are humans so self-critical and self-conscious? Scientists have long studied body dysmorphic disorder, a phenomenon in which some quite normal people see themselves as ugly, even disfigured, resulting in extreme and recurring plastic surgery and higher suicide rates. It turns out that people suffering from this disorder see themselves with a disproportionate amount of the left side of their brain, stuck in a place of logical analysis and over-thinking even the smallest details.

This may be the same pattern of thinking that causes some of us to judge ourselves so critically. When we think about ourselves, our appearance and our performance, and when we are stuck in over-analysis and detail, maybe we may just be stuck in wrong side of our brain.

Scientists believe that sufferers of this disorder may be able to be re-taught. For the rest of us, perhaps this simple awareness may be the key. See the December 2007 *Archives of General Psychiatry*.

Most speakers are not *good* speakers. Most are boring and uninteresting, some are pompous, and others lack credibility. When it comes to speaking, your competition is quite average, and you really have nothing to worry about. Typically the worst that can happen is that you will be just like most other people.

Speaking, however, is your most important workplace tool. Those who do it well can be tremendously successful with almost no other positive traits. Great presenters, advocates, and negotiators can make entire careers out of saying the same thing over and over to offer a clear message, easy recollection, and distinctive branding, as with politicians who have learned to win elections repeating the same speeches and buzzwords.

Skills of great speakers

Great speakers are patient and thoughtful. Many choose to speak more slowly, getting to the point in a leisurely way and making people feel as though everything is okay and in good hands. Great speakers are comforting, inspiring, and connecting.

Speaking skills can be mastered. Improving requires learning what you do and don't do well and having the patience and thought to incorporate these lessons.

Speaking in front of others is a craft, and it takes practice and care, so that when you speak you do look as spontaneous and unself-conscious as possible. Many executive coaches videotape their clients. For instance, you can learn to avoid the use of words such as "uh, um," and all of those other trip-over words, but it takes practice.

In impromptu business conversations, learning how to listen carefully and think before you speak—so that when you open your mouth, you are coherent—can be one of the greatest challenges of all.

When it comes to more formal presentations, it is helpful to remember these few truths:

First, most presenters are not good speakers. On your worst day, you will be average.

Second, everyone is nervous and self-conscious to one extent or another. The audience wants to see you do well.

Third, prepare! If you are prepared to discuss your subject, you are 95 percent of the way there. Moreover, being an expert is a cure for most nervousness.

Fourth, outline. Regardless of your subject, make sure your material flows coherently, one point into the next, and that the entire presentation has a logical sequence.

Fifth, it bores your listeners to read the materials you provide, so don't put your whole talk on PowerPoint slides. Summarize. Say something that your listeners will find interesting and valuable. Send them away with knowledge, insight, commitment (yours, the company's), or something else that they didn't have before. And here's the real secret: everyone wants to be told a story. Tell stories, and let the stories bring life to the facts. Oh… one more thing… if you keep some secrets off the materials but still within the spoken comments, your audience will need to keep coming back to you.

Sixth, don't pretend to know what you don't know. If you are asked a question that you are unprepared for, tell the group that you'll get back to them when you learn the answer.

Seventh, great speakers listen and pay close attention to their audiences. A speech is not a monologue but a conversation. Great speakers notice eye contact changes, seat shifting, and people who are interested in responding and/or disagreeing. The speaker feeds off of his audience's responses.

Eighth, humor is your best friend and worst enemy. While a bad joke can make your message much more difficult to deliver, a well-selected personal anecdote can ensure an attentive audience. But be careful—an inappropriate joke told to a group can instantly destroy your career or credibility.

Ninth, control the room. If you are speaking, you decide when the room should quiet down, and whether, when, and how to take questions. Only you should decide what you should discuss and say. Do not let your audience bully you.

Tenth, quiet down. There is no need to scream. Project your voice and presence, but remember that higher volumes tend to push people away. A quieter speaker (not too quiet, of course) tends to bring the listeners closer as they *reach out* for the words. Watch stage actors to see how they reach the entire audience without shouting or straining themselves.

Finally, relax. Everyone always survives the experience just fine. Take long breaths and pauses when you need to. Your pauses will bother you more than your listeners, and will create a sense of anticipation in the room.

In general, a fear of speaking often starts when people are more focused on themselves than on their listeners and the message. Fear is self-centered. If you can find the ability to focus on the group or your message, your fear can magically disappear. If that doesn't work, as the old adage says: picturing everyone in the nude might be your next best option (it may certainly be the most fun).

GIVING YOUR PRESENTATION ON *YOUR* TERMS

The true genius shudders at incompleteness – and usually prefers silence to saying something which is not everything it should be. —Edgar Allan Poe

If you are not ready to speak on a subject, don't. Do not let people pressure you into revealing what you think until you are absolutely ready to speak about it. Speaking prematurely is a key to disaster. Your early stumbling reflects a lack of preparation and skill and will impact your credibility and message, and any assumptions that turn out not to be true will reflect negatively.

It can take great willpower to avoid this premature lip flapping. It is very hard to tell your boss, higher-ups, or groups of people that you are not prepared to reveal even the most basic and preliminary thoughts and observations. But you must. *If you want your hard work to matter, you and your presentation, when you give it, had better be ready.*

MEETINGS, DAMNED MEETINGS

Say as little as possible while appearing to be awake.—William P. Rogers

Some meetings are essential, or at least helpful. It is certainly true that some things require face-to-face interaction. Most things, however, don't. There are statistics that show that some companies spend more than 20% of their payroll on unproductive meetings. When there are too many meetings or if meetings go on too long, a business can stop functioning.

Most meetings, including most meetings I've been a part of, just fade away, having been called for well-intentioned reasons but leaving the attendees with ambiguous messages, points lost and follow-up items never followed up on. We're too busy holding meetings to follow up on them.

Your strategies for better meetings

In order to make meetings more efficient, you must show up on time and look interested. While the person who shows up late may be trying to flex political muscle, it is disrespectful and condescending, albeit at times appropriate (e.g., if he/she is the highest-ranking person there).

Always have a pen and paper or if you are an e-note taker (in an e-note acceptance culture!), your proper device. *Pay attention.* Do NOT do other work or glance at your cell phone/PDA;* it makes you look more like a brat than a person of import.

Running a meeting is in many ways a mere exercise in trying to avoid failure. When you are hosting a meeting, prepare an agenda and keep order. Have a firm conclusion or goal in mind and offer that to the group at the start of the meeting.

When you are attending a meeting, remember to speak only when you need to. Defend yourself as vehemently as you must. But remember: the more often people hear your voice, the less they want to—and the less weight each word will carry.

Timing is key. If you speak at the very end, when a meeting is winding down, you'll just end up frustrating your colleagues.

THE MAN WITH THE SOFTEST VOICE

If A equals success, then the formula is A equals X plus Y and Z, with X being work, Y play, and Z keeping your mouth shut. —Albert Einstein

Some of the greatest CEOs and leaders of all time would attend meetings and not say a word, sometimes for months or years on end, letting the people beneath them sort out the facts and fight for their positions and ideas. They let the children squabble, so to speak.

The great power of the silence is revealed when the silent one decides to speak, and the words become holy, guiding, definitive, and meaningful. Sometimes that powerful voice is also the quietest, requiring that everything else in the room stop so that people have to reach out to practically beg to hear what is said.

---

* See, for example, the *Forbes* article on why successful (super busy) people stow their smartphones at meetings: http://www.forbes.com/sites/kevinkruse/2013/12/26/why-successful-people-never-bring-smartphones-into-meetings/#!

While speaking softly may also be a sign of weakness, including fear or intimidation, much of the greatest power is found in the silent person with the rare deliberate and thoughtful delivery. (Then again, the quietest person might also be the stupidest. I've seen it go both ways.)

SILENCE, PATIENCE, AND BALANCE AS TOOLS

It is a well-known proposition that you know who's going to win a negotiation: it's he who pauses the longest. —Robert Holmes a Court

As a negotiating or interrogation tactic, silence is perhaps the most powerful tool we have. If we want someone to speak more, all we have to do is not say anything. If we are looking for a negotiating concession or an admission, often all we have to do is be patient enough to decide that there is no need to speak.

When no one else talks, people have a tremendous desire to fill in the blanks. People hate silence, they can't shut up, and so they don't take the time to think.

It is okay to take all the time you need to think. It's okay to ponder and contemplate. It's okay to diffuse stress and anxiety by indicating that you are not in the midst of a fire drill. Don't let the vacuum of silence suck words out of you or force your hand or your ideas before you are ready.

When I first started practicing law, I worked for a partner who liked to listen to what I had to say. Then he would sit back to think, sometimes for several minutes. It was torture for me, since at that point I was not permitted to move or write or speak—and he'd get angry if I did. Perhaps he was just making a point, but he was always tremendously articulate, and the lesson was clear.

STUPID PEOPLE DON'T ASK QUESTIONS

My greatest strength as a consultant is to be ignorant and ask a few questions. —Peter Drucker

Many people want to prove their intellect and, if necessary, pretend they know answers not merely before they've stopped to learn all of the facts, but even before the problem has been stated or information has been thought through. The brain just tries to fill in the missing blanks on its own. The solution isn't merely to slow down, listen, and think, but also—of equal importance—to make sure that you have all of the necessary facts.

And yet, the wisest and most experienced people always ask the most questions, constantly learning and listening and assuming that the facts that they have been presented with are only the tip of the iceberg, or are presented/explained by inarticulate souls.

The importance of asking questions

True experts understand how each fact might impact the answer and recognize the need to pry. Questions also entice the speaker to become more engaged and forthcoming. In addition, for those of us who could use some extra time to process the information we are given, asking questions allows us valuable time to think through our responses.

There are other reasons to ask questions. Questions fill in quiet or awkward moments. They allow others to feel important, and they create a bond. They can be teaching tools to get people to think through issues for themselves. Simple questions, such as "What else?", can be used to create an open and creative atmosphere for brainstorming. There are always other points of view, and probing questions can help to reveal them.

There's nothing wrong with requiring yourself to always ask a few questions before proceeding.

When NOT to ask questions

People who ask questions are usually perceived to be more helpful to the business. There are, however, four very important moments when you should not ask questions.

The first is when you don't need the answer and the question can be interpreted as a waste of time; second, when your question resembles more a challenge to authority than an innocent inquiry (unless the challenge is your goal); third, when the question would convey a sense of weakness; and fourth, when you would rather not have the answer.

Executives, even those who despise being put on the spot in meetings and public settings, are expected to know exactly what masterful thing they should say next. When they (or you) don't know what to say, remember that there is almost no occasion in which a question or two would not suffice in place of a brilliant comment. Help yourself by memorizing an assortment of standard questions in advance. Many are applicable to almost any situation. Remember such golden (meaningless) favorites as:

"Can you elaborate a bit more on that?"

"How are we going to pay for that?"

"Do we have the resources?"

"What is the time frame for completion?"

"Is there any flexibility there?"

"What else do we need to know?"

"Are you getting what you need from my group?"

"Who else has been involved in this?"

"Who else do we need to get involved in this?"

"Are there any deal-breakers?"

"Do we have management buy-in?"

"Are these decisions final?"

"What are the open issues?"

"Can you give an example of what you mean?"

"Have we thought about . . . ?"

"How will we handle . . .?"

"Are there any other options?"

"What are we hoping to achieve by . . . ?"

Any of these questions can make you look engaged, competent, and necessary to the process. However, if none of these work, just come up with problems.

While detractors can be big problems for a business, all problems must be discussed and contemplated (until dismissed or resolved), and raising questions can help you look like a hero unless you were expected to be the authority on the point of your question—or the question itself is politically unwelcome.

STUPID PEOPLE DON'T REHEARSE STUFF

If I am to speak 10 minutes, I need a week for preparation. If 15 minutes, 3 days. If half an hour, two days. If an hour, I am ready now.
—Woodrow T. Wilson

Practically no person alive, no matter how brilliant, is able to speak intelligently and be captivating on any subject without thinking through, and in some way rehearsing, what he is about to say. Some people can rehearse on the spot and in their minds, but most others rehearse with written statements, outlines, or note cards. Some keep a list of single words that are trigger topics for discussion.

No matter how they get there, the best speakers and thinkers rehearse. The rest just tend to look like amateurs.

WRITING WELL

What is written without effort is in general read without pleasure. —
Samuel Johnson

Many very smart people do not know how to write well, and a surprisingly few know how to spell or use punctuation with consistent correctness. The most significant cause of bad writing is not reading, never mind proofreading, what has been written.

There are tools embedded in word processors and email systems that help with grammar and spelling, but they are not enough. You, or someone you trust, must read (perhaps aloud) what you write. Sleep on it (whenever possible). It's always best to see something with fresh eyes if you have the time.

Broader issues of clarity and coherence are just as important as mechanics, If not more so. Make sure that each sentence Is internally clear—and clearly connected to the previous and following sentences.

Another pair of eyes

Also, ask another reader to critique your writing. Many top executives ask each other and people they trust to review their drafts. (Since I am their lawyer, many executives provide their memos to me for my thoughts.)

We are all part of a team that wants everything we put out there to be well-written, and as a team, we review each other's key letters and memos. We have learned that our own eyes are not our best allies. And with the written word as important as it is, writing without reading can produce disastrous results.

Good writing is so essential and integral to your success and that of the business that the constant improvement of your writing should be a lifelong endeavor. Clarity, organization and conciseness are essential, and your ability to inspire and persuade with the written word is a brilliantly powerful tool.

I regularly use a text-to-speech program that I purchased for $30 (Nextup's *TextAloud*) to read with exceptional clarity the documents that I write or need to review.

Hearing the document aloud helps me stay focused, and I am far better at detecting problems and errors that I hear long after my eyes have glazed over. Of all of the investments that I have made in technology, this little program has kept me out of the most trouble.

MEMOS, EMAILS AND VOICEMAILS

A memorandum is written not to inform the reader but to protect the writer. —Dean Acheson

If you want to be effective, remember that no matter what you have to say, don't expect anyone to actually read more than a few paragraphs of what you write, and no one should be expected to listen to a long voicemail message (most of us delete messages very quickly).

The written word lives forever. It is saved and passed around. In many cases the words outlive us. Once we release them, they're out of our control. And with all of the stuff that people have to read these days, even a two-page memo might take a month for someone to get to, and when the item is finally read, the reader might not even get beyond the first couple of paragraphs.

Get to the point and wrap it up.

Put your words out there with these caveats in mind. Get to the point. What do you want? What are you trying to say? What is the next step? What do you propose? How will you follow up? Wham bam. Wrap it up.

What you write and say has permanence. Never leave a note or message that you wouldn't mind being broadcast around the world.

PLAYING WELL WITH OTHERS (TIME, ATTENTION, AND GIFTS)

If you want to build a ship, don't drum up people together to collect wood and don't assign them tasks and work, but rather teach them to long for the endless immensity of the sea. —Antoine de Saint-Exupery

We rarely get to choose who we work with. Some people have a natural charisma that makes connecting with people very easy and carefree. For others, particularly people who are socially awkward, this social thing can be a terrible experience. Because our communication styles and human interactions are so innate and ingrained in our personalities, the only way to change or improve them is to take a step back and gain as objective a view as possible.

Fundamentals of team play

Experts agree that the key to getting along with people is to let them know that they matter to us. Appreciate the fact that we are not the center of their universe and are mere players in their lives. We are no better than they are, and they are working hard as well. Give them our time and respect.

First of all, lower your voice. Loud people come across as trying to jam things down other people's throats. Don't stand over or too close to other people in a power/dominance position. Listen. Don't interrupt—don't even look as if you want to say anything. Being antsy to jump in is just as distracting as actually interrupting.

Recent reality shows such as *The Apprentice* are effective models of the characteristics that work for leaders as well as team participants. A specific etiquette and protocol go into successful team playing, and these can be learned by observation and practice (now more than ever, given the advent of reality television). Note: being an aggressive businessperson is not necessarily incompatible with being soft-spoken, respectful, and trustworthy.

Let other people win from time to time. This is one way to allow your shared activities to strengthen your friendships. Losing to people of authority allows them to assume the mentor's role, keeping them exactly where you want them.

Let people think you've revealed a secret to them. Knowledge is power, and people love to feel confided in.

Pick your battles. It is okay to avoid challenging every single point and issue. Everyone needs to find a victory here and there.

Finally, *contributions and gifts*. A "contribution" is not a personal gift, but something that makes the group's job easier (I'll talk about personal gifts elsewhere). Something as small as bringing donuts to a meeting instantly causes you to be recognized as an other-people-centric person.

Of course you don't want to be perceived as a sucker or pushover, but endearing yourself to other people, particularly people who intimidate you or to people you intimidate, is often accomplished with something as simple as a donut.

Gifts do matter. They single-handedly accomplish two goals: They let the other people know you are thinking about them, and people who receive your favors and gifts become psychologically indebted to you. It is hard to not like, or at least feel a need to repay, someone who has given you a gift. This includes acts of friendship, such as invitations to parties and social meetings.

The power of bribery

Yes, in business we bribe people to be our friends. And we are happy to be bribed. Not with outright cash of course, but with things like drinks, meals, sporting tickets, birthday and holiday notes, and spontaneous/unsolicited favors. Unless there is a legal or moral conflict, business bribery is a perfectly acceptable and powerful tool.

THE GRANFALLOON - THE KEY TO ALL GROUP FORMATION

When Kurt Vonnegut first created his fictional concept of the Granfalloon (in his 1963 novel *Cat's Cradle*) he perhaps defined the entire dynamic of how groups form and relate to each other in politics, business and friendship, and it is embodied within every war that has ever been fought. If it's not yours by blood, someone has to grant it to you, and we grant things to people with whom we share a bond. The Granfalloon reflects this bond.

The Granfalloon is a connection among people, otherwise similar, *based on nothing of any real significance.* The "Granfalloon Technique" is a method by which people are persuaded to join a particular social group or Granfalloon. Henri Taijfel, the British social psychologist, defined the "minimum group paradigm," in which total strangers naturally form into groups often on the basis of entirely inconsequential criteria (in one case, a coin toss). These new groups immediately developed in-group/out-of-group bias, affiliations, friendships, loyalties and enemies.

Simple examples of modern groups of strangers include the Harley Owners Club - buy a Harley and you get a million new friends who will each look out for you (and you are expected to look out for them). BMW owners have a very tight connection as well. So do VW Bus and VW Bug owners. PC and Mac owners. Canon and Nikon users. The products can be of equivalent quality, but the rivalry will define loyalties. Customer loyalty and fan clubs of all kinds (e.g., frequent flier programs), with their token preferential benefits, exist for this reason—ensure loyalty by offering a sense of commu-

▶

ASSEMBLE THE BEST PEOPLE

The best executive is the one who has sense enough to pick good men to do what he wants done, and self-restraint enough to keep from meddling with them while they do it. —Theodore Roosevelt

I'm pretty sure that neither you nor I would be considered the best in the world at any one thing, although I do hope that each of us is reasonably good at something. *Many of the best businesspeople in the world are where*

nity. Each group member feels a bond and its members would defend each other, otherwise total strangers, in a bar fight against their perceived unified enemies. The connection establishes the the bias.

In the 1950s, a teacher conducted a study exploring the basic tenets of discrimination, separating her elementary school class into students with brown eyes and blue eyes. Two groups each quickly formed tight bonds with their members and soon began to compete and even fight against one another. These otherwise similar students began to hate one another merely because of their arbitrary affiliation.

This social bias, along with other propagandistic techniques, may explain why Nazi Germany was so successful at convincing otherwise moral and good people to become unified in the most immoral and disgusting acts perpetrated in modern history. A sense of belonging, particularly when coupled with fear, is a powerful drug. The Granfalloon is one reason why citizens agree to go to war for their country in circumstances that do not directly affect them, at great personal sacrifice, and for causes they may not believe in; and it is the reason why we will sacrifice our fellow citizens and children for a cause that otherwise has little or nothing to do with us (as individuals).

The Granfalloon is a powerful business tool as well, not only via its marketing potential (that is, its potential to cultivate the brand loyalty) but in the way a business can create a culture by disseminating these points of contact, whether real or insignificant. Perhaps you have sports in common, play poker together. I had a former boss who was in her position because she was the person who fixed up the CEO with his wife. When we say that it is "who you know," it is not critical to find old friends as it may be to identify a bond (*e.g.*, looking for a job with a person who graduated form the same school we did). We'll do anything if the bond tells us we're supposed to.

they are only because of other people. They live by the philosophy that the smart-est thing anyone can do is to surround himself with people who are better than he. Then, without hesitation or ego, they get out of the way and let these brilliant people be brilliant.

Being more effective means not having to learn everything from scratch, thus risking mistakes and an awkward learning curve. Don't reinvent the wheel if you don't have to. Work with the smartest and best people you can.

When you go to conferences, collect business cards. Build a network of colleagues; pick up the phone and call them. And for goodness' sake, ask them questions and listen. Leave the ego at home, and remember that they are better and smarter than you at certain things, and if you let them be as great as they are, they will leave you far better off.

CHANGING HEARTS AND MINDS

You can make more friends in two months by becoming more interested in other people than you can in two years by trying to get people interested in you. —Dale Carnegie

Why are people unwilling to change their minds even when proven wrong? This is basic human nature. We are stubborn. We are defensive. We suffer cognitive dissonance. We are always convinced that our ideas are the best, because . . . well, we just are.

We become wedded to the things we care about or spend time and en-ergy on. We pay more attention to people and information we already agree with; this is called "confirmation bias." We save face and protect our egos. We feel exposed, revealed, defensive and even hurt when new ideas or people come along.

The basics of strong business relationships

The following is the backbone for practically every strong business rela-tionship and negotiating technique. When it comes to working with and influencing other people, here are some of the most critical factors:

1. *Like and be liked.* People want to be around, work with, and help people they like. And as the old adage goes, we like people who like us. If you want to be liked, like other people.

2. *Trust and respect your colleagues.* People want to feel listened to and respected. Anyone who receives respect is more likely to be forthright, honest, and open. So you must be open to the other person's ideas as well as your own.

3. *Align interests.* If your interests are shared, you are far more likely to get others' attention. Most negotiations fail not because people disagree, but because people's interests are not aligned. For instance, when you want to buy a car and a car salesman wants to sell a car, it would appear as though both of your interests are aligned. But the car deal is not about the car but the money, and in that way you are interested in polar opposite results. If you can change the dynamic so that both people care about the same thing (*e.g.*, clearing a car dealer's lot so that new inventory can be brought in), the problems may solve themselves.

4. *Reduce or eliminate risks.* Most people (and businesses on the whole) are risk-neutral or risk-adverse—they avoid risks wherever possible. Even great risk takers don't take unnecessary or imprudent risks. The fewer the risks in the new idea, the more likely it is to be considered. This is why product warranties matter.

5. *Increase risks related to the old idea.* Everything is relative. Revealing the risks of the alternative ideas, particularly when compared to your *less risky* idea, makes it more likely that the new idea will be considered and selected.

6. *Reduce personal exposure.* No one wants to be embarrassed or humbled for his or her choice. Minimize others' personal exposure and you make it more likely that they will be willing to consider your idea.

7. *Increase personal reward.* Obviously, if you can reward a person for making a choice that you are trying to inspire, you are more likely to sell your idea. Even a small token (such as acclaim) may be sufficient.

These points work to influence and connect with people because they are the things people care about. Not all apply to every situation, and in many cases only one will matter. Deciding which rules to apply and how to apply them is just a game predicated on simple human nature.

THE GROUP DYNAMIC: BEWARE OF DECAPITATION

Our meetings are held to discuss many problems which would never arise if we held fewer meetings. —Ashleigh Brilliant

The study of group dynamics can encompass entire careers. A truly complete discussion would include sociology and psychology and their insights into the way people behave and communicate within the group setting. Let's simplify.

A group is not a collection of individuals but a singular creature. Every group has its own cadence and character, and individuals modify their communication, behaviors and styles to suit the group. The result has been called *groupthink.*[*]

This phenomenon results in a group's decision making process being... let's just call it... inefficient.

The group decision-making process

Decisions are reached often by consensus or majority rule without adequate research or critical thought (or by dictatorship, if there is a more senior leader present). Participants might *gently* test theories outside of their comfort zones, but *the group, and its members, ultimately finds comfort in those outcomes that provide the least frustration, anger and conflict among the most people.*

No one wants to look foolish or incompetent. People with good things to say may choose not to offer their thoughts.

The resulting decisions often display all of these flaws in group dynamics.

The swinging pendulum of groupthink

Groups *think* in the same way a pendulum swings. They swing in one direction with new ideas and opinions, gaining speed and momentum on

---

[*]   William H. Whyte, *Fortune* (1952).

the downhill, only to ultimately slow down when the idea or opinion has been vetted and participants have run out of things to say.

New opinions are then offered, pushing the pendulum back into motion. With new ideas come increased participation and enthusiasm. Then the idea gradually exhausts itself as opposition and reason find their voice and the pendulum slows, only to swing again.

Unless you are a person of significant power, avoid trying to affect the pendulum's direction with any sudden motion. No pendulum stops on a dime, and you can find yourself decapitated by the blunt force of the pendulum's momentum. If you have a counter-idea, wait until the time is right and the pendulum has slowed. Then with your idea you are able to give the group a gentle shove in a new direction.

If the group is swimming aimlessly, behaving recklessly, or even coming up with a decision contrary to your needs and desires, seek to delay or temper any final decisions rather than engage in outright battle against a group. You might offer questions that need to be resolved or introduce people who need to be consulted. If the pendulum can be brought to a peak comfortably, do so. Otherwise, live to fight another day.

Other valid excuses for delay: the meeting has run out of time; you need to check information or resources; you need certain other participants or management/department buy-in, or the like. Once out of the group setting, the laws of politics and lobbying can once again proceed unhindered.

Personalities and styles can be easily diminished, modified or magnified in the group setting, where we also find dominant individuals, advocates, wise leaders and ignorant followers, those who like to embarrass and humiliate others, and the weak who buckle under pressure and don't speak their minds.

So: *Slow down, keep calm, talk less, listen, observe body language and be watchful for that swinging pendulum.*

ARGUING IS FOR LOSERS

The thing I hate about an argument is that it always interrupts a discussion. —G. K. Chesterton

I used to love to argue. It's was fun (although not so much anymore). And while I believe that I've been right, articulate, and persuasive, most (if not all) of the time, I don't know for sure if I've ever changed a single person's mind.

No one ever really wins an argument. People entrench themselves. Between their opinions and their defense mechanisms, no one ever yields, at least not in the moment. What you win forcefully, hurts; people resent being pushed around and shown up. Instead, *change minds by offering facts and permitting others the room to "evolve".* Psychology often prevents people from instantly backing off of their positions.

Give people a way to change their mind without having to admit their fallibility. When they discover their own wisdom (even if you secretly give it to them), they are more likely to come around in their own time and on their own terms.

ANYONE CAN HURT YOU

The Bible tells us to love our neighbors, and also to love our enemies; probably because they are generally the same people. —G. K. Chesterton

If you are going to trust and rely on people, then it is important that you be a good judge of intellect, character, capability, and commitment; even so, you will be fooled from time to time. While not every person can help you, everyone has the capacity and capability to hurt you, even people who are far junior or your closest allies. This risk can be managed, but the point is this: *take no one for granted. Cultivate every relationship.*

ASK, DON'T ACCUSE

It was one of those rules which, above all others, made Doctor [Benjamin] Franklin the most amiable of men in society: never to contradict anybody. —Thomas Jefferson

If you accuse someone of something, you'd better be right—and it better be necessary. If you are wrong (and even sometimes if you are right), unless you are quite powerful, you might just find yourself grossly disadvantaged.

Some managers behave in an accusatory manner to motivate, while others use accusations to demonstrate power, control, or the capability to humiliate. Regardless, when it comes to an effective and efficient work environment, there's usually a more productive way.

Direct accusations are often better made in private. Subtle inquiries and a knowing glance are often enough to convey your awareness of a problem, permitting you the opportunity to make your point while still keeping you from embarrassing or otherwise hurting the other person. Typically, the person who has been let off the hook will feel as though you are kind and decent, and you will have acquired an ally.

Nonetheless, there are times when it is wrong to let a person off the hook. We'll get to that.

FIX THE PROBLEM (NOT THE BLAME)

If you ever have to steal money from your kid, and later on he discovers it's gone, I think a good thing to do is to blame it on Santa Claus. —Jack Handy, Saturday Night Live

There is great power in the motto "Fix the problem, not the blame." Many of the most respected and powerful executives I have worked with do not care who is responsible for causing problems. In such a case, the whole company can work toward overcoming obstacles. Other managers and many employees (most commonly, highly aggressive employees, or employees who feel threatened or disgruntled), however, are not as decent.

Problems need fixing.

Does it really matter who erred in the first place? Blame is an enemy of efficiency.

It matters, unfortunately, if you are the one at risk. Then, of course, you might choose to sacrifice efficiency for personal interests. In that case, it may be better to create your alibi before getting dragged in.

RESOLVING CONFLICTS

Peace is not the absence of conflict but the presence of creative alternatives for responding to conflict—alternatives to passive or aggressive responses, alternatives to violence. —Dorothy Thompson

Conflicts are inherent in any relationship, since we all have different personalities, wants, needs, and values. The less emotion you bring in, the more likely the conflict will be resolved in a manner that allows all parties to feel that there was a positive result.

Conflicts, however, are rarely logical. In essence, resolving them often requires one or more acts of humility, which many people are not willing to give. *Pay attention to those situations in which people, whether for good or bad reasons, dig in their heels.* Be careful not to cause the other person to entrench even further. Once that happens, logic may not be sufficient to resolve the issues. Change tactics.

If you make a concession, do so in an obvious way and ask for one in return.

Mediators will often keep the opponents in conflict separate and will go back and forth, practicing shuttle diplomacy, working to loosen everyone's entrenched positions. Others will require a group hug. Whatever it takes.

STRATEGY AND ITERATION (*I.E.*, DOING THINGS OVER AND OVER)

I think and think for months and years. Ninety-nine times, the conclusion is false. The hundredth time I am right. —Albert Einstein

Every problem requires a solution, and solutions take time.

In the legal world, simple problems often have extremely well-thought-through solutions. And as other people act and facts change, solutions must constantly adapt to the new playing field. I might change my mind and vary my strategies countless times. I go to sleep feeling as if I've got it, and I wake up with a whole new outlook.

There is no need to have the perfect answer the first time. Immature minds try to do that. Wise people learn when to stop, think, relax, and allow themselves to change and adapt. Don't end up doing the wrong thing because you couldn't wait or wouldn't allow yourself the flexibility to let your mind do what it is supposed to do: think.

Iteration is essential

The modern business model is based on this repetition. Tasks are delegated down, then reviewed, redone and eventually presented for renewed review and reconstruction. This vetting process offers fresh ideas, fresh eyes, fresh minds, and changing circumstances.

Admittedly, it is sometimes frustrating to have to solve the same problem over and over again. But remember: that *is* what you are paid to do. It *is* your job. It *is* what keeps you gainfully employed. All things are done and redone. Ditches are dug, filled and dug again. It is, quite literally, the job you are paid to do.*

---

*　There is an adage for writers: "There is no great writing, only great re-writing" (Justice Louis Brandeis). This book, like all books, is an example of this repetitive process. It would be striking to show how vastly the manuscript has changed from the first draft to the present.

NEGOTIATION AND THE SEARCH FOR A RISK-FREE LIFE

Negotiating techniques do not work all that well with kids, because in the middle of a negotiation, they will say something completely unrelated such as, 'You know what? I have a belly button!' and completely throw you off guard. —Bo Bennett

Life is negotiation.

Every time you and your loved one decide which movie to see or which restaurant to attend, you are negotiating, and you are making concessions. Every advertisement on television is a part of a longer negotiation, and every assignment you are delegated, project you take on, and request that you make includes an aspect of negotiating, whether it is in the allocation of project scope, time, priorities, resources, or attention.

Negotiation as win-win

In the workplace, the vast majority of negotiations are seemingly "win-win," that is, both parties feel that they have ended up with as much as or more than they started with. Negotiation happens with the realization that future negotiations will follow. When everyone gets what he wants, relationships become stronger, and future needs can more easily be satisfied.

When a customer has a complaint, the business, hoping for a win-win, gives the customer what he or she needs so that the business gets to keep the customer, its reputation, and the likelihood of future business; everybody wins.

The zero-sum game

The opposite kind of negotiation is the competitive style, or "win-lose." In this case, both parties are seeking to get as much as possible, regardless of whether the other person has anything left at the end. This is more common in situations in which the parties are not dependent on one another and are less likely to be negotiating again in the future.

This is called a "zero-sum game," after which the participants might end up not trusting each other at all.

In a competitive style, the result is the only thing that matters. But both styles are quite appropriate at times and might even be built into the same discussion. For instance, in business, many win-win negotiations are somewhat false: each party really wants the other to win only in the event that he himself wins personally (even at a cost to the business).

No matter what style you are using, *it is critical that you not be tricked into believing you are in a win-win when you are really in a win-lose, and it is essential that you not give away concessions gratuitously* (and don't give away something without getting something in return).

The importance of negotiating skills

While some people are quite skilled at negotiating, it is important for every person in business (and in life, for that matter) to take the time and energy to become more knowledgeable about the process and craft of negotiation.

Often your most powerful tool is having good alternatives and knowing in advance what you will do if the negotiation does not work out; that way, you know that your business (or your life) will not come crashing down if you are unable to come up with a successful result.

Negotiation as a dance

When it comes to the negotiating process, your most powerful defense starts with an awareness of the negotiating tactics being used against you.

In the end, the process of negotiating is much like a power and relaxation game, and it is often the person with the most power (or the most apparent power)—and/or the one who seems to care the least about a successful result—who usually wins. Ironically, *the person with the most power is often the weakest or the minority combatant—since the powerful are seeking to retain power, the weak are left to utilize every tool in the shed.*

Often the best defense against a tactic is to describe it to the person using it, *e.g.*, "You're trying to nickel-and-dime me right now. I know that tactic. Let's not do that." No one wants to get called out.

A negotiation is just a dance, and as long as you're dancing, you're doing just fine.

NEGOTIATING TACTICS

Here are the most common negotiating techniques happening around us every single day. Each is used so regularly that your ability to recognize the tactic you are seeing is a business prerequisite.

Deadline Games: One of the most effective negotiating tactics is the use of deadlines. If the other person's deadline is closer than yours, or is thought to be closer than yours, and missing the deadline has some real impact on him, you are likely to get some great concessions as the deadline approaches. In this case, delay. Do not let your deadline be known, or if it is known, diminish its meaning. Add deadlines of your own for the other person to chew on, *e.g.*, "If you accept by 11:30 A.M., then..." or "I'll be going on vacation tomorrow night for seventeen weeks."

The Boss-Is Gone: This common technique refers to a person's position, regardless of seniority, as a mere messenger or lackey, *e.g.*, "I think that would be okay, but I'll have to check with my boss." The boss (or hypothetical boss) then seeks additional concessions.

The Divide-'em Up: This is the backbone for most corporate politics. Persuade each person separately, and then use the consensus against any person who has not agreed.

The I'm-an-Idiot: Play the role of an inexperienced person to reduce the threat to other people. If you can get the other person to assume the role of a teacher or mentor, you will not only take away his aggression—you might even find him looking out for your position in the negotiation. This technique is very powerful and often helps get things done in a nonthreatening way.

The Are-You-Stupid?: No one likes to look like an idiot. This tactic is often used by a fast-talking negotiator, particularly against young people or those who care deeply about how they are perceived. The tactic presents complicated thoughts as if they are foregone results in order to force the other person to either (i) say that he doesn't understand what is being said, which is embarrassing, or (ii) allow the negotiation to charge ahead, and thus become a victim of the process.

The Non-Negotiable: Explaining that some things are simply not up for negotiation is sometimes enough to convince others that they just have to accept the deal on your terms.

The But-It's-Typed: Present documents in a way that looks as if changes are impossible or highly inconvenient.

The You-vs-You: Say, "That's not good enough," to make a person up his/her offer with no corresponding concession.

►

The Gossip: If someone doesn't act in a cooperative, fair, or decent manner, let that person think that you will tell others. No one likes to be told on—at any age.

Other, Better Deals: Suggest that you have better options elsewhere and don't have any real vested interest in the outcome of this discussion.

The Prostitute: Get the money or a big deposit or commitment upfront to lock the other person in.

The Square-Dance: Add another person to the negotiation, and start talking again about the things you don't like.

Only the Facts: Have and use data, numbers, and statistics to support your objectives.

The U.S. Congress: Fuzzy math and the ability to pick and choose only the numbers that can help and to frame those numbers only in ways useful to your cause—these can allow you to come up with practically any mathematical result you want. The more complicated, the better—and the more difficult to refute. Use your numbers both to support your position and to prove the other person's position is incorrect.

The Lowball: Start at one extreme to set an overly favorable ending point and test your opponent.

Paper Mountain: Overwhelm your opponent with too much information.

Revealed Secret: Create trust or a bond by offering a secret that the other person thinks is confidential.

Revealed Secret II: Let the other person think that a secret of yours has been accidentally revealed, a secret that they can take advantage of or that you can feign offense. Of course, this is all according to your plan.

The-Important-But: Make something seem valuable, and then concede it in exchange for a concession from the other person.

The Ultimatum: Take it or leave it. Force the other person to decide whether the items remaining in dispute justify walking away from the discussion. This is highly effective once a substantial amount of time or confidence has been invested in the outcome.

The Plea Bargain: Offer a way out to the other person, often personally, to avoid the consequences of a worse experience if they don't go ahead.

Good Guy/Bad Guy: A person will bond and connect with a more pleasant person or experience, then begin to take measures to avoid being again subjected to an uncomfortable setting. For instance, this tactic is most often associated with a police interrogation when one officer is terribly mean and the other seems to befriend the person being interrogated and offers to protect that person from the bad experiences. P.S.: it is possible to be both good guy and bad guy, but the tactic is most often employed by two or more people.

The Split-It: Set a final point midway between two positions in order to get one last concession out of the other person.

The Good-Deal: Offer only options that already have everything you want.

The Steamroller: Threaten to crush the opponent personally or professionally if he doesn't agree.

Walking Away: This is another form of the ultimatum. Prove that the other person cares about something more than you by walking away or threatening to walk away. This can evoke a concession—or create a desperation to keep the negotiation alive by any concession necessary.

The A-la-Carte: Negotiate everything separately.

The Fixed Price: Require that everything be negotiated together.

The Nickel-Dime: After the negotiation is over, bring up small things to negotiate in hopes of extracting more concessions.

The Oops-Forgot: Bring up one last thing as the deal is being signed.

The Savior: Show how much they need you and how you can save them.

The Armageddon: Paint a horrible or out-of-control picture that will result if the other person doesn't agree with you.

The Got-No-More: Say that you can't afford it and appeal to your opponent's decency.

The Don't-Do-This: Appeal to the other person's human sensitivities and explain the trouble or position you are in if there is no favorable agreement.

There are many other negotiation strategies, each preying on relative and perceived power differences, each concerned with the things you want or need, your fears, or the risks you want to avoid. Recognize the tactic. And study this stuff... it's important.

RELIGIOUS, POLITICAL, SPORTING, AND OTHER CONTROVERSIAL VIEWPOINTS

It means nothing to me. I have no opinion about it, and I don't care. —
Pablo Picasso

It is possible that you might be more effective with certain people if you share your differing viewpoints (see *Arguing...* above). But it is far more likely that you won't be.

Respect and dignity in the workplace, when it comes to anything personal and controversial, are founded on non-disclosure.

Even in my workplace, where everyone has strong opinions, most of us don't even know each other's political views.

Why you must play "keep-away"

Religion, politics, sports, and other common/shared topics of conversation can offer common ground and even bonding opportunities. Relationships can be built upon healthy, enjoyable debate. However, *when someone feels alienated or offended (most notably the people overhearing and not participating in the discussion), they seldom speak up about it. Rather, they silently stew in anger or plot passive-aggressive revenge.*

Take sports. Discussions can get loud and highly technical, with last night's scores, player trivia and gossip, team preferences, and so on. There is no limit to the duration of a sports discussion—which is unfortunate for the people in the neighboring area who don't care about it.

Like religion and politics, sports is a controversial topic that alienates the people who disagree; it ends with that Yankee fan (me, for one) debating a Red Sox fan over something that causes us to not want to work together for a while (at least until after the season). Or it simply excludes others who then feel left out.

Take religion. There's nothing wrong with demonstrating values, and even some symbolism that is important to you. People who talk about religion (in the typical workplace) do risk alienating others, even those of the same religion.

And if you talk too much about any of these hot-button subjects, you'll sound distracted and disconnected. Strong opinions on non-business topics get in the way of business. And nobody likes a fanatic.

SCHMOOZING IS A JOB REQUIREMENT

All lasting business is built on friendship. —Alfred A. Montapert

Effectiveness means avoiding certain topics—but business is about engagement. You must schmooze.

The word "schmoozing" sounds disingenuous. Good schmoozing is not. The more people you know, the better and more efficiently you can do your job.

Books on schmoozing tell us that we are all human, regardless of position, stature, or résumé, and that humans like to talk. Ask a question and you'll get an answer.

People who meet celebrities are always surprised when they realize that the celebrity is actually smaller than they'd imagined—and friendly, approachable, and really quite fallible and real. Visit a major business or political leader at home, and the person seems just like any other nice neighbor or relative that you would visit.

Basics of schmoozing

Talk to people. Ask them questions. Don't tell them things. Get them talking, and find things you have in common. Give a genuine compliment and ask a question. If you don't know what to say, then memorize a bunch of possible introductory lines. And in the words of Benjamin Disraeli, "Talk to people about themselves and they will listen for hours."

I know it's hard, but approach people of greater stature than you. That super-important person might even enjoy your conversation, but the worst that could happen is that he won't remember you. There is nothing to be embarrassed about. Just be polite, and you will either find opportunities or end up right where you started—never any worse.

Then follow up.

And then follow up. And then follow up quickly and with the idea of building a relationship. This is the key add-on to schmoozing—and the most common failure. *The connection is built not during the conversation but in the first interaction that immediately follows*, because people tend to forget you within hours or days. As far as contacts go, even when you get blown off, you've made the contact. Send an email that says, "We met at ..." and you will instantly have a tool to help break through that ice.

Schmoozing can be fun. Remember that.

ENCOURAGING FREE SPEECH

> *It is by the fortune of God that, in this country, we have three benefits: freedom of speech, freedom of thought, and the wisdom never to use either. —Mark Twain*

I'm not suggesting that you spend your time gossiping. Well... I am, actually within strict limits.

You need to know what is going on around you, what people are thinking and doing, and whether your people and others around you are happy or miserable. Gossip, more theirs than yours, is how you find out what work is coming and what your employees, manager, and other executives might be concerned about.

Like corporate politics, gossip affects every aspect of the workplace and directly relates to the things you are responsible for. The more you know, the more you know how to navigate your business.

You need to have something to offer in order to get gossip. It is a *quid pro quo*.

Gather input for your gossip

It's true: information really is power. Any information, including the news, can easily make you more effective, so don't just limit your information-gathering to the office.

If you can, run a few web searches when you first arrive in the morning to find out if your company, your competitors, your products, or your field of expertise made the news. When you find something of interest, send around an update to prove that you care about your subject matter and are engaged. If the information proves helpful, you may find yourself right on the cutting edge.

Why we love gossip

What makes gossip and information exchange so effective? Somewhere in our subconscious we take an interest in the lives of others (witness all of the entertainment channels and tabloids), as well as joy in the misery of others.

Taking joy in others' pain is known by the German word *schadenfreude*. It is rooted in the same part of the brain that shows delight in food and sex and enjoys gawking at car wrecks while we drive by. We love rumors, even inaccurate ones.

So it's no surprise that few people can keep a secret, and the worst information always gets out. It is entertainment, and it spreads as quickly as a virus. Everybody talks, even those we trust. Everything gets out. With every person, no matter how close, there's the likelihood that they'll reveal the

---

ESSENTIAL GOSSIP

Is there any way to keep gossip out of the workplace? No. Try as you might, you will lose. While some environments may suffer the negative consequences of gossip, healthy organizations tend to gossip just as much. Gossip is as much a bonding experience as it is divisive.

Psychologists have revealed that we humans are actually hard-wired to gossip. Gossip, both the good kind and the backstabbing kind, is used for a wide variety of reasons, including networking (looking for personal opportunities), gaining influence (maintaining social position) and social alliances (friendships), exploring other people's motivations, and determining whether or not that person belongs with a particular group. See "The New Word on GOSSIP" by Nigel Nicholson, *Psychology Today*, May, 2001.

---

things you've confided with them—at least to someone. (As Ben Franklin said, "Three can keep a secret if two of them are dead.")

So keep your ear to the ground. Gather what you can, but be very careful what you say. And trust no one.

THE ART OF LOSING YOUR TEMPER

He who angers you conquers you. —Elizabeth Kenny

Losing control of your emotions is a terrible thing to do, and a true temper tantrum or anything suggesting violence is absolutely inappropriate in the workplace.

However, *looking as if* you have lost your temper can be a valuable tool when used properly (though it carries a substantial risk of misuse). As you grow more powerful, your temper (even an irrational one) may even become an asset (provided it is not on social media). People respond to emotional outbursts, and if controlled and used thoughtfully, particularly if you are in a position of power, an apparent loss of control can be effective.

Many of the best negotiators will plan their temper tantrums and even rehearse their "spontaneous" lines.

BEING BORED AND UNINSPIRED

If you don't like your job you don't strike. You just go in every day and do it really half-assed. That's the American way.
—Homer Simpson, The Simpsons

Boredom happens. There is not much you can do about it. Keep it to yourself. Build and try to follow a to-do list. And get over it before anyone notices.

LIES, OMISSIONS, AND CONSPIRACY THEORIES

If anyone at all is to have the privilege of lying, the rulers of the State should be the persons; and they, in their dealings either with enemies or with their own citizens, may be allowed to lie for the public good. — *Plato*

I have learned not to trust people in general. It's not that I think that everyone is intentionally lying to me. I merely believe that what I see and perceive is more a presentation than a complete truth. I believe in self-protection and personal bias and that most lies are not conscious but are the product of unique perspectives and vantage points.

The ubiquity of lying

If we define a "lie" as anything that is said *on purpose* that is *not the truth* (including half-truths and lies by omission) and with the intent that the statement be *taken as truth*, then everybody lies every single day, albeit often without intent or malice. Nevertheless, these *lies*, particularly when others end up relying on them, can cause all kinds of problems. The effective business person sees these lies for what they are—not good or bad, just common.*

Of course, we lie to ourselves. We say things driven by the psychological need for self-protection, which creates defensiveness or bias. Examples include down-and-out people who believe that the whole world is against them or employees who perform poorly but believe that the fault belongs to everyone else.

Cognitive dissonance and self-deception

Cognitive dissonance leads to other psychologically-driven lies and beliefs that create our biases—for example, people who believe, without regard to objective data, that their child is the best because it is the one they birthed...

---

* Studies have demonstrated that individuals lie at least once per day. A 2002 study by the University of Massachusetts Amherst (June 10, 2002) demonstrated that 60% of adults couldn't go ten minutes in a conversation without lying. Interestingly, many lies about happiness result in an increase in happiness. Lies about student GPAs translated into many instances of an increase in subsequent GPAs. See also, U.S. News and World Report, *We're All Lying Liars: Why People Tell Lies, and Why White Lies Can Be OK* (May 18, 2009) or that whatever restaurant costs the most must have the best food…or that the umpires' calls in sporting events are always wrong when assessed against their own team…or that the politicians one supports are always right on every issue when every other politician (and party) is always wrong. We eventually even buy into our own arguments, no matter their validity.

Then, via a process I referred to as "confirmation bias," we seek out and believe only that which supports or confirms the views we already hold. There are so many other bases for formulating ingrained positions. Generalization bias allows the current perception of truth to be drawn from circumstances of the past. "I love you" bias (named by the author) is the

COMMON LIES IN BUSINESS

Here are a few very common lies told daily around the workplace. These are real lies because they are untrue statements told in a manner suggesting that they are true. Business relies on these lies to its detriment every day.

1. The "Bold Faced" Lie: Perhaps the least common but the only lie that is absolutely inappropriate. This is the blatant, intentional and perhaps malicious lie. I place in this category people lying for personal benefit, or more maliciously, to start rumors, hurt others, or cover their butts.

2. The "Innocent, Philanthropic (White)" Lie: This is perhaps the most common and acceptable lie told throughout all of society. It is a lie designed to avoid harm and offense. Examples include telling someone in a hospital that he will be okay, or telling someone that the new hairdo looks good when in fact the do is not so good. The lie causes no serious harm if revealed.

3. The "You Can't Handle the Truth" Lie: This is the kind of lying told by managers when they are planning to lay people off but don't want to cause an emotional scene.

4. The "You're Not Ready for the Truth" Lie: This is the kind of lie told by a manager to an employee when the manager is still thinking about how work is going to be divided or who will be promoted, e.g., "We haven't decided anything yet." Also, this is the lie told by employees who are interviewing elsewhere when they explain that they are merely going to a doctor's appointment.

5. The "I'm Protecting You" Lie: This lie is told (or information is withheld) to protect a person's feelings—perhaps not revealing what others think of them or telling someone that everything is fine when that person is on vacation to help him or her have some nice time off when if fact the building is burning down.

6. The "Negotiating" Lie: This is the lie told in a business negotiation when someone says, "We have no budget for that" or "I can go no higher than $25,000," or "I don't have the authority to agree to that; let me check with my manager."

7. The "Interrogating" or "Forced Admission" Lie: This is the lie told when someone is trying get to the bottom of some facts or looking for some scoop. For example, a manager knows that an employee has violated a rule, and the manager either decides to learn more facts, pretending not to know anything and thus not tipping his hand, or tries to get the employee to admit the mistake or cover-up.

8. The "Keep a Secret" Lie: This lie is told when you are trying to explain to someone that you know nothing about something (such as a secret) that you actually are quite familiar with. This lie is different from the bold-faced lie, although told intentionally and with the intent of lying, because the intention, while lying to one person, is to keep a promise by telling the truth to another (i.e., that you would keep a secret). This liar, by societal standards, is doing the just and principled thing, and that on balance the truth weighs more than the lie.

9. The "Simple Mistake" Lie: Also known as the "Stupid Customer Service" Lie: This is the lie typically told by someone who thinks he's telling the truth, but is totally wrong— it's often something told as absolute fact though based on incorrect assumptions. This lie can be as innocent (albeit possibly expensive and inconvenient) as someone giving you the wrong time for the departure of a plane – or as serious as a mistake that affects the business or relationship with a customer. It is a lie because it is intentionally told, incorrect, and, although now too late, could often have been easily fixed with any attention to detail. Here, the lie is in the misrepresentation of assumed knowledge.

10. The "Omitting" Lie: This lie is something that is technically true but misleading because a key piece of information is left out. This is the lie told by hotels when they give a room rate before actually charging extra mandatory fees for a recreational facility that you didn't even know existed.

11. The "Wild Guess—Lazy" Lie: This lie is told when someone is too lazy to find out the facts and they (often quite eloquently) take a wild guess and represent their statement as having been researched, e.g., "Yes, I looked into that and ..."

12. The "Get Off My Back" Lie: This lie consists of whatever will get you off someone's back. Perhaps this might be something such as, "You can call me on the cell," when there is no intention of ever picking up the phone when it rings, or "Let's talk on Thursday to plan a time to speak," when there is no intention to plan a meeting. Common behavior associated with this lie might also include dodging phone calls or other delay tactics.

13. The "It'll Be True Before You Realize It's a Lie" Lie: This might be something such as "It's done," when the person intends to stay late or get in early the next day to finish the job.

14. The Braggadocio Lie: The lie of bragging is designed, whether by exaggeration or untruth, to bolster one's reputation for egotistical or professional purposes. This lie includes shameless self-promotion and might extend to the creation of an artificial persona.

15. Obvious Transparent Lies: Lies such as exaggeration and sarcasm are intended to be received in the same form as offered, with transparent obvious overstatement or for ironic wit or point. The listener is left to guess how much these hyperboles stretch the truth.. Euphemisms designed to hide sexual or other meanings from children may fit into this category, although from the child's perspective the lie, if discovered, may be less innocent.

16. Other Lies: Other categories of lies include lies designed to benefit the victim (such as telling someone that you need to make a stop when in fact you're going to a surprise party), or to prevent great harm (not telling a neighbor that his wife is having an affair).

requirement that we side with and accept the positions of our friends and those we like (and do not wish to hurt). "Anchor bias" is what causes us to hold onto an initial position, defending the position even after it has been discredited. "Lazy bias" (again, named by the author) is the acceptance of facts which lead us to the path of least effort or work. There are so many other platforms for self-deception it is rather scary to assemble them all in one place.

One important note—we are not talking about outright deception, but reasons why our brains trick us into making a decision which may or may not have been the right one. This is subconscious. The lie is told to ourselves by ourselves, and we buy right in.

Our inability to overcome these innate obstacles keeps us from changing our minds, learning and growing. Thus we humans are all kept at least one step away from total honesty.

If you don't think that people are truly capable of lying to themselves, take a few minutes and watch the *People's Court* on television—or for a more hands-on experience, visit your local courthouse.

Lying and effectiveness

At some point, the business world concluded that certain lies are acceptable to one extent or another. The public has long tolerated all lying of all kinds, and while particularly evident in politics and business, these same lies are evident in daily interactions with our families and friends. Society not only tolerates such deceit, but rewards it, insofar as we reward the people who play the game better—regardless of the lies told on their way up the ladder.

Improving your efficiency and effectiveness means being better able to recognize and see through human behavior to get at the facts and truth. Question everything. Find the bias and personal interest. It often takes just a single innocent follow-up question to reveal that the original statement was entirely unfounded or unresearched, and anyone who relies on a single unsubstantiated thing told to them can get into some really big trouble.

With years of experience, I have learned to question nearly everything that is provided to me and ask for explanations when I can't actually see what makes up the underlying substance. There is always another side to every story. This insight is offered without cynicism (well...maybe a little) but instead with a love for business and a rudimentary understanding of human nature.

So really, defending lying and politics is just a defense of all of humankind.

There are four ways, and only four ways, in which we have contact with the world. We are evaluated and classified by these four contacts: what we do, how we look, what we say, and how we say it.
—Dale Carnegie

PERCEPTION & SELF-REFLECTION

PERCEPTION IS SURVIVAL. It is, as they say, reality. It is all we know.

Success in business is based largely (if not exclusively) and perception. This is not surprising, for we tend to trust, respect and promote the people we like and not trust the people we don't.

In these considerations, we tend to like the people who we believe are helping us—and dislike those folks that might be hurting us (whether in performance or politics). And we tend to like those people who are funny and fun to be around, and we're indifferent to people who are not enjoyable company. These determinations, while entirely subjective, are important in defining the fabric of our relationships and potential.

It's a popularity contest.

In the end, success in business is very much a popularity contest, and people will go to great lengths in order to be liked more than someone else.

In many ways, this all makes sense. A person's ability to be effective can be greatly improved if there are established relationships to draw upon. Are you someone I trust? Are you competent? Are you a decent person? Would

I let you date my son or daughter? Who are you, really? And who are you to the people around you?

I will base my conclusions on everything I know about you, including how you look, dress, smell, act, and move, the people you associate with, all of our past experiences, and all rumors and gossip.

See yourself the way others do.

How many of us perceive ourselves as others do? When we look in the mirror, we see an image colored by our deepest held beliefs—or fears—about ourselves. But when others look at us, they may see someone fatter or thinner, with more or less hair and wrinkles than we see. We sound different to ourselves than we sound to other people (actually, this happens for anatomical reasons).

And when it comes to our personality, we are often equally blind, not realizing when we are going a bit too far, being offensive or losing the connection with the people around us. We color the world with our own lenses, and we see the world and ourselves through the limited perspective of our own lives.

Quite simply, we are not the people that others see. And we see other people differently from the way they see themselves.

One of the most important skills a person can have is the ability to see oneself and all of one's problems through the eyes of others. If you can find a way to do this, you can become easier to connect with and work with, and you will find fewer obstacles to influencing the people around you.

Perceptions as promises

On the other hand, other peoples' perception of who you are becomes an inadvertent promise. If you are perceived to be honest, for example, and are later revealed to be a liar, people's resentment will magnify. This is why priests and police officers have it so hard when they go astray.

Here are some initial thoughts to get us going:

First, take an interest in understanding how others perceive you. If you are perceived to be a leader, then you are. If you are perceived to be a hardworking, dedicated and committed person, then you are. And if you are perceived to be lazy, then you are.

Second, if you are perceived to be virtuous, honest, decent, and hardworking or any other wonderful thing, then you have an obligation to live up to that standard. It is unfair sometimes, particularly because you never intended to promise to be anything special in the first place. You are regular-human, not superhuman. But letting people down when they think you are superhuman can be very harmful and serious.

Third, remember, other people are not necessarily as you perceive them; the one thing you know for sure is that they are all flawed, just like you. They walk, talk, sleep, poop, work hard, fight with their significant other, have problems with their children/parents, get in trouble for not doing things around the house, and everything else you can imagine, all just like you. And like you, they are the beneficiaries and victims of their own perceptions and are working hard to manage them, just as you are.

Remember, perception accompanies age and position. For instance, no matter how much I like to joke around, I am an experienced lawyer. The younger employees and other business professionals should not see me as anything other than a person of authority.

While I do like beer and wings, if I act young (even if that's my true self), I will never be perceived as one of the gang, but just as a weird, creepy, erratic, immature lawyer. Being perceived as an authority figure is an essential prerequisite for me to succeed at my job, but it means that success in my profession means hiding away a part of my life that I quite enjoy. Perception wins.

BEING A CARING, PASSIONATE, TEAM-PLAYING, THOUGHTFUL, CORPORATE-PREACHING, SHOWING-UP, FINISH-THE-JOB KIND OF PERSON

It is amazing how much you can accomplish when it doesn't matter who gets the credit. —Harry S. Truman

Many of us aspire to be a unique individual with personal interests and private lives, but despite what they say, businesses rarely want true independent thinkers (except perhaps for creative, out-of-the-box problem solving).

It would be more accurate to say that *businesses that value true independent thinking really do so only when it comes from people who have earned the credibility to speak on their subjects.*

For instance, I don't want anyone to tell me what the law says until that person has developed a thorough understanding of the laws that apply. Until that point, I want followers. Learn first, and then open up your mind.

Cheerleaders, team players, and the company's values

Businesses, on the other hand, want cheerleaders and team players, people who sell their souls to the collective and their manager's cause and give up the rest of their lives and personal aspirations to share in the business' thinking. While individuals within the company may have different personal values, the good corporate employee adopts the company's values in his primary daily activities. Participating means conforming.

Employment is a voluntary servitude of sorts. Following instructions and being loyal and committed are mandatory, and absent conduct that violates legal standards, your remedy to workplace injustice is either conformity or departure. Your job description, while negotiable, is entirely dependent upon the will and the needs of the business.

The perils of individuality

Individuality and strength of mind can quite literally get in the way. If you want to do things your way, go open your own business. Managers want sweatshop workers, either capable of production without supervision, or closely monitored for productivity. And they want people willing to be in the office, no matter what. *So it is in your interest to be perceived as this hardworking, caring, team-playing, showing-up, finish-the-job, corporate cheerleader who makes their life easier.* It's a bit of a personal charade.

I'm all for individuality, but as a general practice, depending on your business and culture, it may be quite inconsistent with the corporate conformity mandate.

SPIRITUALISM, HIPPIE-ISM AND ARTISTRY

Be yourself is about the worst advice you can give to some people. — Thomas L. Masson

I am a spiritual and artistic person. I keep that at home.

Most workplaces, even many of those that require creativity, do not understand spiritualism and art. Neither does the average business understand bare feet, tie dye, incense, aromatherapy, meditation, massage, nude resorts, communism, peyote, ESP, UFOs, earrings, tattoos, or body piercings.

The average person falls somewhere in the middle of the political and social spectrum. They are middle people, with middle-of-the-road levels of interest in "normal" things. You can love your art, nudity, sexuality, communal living, and meditative chants, but the more you are able to keep them out of the office, the better.

Even the most non-conforming workplace behavior conforms in its nonconformity. Non-conforming behavior is not reliably viewed as individualistic or quirky but as freakish. There is, without any doubt, such a thing as "normal."

OFFICE DECORATIONS (THE IMPORTANCE OF PLANTS)

Never go to a doctor whose office plants have died. —Erma Bombeck

Your office/space décor has two requirements. The first is to say, "Yes, I'm here to stay!" And the second is to say, "Yes, you've come to the right place. I will get the job done, trust me."

Your physical space must convey roots (even if you are planning to move). Plants are a powerful way to do this. The person with nothing on his walls conveys a transient existence; seemingly capable of departure at any moment.

Bookcases filled with books are great. Photos on the wall are wonderful. Real artwork (not company poster prints) can do you a world of good. It says that work is important enough to you to bring a piece of yourself to the office.

The state of your desk is critical. Some people build their reputations on their messiness, and if that's how they want to live, great. I'm messy at home. But I'm generally convinced that people who have piles of paper on their desk are bound to lose a paper or two (and history tells us that many of these piles will not be looked through for years).

A line from the movie *Bull Durham* is relevant here:

> *"Your shower shoes have fungus on them. You'll never make it to the 'bigs' [big league/major league] with fungus on your shower shoes. Think classy, you'll be classy. If you win twenty in the show, you can let the fungus grow back and the press will think you're colorful. Until you win twenty in the show, however, it means you are a slob."*

GOOD ATTITUDE AND POSITIVE SPIN

> *The greatest discovery of any generation is that a human being can alter his life by altering his attitude. —William James*

What makes your boss the happiest? To know that you, as an employee, are capable, trustworthy, and self-sufficient. Bosses don't like employees with problems. People with personal problems are problem employees. They are like babies, and bosses don't want to baby-sit people who are not their children, especially people they are paying to be professional, performing, and easy to work with.

If you are not happy, your boss will feel frustrated with you. Anyone who is not happy is a potential problem, inefficient and distracted, and at risk of causing some workplace disruption—or simply leaving. If you appear to have a good attitude, not only are the manager's concerns alleviated, but also you will be more likely to foster the trust of your peers and the people around you.

This means *NO complaining. Keep a positive attitude, or fake one. If you are unconvincing, your road, as well as theirs, will be all the more difficult.*

THE IMPORTANCE OF SHAKING HANDS

The biggest danger for a politician is to shake hands with a man who is physically stronger, has been drinking and is voting for the other guy. — William Proxmire

A good handshake is an important tool, allowing for bonding and connecting. One reason why the handshake is so vital is that human beings *need* some form of touching, and the single-hand handshake is the safest form of business touching. Many effective business people shake hands with practically everyone all the time—even the people they see every day.

Handshakes (in the United States) should be firm, signifying respect for one another and reminding the other person of your own self-confidence. A weak, moist handshake (again, in the United States) is distracting, and even kind of creepy. Always shake hands while standing or at least after rising a bit off your chair. Then the inside web of the thumbs should meet, followed by a gentle up and down motion. Release easily. Do not hold for too long unless you are showing a position of dominance.

It is common for people who are familiar with one another to stop shaking hands in the workplace. But professionals shake hands. Shake hands more, and you will be surprised how quickly it helps you build a better bond, even with routine coworkers.

Hand-shaking don'ts

Unless you are very comfortable with the other person or are trying to make a dominant point, do not bring the person in close by the hand or squeeze too firmly. Never hurt the other person with your force. And during the entire handshake, the eyes should be in direct contact with the person whose hand you are shaking. Wavering eyes can come across as just weird.

Be careful of the two-handed handshake or the non-shaking hand touch to the shoulder. This, like a hand on the shoulder or back, can be misinterpreted, particularly between sexes, or seen as patronizing. Remember, the person whose hand you are shaking (or whose shoulder you are touching) is, just for a bit, being held captive.

Touching in business interactions is, pardon the expression, a very touchy area. For example, a same-sex superior can rest a hand on your shoulder for a moment as a sign of bonding, but the reverse is strictly forbidden. Observe the rules and limits very carefully.

(DIS)RESPECTING THY ELDERS

I have been driven many times to my knees by the overwhelming conviction that I had nowhere to go. My own wisdom, and that of all about me, seemed insufficient for the day. —Abraham Lincoln

We respect older people for their maturity and experience, and we doubt the young for their lack thereof.

Although you can't fake your age, demonstrating maturity at any age is important. It's not just the age that we respect, and more than a fair share of older people behave like children, but the accompanying characteristics, such as thoughtfulness and the ability to listen and ask questions that tend to come with experience. Characteristics that reflect youth, such as standing with your weight on one foot, rolling your eyes, reacting emotionally, giggling, cursing, using slang or erratic movements, smiling at the wrong moments, flirting, and so forth, mark you as immature and undermine any attempt you are making toward building trust.

Our wise elders do not put their feet up on chairs or on the desk, lean over other people's desks, mill about aimlessly, become emotional, or use slang or immature language (such as the words "like", "dude", "whatever" or "goes", *e.g.*, "Dude, I told the boss that we're having, like, a good month so far and the boss goes, 'Yeah, whatever'.").

Our elders (or leaders) tend to dress well, look older and cause others in their presence to change (and improve) their respective behavior. Even in the most informal settings, the leaders tend to incorporate a more refined tone.

WISDOM, EXPERTISE, EXPERIENCE AND AGE

Is it wise to respect our elders? Of course. Do years of experience equate to wisdom? Occasionally.

Time does not necessarily equate to wisdom or even experience, but time can offer greater sensibilities rather than core knowledge. The one thing that experienced people have going for them is *apparent* experience. The use of the word *apparent* means that time allows a person to have been present—but simply being present does not mean learning. Experience alone is not wisdom. Experience, in many cases, creates just the opposite.

Every person evaluates and manipulates information in his own imperfect way. Bullheaded individuals (a side effect of years of experience) reject knowledge and information. A stubborn mind tends to be closed. The bull has a diminished inclination to notice or learn anything contrary to what he already thinks he knows.

Fatigue or boredom breeds contempt and disconnection.

Subjective or one-off experience can not create wisdom either, because a person's education, while accurate, are limited only to special and/or unique circumstances which are not a reasonable sample of the accurate truth. A new mother might claim, "I can tell you firsthand, childbirth is easy—labor takes only a few minutes and really doesn't hurt." Subjective experience is so narrow in scope as to not be statistically accurate or even connected to a broad reality.

Even scientific experience can be its own obstacle to progress. At the point at which a theory is adopted, new experience and knowledge are no longer valuable and are even refuted. A perfect example is Einstein's resistance to quantum theories that contradicted his prior theories. Eventually the new overcame but resistance came from experience.

Wisdom tends to show itself in funny ways. For instance, there are scientific studies that show that nice people tend to be less engaged, informed and even less smart than edgy (mean) business people. Smart people tend to become frustrated and impatient with others' inabilities to understand and evaluate information. This too explains why "nicer" does not necessarily mean "smarter."

The age thing is not within your control. The maturity thing, however, very much is.

PEOPLE WHO TELL YOU THEY'RE BUSY ARE LYING

Being busy does not always mean real work. The object of all work is production or accomplishment and to either of these ends there must be forethought, system, planning, intelligence, and honest purpose, as well as perspiration. Seeming to do is not doing. —Thomas Alva Edison

"Everybody works all of the time." "Business never sleeps." "In the global world the workday is 24 hours long."

It's nonsense. We do a better job pretending to be busy, and if we pretend long enough, we eventually believe that we really are this busy.

Being busy, walking fast, appearing hyper, and acting important is a part of our modern culture that allows us the excuse to not call people back, to miss deadlines, and to avoid taking on more work. In the end, most people work hard but still go home at the end of the day, go to the movies at night or on the weekends, and find a great deal of time to socialize with their family and friends.

Everyone is guilty of this exaggeration to one extent or another.

Everybody pretends to be busy.

In the business world, people walk fast down the halls carrying lots of paper, diving into their offices, hiding behind closed doors. Then they promptly get on the phone and engage in small talk for a while before getting down to business, or they have a conversation that is not work related, or they check their personal e-mail. Then perhaps a cup of coffee?

Many people act hectic and frazzled because that's what they believe that is expected. Busy-ness is perceived as justifying existence, salaries, and bonuses. Or perhaps we just don't wish to have any other obligations placed upon us. We sometimes forget to get back to people because we are busy—but we're not really *that* busy, just busy enough to forget. More often than not, the reason why we don't get back to people is that we don't want to. When we don't call people back, it is most often because the person asking something of us (or his or her project) is not a sufficient priority and therefore not worthy of our time.

Or maybe we're disorganized. "Disorganized" is not synonymous with "busy." Instead, being busy is the guise for disorganization.

What I am saying is this: No one (including you) is so busy as not to have time to return a phone call.

Perhaps looking busy is a good thing. It keeps the bosses happy if they think you are grinding it out. It lets others perceive you as being valuable. Employees who appear to be less busy, whether or not they truly are, are perceived as not having enough to do. People who have been around the block should see through this charade—although they too might be too busy looking busy.

Looking busy and rushing around, however, do not help you get the job done. The most effective people are often the calmest, and they are dismayed and perhaps disappointed with the employee who can't stop running, checking messages, or engage in an uninterrupted conversation.

In any event, no matter how busy you want to look, the person who doesn't return calls is not professional. Return your calls.

NEVER RUSH

Haste and rashness are storms and tempests, breaking and wrecking business; but nimbleness is a full, fair wind, blowing it with speed to the heaven. —*Thomas Fuller*

In fact, in sharp contrast with the people who look busy, many of the people who actually the busiest are best at looking graceful under pressure and often appear the least busy. They might even have the cleanest desks.

We don't promote, or even trust, people who act frazzled and busy. CEOs don't look frazzled. Frazzled people are grunts, perhaps good at what they are doing now, but incapable of handling any more, and certainly not anything too important. They're just too busy.

UNDERPROMISING AND MANAGING EXPECTATIONS

Punctuality is the duty of subjects and the politeness of kings. —Louis XIV (also attributed to Louis XVIII)

Deadlines are for real.* The word "deadline" originally referred to a physical line that was drawn around prisons. If a prisoner passed the line, he could be shot.

One thing that infuriates colleagues and managers more than anything else is expecting something in a certain way or before a certain time and not receiving it by the deadline. Absent political motivations (we'll talk about this in a little bit), never allow a deadline that you might miss to approach without notifying people involved. If you are expected to complete a project in a certain way or come up with an expected product, and you are having problems, speak up quickly, honestly, and concisely.

Manage expectations

Failing at a task does not necessarily require total failure; maybe you simply fall short of another person's expectations of what you would accomplish. It is far more damaging if you fail in a circumstance in which you were expected to succeed—and far less damaging if you weren't. True accolades, including hero worship, come from achieving results thought impossible. Always manage expectations downward: prime your manager or client for failure—and then blow their doors off.

---

* Deadlines, while key to performance expectations, are, in actual practice, generally not immutable.. I have rarely been witness to a deadline in the business world that could not be extended or adjusted. Deadlines, however, are terrific motivational tools and establish objective criteria for performance evaluation.

GEEKS CAN'T BE COOL (UNLESS IT IS COOL TO BE A GEEK)

Even with a billion dollar industry and fitness facilities on practically every block, we can't even change our diets. In many ways, we are genetically, psychologically and physiologically resistant to change (note for instance: psychological scarcity, the instinctive desire to aggressively hoard supplies and protect existing territory). That is not to suggest that we cannot modify certain aspects of our behavior. We can, but we usually revert to type.

We talk about perception as a thing that can be manipulated to a certain extent; fake it till you make it. Our style of communication and dress, and our sense of humor, mannerisms and quirks are fundamental to our identity. Be sure to recognize the limits of artificiality. However, avoid artificiality. Geeks however are geeky, even in fancy LA shiny shirts.

I spend a great deal of time teaching about the craft of negotiation. Authenticity is relevant. Although each student is vastly different from the rest, the same pattern tends to emerge. In the beginning of the semester, the most assertive students always win. The meek students, including those who tried to be assertive, lose practically every negotiation. Yet by the end of the class, no one type of student was any better than any other. In the heat of the battle, there are different tactics best matched to different personality types. For instance, the quiet person's best tool is actually silence. How about that! By being yourself, you are best able to match your strengths with the tools available to you.

DRESSING FOR RESPECT (OR REACTION)

Eternal nothingness is fine if you happen to be dressed for it. —*Woody Allen*

Wear clothes that fit. If you are gaining weight, make sure that your pants are gaining waistband right along with you. No overly baggy clothes. And watch out for the rules of stripes and plaids. If you are not sure how to show off your strengths and de-emphasize your weak points, seek out an executive coach or wardrobe consultant.

The parameters of conformity

Ultimately, individuality is not what makes a leader. When it comes to looks, conformity to *leaderly* standards is an important factor. Many businesses permit employees to "dress down," some just once a week and others for certain time periods or special occasions. Some are casual all the time.

But regardless of whether "dressing down" means "business casual" or truly dressing for super comfort, wearing anything that looks more messy or sloppy than the average person in your company will reduce your stature. You carry an aura, and you must emit confidence and respect. In most business environments, when you are dressed poorly, you are seen as less mature, sloppy, and unprofessional.

That is not to say that you should be the best dressed person either. That can come across as pretentious and can be counted against you if it looks as if you are trying too hard. But no matter what, you should never, ever look the worst.

One piece of awareness advice: if you decide to change your outfit to look especially nice one day, your boss might think you are interviewing elsewhere. And whether the boss is right or wrong, your excuse that you have a doctor's appointment will only act to confirm these suspicions.

REACTING: AVOIDING "AL GORE EYES" AND KEEPING A POKER FACE

How people treat you is their karma; how you react is yours. —Wayne Dyer

Your eyes and facial expression reveal more about what you are thinking and feeling than your words ever could. And while we all know that these "tells" can be your downfall in poker, as former Vice President Al Gore knows all too well from the one moment on television during a campaign debate, the simple act of rolling your eyes looks immature and can provide a basis for very real problems.

Controlling your reactions

In business, any reaction can be bad. From a negotiating standpoint, reacting can be your downfall. Be still. When you are listening, maintain eye contact and do not move or shift at all. No comments or groans. Keep your eyes still, neither moving them up or down or off to the side. Keep your face, eyes, and mouth still. Listen carefully and wait for your turn to speak; wait at least a full beat if not more after the other person stops speaking.

Patience and dignified silence are powerful tools. If you wait your turn, you'll get your turn, and you will not reveal your thoughts or look like a child in the process.

CRYING IS FOR BABIES

If you think a weakness can be turned into a strength, I hate to tell you this, but that's another weakness. —Jack Handy, Saturday Night Live

There is only a handful of studies on crying in the workplace, some focusing on productivity and others on frequency and perception. Some writers have suggested that there is an increase of workplace crying and have attributed this trend to higher-stress work environments and lower-stress childhoods in which children are not exposed to the same stresses and personal accountability as children of previous generations.

I disagree. There's plenty of ambient stress today: school shootings, violent video games, child predators, competitive dynamics, working/divorced parents, graphic news, and, of course, the Internet.

But that's neither here nor there.

Crying is simply a sign of weakness, and it makes people around you feel uncomfortable. Babies cry. Leaders don't. Crying reveals to others that the work and your environment have gotten the best of you. We don't trust people who can't handle their work, and we don't trust weak people to be our leaders.

Although the act of crying is usually involuntary, keep it out of the workplace (that includes the related acts of moping, stuttering, and shaking). Unless you are looking for sympathy, which you probably won't get anyway, crying will do you no favors.

SELF DEPRECATION

> *A man should be careful never to tell tales of himself to his own disadvantage. People may be amused and laugh at the time, but they will be remembered, and brought out against him upon some subsequent occasion.* —Samuel Johnson

How you are perceived starts with how you perceive yourself. If you don't perceive yourself as worthy, then either fake it or settle in for a self-critical, underachieving life.

This is not to suggest that being overly confident is good; it's not. But the simple ability to walk tall, feel proud, and work hard will cause others to perceive you favorably. If you are not confident, or do not exude a positive feeling, you will not be regarded favorably or be able to effectively fit in. As we will discuss shortly, self-esteem is one of the most significant characteristics of successful people.

Confident humility

Using self-deprecation as a tool requires a *confident humility*. The intent is to disarm other people by injecting levity and by offering a bit of a compliment to others.

Statements like "I'm not really an expert on that, but I was just noticing that…" are easily accepted because they are less threatening—the speaker puts himself down a little bit in order to get the message across in a non-threatening manner. But notice that there is no breakdown of confidence here—just an acknowledgement that the person speaking is not perfect and doesn't know everything.

Self-deprecation, when used correctly, comes from a position of inner strength. When used incorrectly, self-deprecation is just a sad person lacking confidence.

Nonetheless, we all like (and need) reassurance, and when we put ourselves out there, we really depend on the old pat on the back to let us know that we are doing okay.

Many people never get the reassurance they need, so they try to solicit this affirmation by asking for confirmation that they are doing well. This, however, is itself a sign of weakness in itself if it is not done in the right context. Ironically, when the person needing reassurance asks, "How did I do?", it may be coming from such a lack of confidence that the individual is unable to accept criticism, regardless of how constructive.

Good days and bad

There will always be good days and bad, and just as the good days don't make you great, neither do the bad make you terrible. The workplace is not always capable of assisting people when they're feeling down, and the people in it generally don't enjoy being forced into a compliment. Don't require or depend on the forced compliments of others. If you do depend on them, you probably don't deserve the compliments in the first place.

RECEIVING ADVICE

If you want to get rid of somebody, just tell him something for his own good. —Kin Hubbard

Some advice is genius. Other advice is really an instruction in disguise (as when the advice comes from your boss). And not all advice is sage or welcome.

When someone offers you advice, solicited or unsolicited, it may well be offered out of generosity and caring, and the best thing you can do in most circumstances is to say, "Thank you, I appreciate the thought," even if you have no intention of taking the advice to heart. Most advice is, in fact, worth hearing.

People like to offer advice; it makes them feel important. While the advice may not be welcome, any real response (including responses such as "I don't really see it that way") will make you look unwelcoming and possibly argumentative and bullheaded.

Of course, there are times when the advice is unwelcome—even insulting. If you absolutely have to challenge the advice-giver, do so quickly and remove any emotion. Something as simple as "I think I'm comfortable with the current approach" will do. Anything beyond that may be regarded as insulting a person who was trying to be helpful. That's not helpful.

Listen to the advice without judgment. Weigh the ideas. Be humble and gracious. Then bite your tongue and move on.

COMPLAINING SHOULD GET YOU FIRED
(EVEN ON YOUR PERSONAL TIME)

Complaining, like other forms of interference with a business, is insubordinate and may be cause for getting fired. Society knows this intuitively, and courts of law know that the best complainers are lying, disgruntled former employees.

Most people do complain in some fashion. Complaining is a form of gossip, not as much voluntary as it is a way in which human beings communicate (see the discussion of gossip). Few can stop. Complaining, like gossip, is actually wired into our brains and serves some valuable purposes for us. We build the right to speak (i.e., complain) right into the First Amendment right to freedom of speech. We value complaining so much we built it into our nation's governing document.

Fewer protections exist in the private sector. Only a few forms of communication are absolutely banned. That doesn't make speaking your mind entirely smart, however.

The Internet in its anonymity is sufficiently for complaining, and employers are more often than ever viewing the postings, blogs and websites of their employees. Moreover, a Google check is now entirely customary in pre-hire decisions. Many companies also peruse employee sites and posts periodically to identify indications of potential office-related problems.

If you don't think it can get you fired, just ask the many people caught complaining about their bosses or co-workers on rant sites. Moreover, if complaining is defamatory, libelous or invasive of privacy, it can even result in civil liability. Of course, the rant may make you feel better, and you may end up with many more hours in the day to re-read your brilliantly articulated post and supplement it with further complaints.

If you don't know how to stop complaining, simply force your lips together. If you seek respect, you must find a way to shut up.

COMPLAINING: DON'T DO IT

The squeaky wheel doesn't always get greased; it often gets replaced. —
Keith's Observation. In 1,001 Logical Laws.

Speaking about problems is advantageous only when it reveals a position
or a message to someone who can help get something fixed. Beyond that,
complaining is a self-important, self-centered, emotional, time-wasting
activity. It is an immature act and something that good employees and
leaders don't do–at least not at work.

Apart from the perception issues, if you are in a position of power and
respect, complaining to or within earshot of anyone with less power is disrespectful. And if you are in a position of envy, perhaps if you have more
power or make more money than the people you are complaining to, your
complaints are insulting and cruel.

BEING COMPLAINED ABOUT

*There is only one thing in the world worse than being talked about, and
that is not being talked about.* —Oscar Wilde

It hurts when people complain about you, and although the message that
gets back to you might lack context, it is hard not to get angry at the person doing the speaking. Your job is to get this behind you with no residual
hard feelings. Either ignore the complaint, address the issue, or confront
the complainer ("I heard that you had concerns about..."). But complaining and judging are fundamental elements of workplace discussions, and
we are all the subject of others' complaints from time to time.

Importance of a thick skin

This is a world built on judgments, and to play in this playpen requires
thick skin and, when called for, an aggressive response. For instance, you
are judging this book right now, and while I sincerely hope that you like
it, particularly since I've put time and effort into it, I can't take your judgments personally. I can listen and hopefully make a better book, but any
thinner skin in this harsh world and I'd be turning into a blithering fool.

RECOGNIZING OTHERS

Men can endure to hear others praised only so long as they can... persuade themselves of their own ability to equal the actions recounted: when this point is passed, envy comes in and with it incredulity. —*Pericles*

Nothing is more honorable and decent than giving credit to others. It is always polite to say "thank you," but make it a point to let people's managers know when their folks have gone above and beyond, and of course, always send a copy of the accolade to the person you are complimenting. This practice not only reflects favorably upon you—it may even come back to benefit you in spades.

WHEN PEOPLE ARE MAD AT PEOPLE

"If you want to make peace, you don't talk to your friends. You talk to your enemies." —*Mother Teresa of Calcutta*

Bad things happen when people are angry. They often stop speaking to each other. They stop calling and start dodging calls. They start making their case to other people, contaminating the workplace. My rule is, absent political advantage, to never let a person stay mad at me for more than a few minutes, although as a lawyer and a participant in the hard-edged business world, this is very difficult, and I have ended up with my fair share of personal challenges (*i.e.*, enemies) along the way.

How to deal with anger (and you must)

Anger is easy to hide behind. It feeds gossip, and it intrigues others in the same way that a car accident is entertainment. Deal with this stuff right away. If you want to let someone sit angry or hurt, decide when enough is enough, and, if you have to, find a way to get face-to-face.

Don't demand an apology, because many people are simply incapable of giving one. Let people off the hook (when you're not disadvantaged by doing so). Try to be sure that people have a way out of any crisis or problem.

If an apology by you is appropriate, find a way to do it quickly, sincerely, and non-publicly. Then move on to small talk, change the subject, and get on with your newly improved relationship.

"HOW ARE YOU?" AND QUESTIONS THAT PROVE THAT NO ONE REALLY CARES

Don't tell your friends about your indigestion. "How are you" is a greeting, not a question. —Arthur Guiterman

"How are you?" is not a real question. Neither is "What's going on?" "How was the weekend?" "What's new?" or "What's up?" And in most cases, questions like "How's the family?" or "How about them Yankees!?" are not real questions either. When a question is not a question, the answer should not be an answer.

Nobody really wants to know how you are. This stuff generally means "hello," so don't try to pretend that the common conventions of the language have somehow changed just for you. The questioner really doesn't expect an answer beyond something equally as meaningless as "fine, and you?" Questions such as "How do you do?" often call for no response at all (sometimes just a purse-lipped smile will do). Society accepts the non-literal meaning of these questions, and offering literal answers will annoy others.

Creativity here is not helpful and being literal is not funny. It's a joke already overtold. Say "hello" back in some other way equally inconsequential.

Then the greeting is over.

EVERYONE HATES MONDAYS AND MEANINGLESS CONVERSATION

Monday is an awful way to spend 1/7th of your life. —Steven Wright

Why are Mondays so horrible that we can sum up the entire misery of our lives and jobs by reminding other people of the mere fact that it is Monday? For example, in response to "How are you?" people respond with "Well…it's Monday" to sum up the fact that that person would rather be anywhere else. Why don't people on Mondays say that it's great to be back in the office?

The purpose of small talk

"Small talk," is by definition somewhat meaningless, although it serves many very important functions. It fills time in otherwise empty situations.

It also allows people to build relationships and find common interests and topics of shared importance. Finally, small talk sets a friendly foundation before more difficult subjects are explored.

The art and science

The art of small talk requires that you be (or seem) interested in the other person. Remembering key details, asking questions, and finding commonality with other people impresses them and makes it easier for you to get what you need.

The science of small talk is an interesting one, as you will see in Dr. Bernardo Carducci's book *The Pocket Guide to Making Successful Small Talk: How to Talk to Anyone Anytime Anywhere about Anything.*

In essence, there is nothing wrong with planning what you will say. Have ten different subjects for small talk ready to go. As the doctor recommends, keep your opening lines simple, plan your introduction and be prepared to discuss common interest subjects, throw out different subjects in search for a connection (this can include news, current events, travel, etc.), elaborate by adding to the subject (not bashing or changing subjects), and then, if desired, end the conversation.

Other key pieces of advice; avoid those corny opening lines, and be careful of holding onto a subject when the other person wants to change topics.

People don't like to get too serious too quickly, and forcing this process suggests that you are not capable of normal conversational flow. The small talk gets us to the big talk. Common bridges must be built or the conversation devolves. Once the bridge is built, other topics can be explored far more easily.

THE ART OF WAFFLING

Mirriam-Webster OnLine defines *waffling* to mean to "equivocate, vacillate, yo-yo or flip-flop, be indecisive or to talk or write foolishly." The most notable derogatory connotation in the United States is to refer to a politician who changes positions in response to political pressures or to solicit political favors.

Because of these negative connotations, many business people (and politicians for that matter) work extremely hard at not waffling. They lock themselves into a position as a *decision maker*, and then stay there without regard for facts or truth later learned or realized.

In fact, waffling as a way of learning is not only good but reasonable, provided it is a means to a thoughtful conclusion and well reasoned discussion. It is a recognition that human beings learn iteratively. With new facts, all things already learned must be re-evaluated as the new learning is appended to the old. Then...when new facts are later learned, the process continues.

The smartest people in the world do this. Einstein spoke at length about the learning process. But the smartest people in the world also hide this.

For instance, scientists, the people most known for learning iteratively, are also the most aggressive at holding their colleagues to a standard whereby hypotheses cannot be found later to be wrong. That has the natural tendency of forcing brilliant minds into holding firm to positions otherwise learned to be wrong. Compound this with a little defensiveness, bias and cognitive dissonance and you have greatly diminished the power of productive learning.

Allow yourself to waffle—privately, so that when you do speak you are intelligent. And do your best to avoid firming your opinion until the last possible moment so you can gather and consider all the facts and everyone else's opinion first.

Then adhere to the requirements of custom in never admitting error, protect your position no matter how wrong you might end up being.

THE ART OF OFFERING TO HELP

I've seen and met angels wearing the disguise of ordinary people living ordinary lives. —Tracy Chapman

We should all help one another.

While this book focuses first on personal responsibility, and while the business world does not always seek to assist poor performers, nor should it, I believe deeply in the ideal so brilliantly expressed by songwriter Chuck Brodsky in his song *We are Each Other's Angels:*

"'Cause we are each other's angels
And we meet when it is time
We keep each other going
And we show each other signs"

In the workplace, however, we don't really *want* to help each other—we're all really just too busy paying attention to our own concerns. But *offering* help can be a magical tool for building trust and demonstrating your care, loyalty, and dedication to the person and the business.

The helper might also be interested in working or connecting with key people or on key projects. Of course, few of us really need or want any more work; therefore, the true art of offering help is to actually not be taken up on your offer.

Regardless, the simple offer can mean the world to the person you asked, indicating with a single question that you care about them and the business and that you are willing to sacrifice a bit of yourself for the cause.

THINKING IS A HIDEOUSLY UGLY ACT

To learn is no easy matter and to apply what one has learned is even harder. —Mao Tse-Tung

One of the first lessons I learned when I entered the practice of law was to make sure that my clients never got to see me think.

The act of thinking is never graceful. It involves learning, considering, reconsidering, talking out loud, testing solutions, and retesting. Ideas and arguments are formed slowly. We are wrong on the way to being right. If we are allowed to think in private, the resulting presentation will be less haphazard and far more convincing and professional.

Thinking: the process

Watching someone think is a glimpse into the processing of information, experiences, and ideas and the forming of logic, which is why we may appear flawed, inexperienced, and unprofessional.

Thinking happens over a period of time. When politicians think in public, they are often dubbed "wafflers" while some (although not the ones deciding on the politically correct solution) are actually formulating final positions.

The same applies to scientists. Einstein's ideas were the product of years of private thought. Brainstorming—and allowing room to think through even the worst of proposals—is the best way to find the best ideas. The greatest speeches and arguments ever made were often developed over the course of many bad drafts and restless nights, typically spanning weeks or months.

It helps to have someone with whom you can privately share ideas. Thinking in a safe and comfortable place with someone who's experiencing the thought process with you can be the most effective and productive way to come up with a result. But other than one or two thinking partners, be certain that nobody else sees you in the process.

LATE MORNINGS AND EARLY EVENINGS

I have a "carpe diem" mug and, truthfully, at six in the morning the words do not make me want to seize the day. They make me want to slap a dead poet. —Joanne Sherman

We call it "face time," the phrase that indicates that it doesn't really matter whether you are working as long as you are in the office. It's an idea that runs counter to everything that society purports to stand for, including life balance and family values. It's clearly undermined by the wonderful technology that supposedly frees us from the office (but tethers us ever more tightly to it).

Yet face time matters.

Why face time matters

Think about it from the perspective of the people around you. Nothing angers others more than someone who gets paid the same amount of money (or more) and who works less. Peers ask why they should have to work as hard as they do if one of them is starting later and ending earlier.

And think about it also from the perspective of the people above you, who ask themselves every day whether you are the right person for a good review or eventual promotion. They are paying you to do something that includes the very simple activity of showing up.

For those of you who work from the office, time in the office might even matter more than what you do when you're there.

PEOPLE WHO WORK FROM HOME MUST PERFORM BETTER

On the fourth day of telecommuting, I realized that clothes are totally unnecessary. —Scott Adams, Dilbert

People who work from home have it pretty good. Even if you are absolutely diligent, those of us stuck in the office are picturing you unshowered, undressed, watching a soap opera, walking the dog and running errands. There's almost no way to avoid it.

If you are telecommuting (particularly in a job in which others have to be in the office every day), other people will be jealous. We all want to wake up late, skip the traffic, work in slippers, and so forth. This is the blessed life of the telecommuter.

Telecommuters and perception problems

This perception problem is something that the telecommuter must work hard to overcome. While everyone should strive to communicate well, the telecommuter should work hard to communicate even better than everyone else, by receiving all calls and returning calls even more promptly, responding quickly via email, and getting work turned around ahead of schedule, proving every day that the mouse isn't spending all day playing when the cat is stuck in some faraway office.

STOPPING BY OTHER PEOPLE'S OFFICES

Fish and visitors stink in 3 days. —Benjamin Franklin

Stopping by someone's office or even calling by phone to say hello is a great way to communicate or get information directly. It is also a tremendous drain on productivity. And one person always wants to end the conversation before the other.

When you stop by another person's office or space, that person, from an etiquette standpoint, is required to let you in to talk about whatever topic you have come by to discuss. While it is polite to engage in this conversation, it is not always what the person hosting the event wants to be doing, and he or she might be under deadline or otherwise interested in getting back to work.

Rules for dropping by

No matter your position or relationship, be excessively polite when you interrupt another person. Maybe ask if it is a good time, and state your reason. Remember that the visitor has all the power because the visitor decides when to end the conversation, whereas the host risks seeming impolite and disrespectful, even though the visitor is the one drawing first blood.

If you are stopping by for casual conversation, or to gossip or complain, say so. Give the person an easy opportunity to defer the conversation. It's nothing personal. Look for visual signs that the other person wants to get back to work, including such signals as turning away or toward the computer screen, beginning to type or read other things, or placing a hand on the telephone or computer keyboard. Immediately depart when you have overstayed your welcome.

And for the host, while there is an obligation to be welcoming, if you wish to put the conversation off, ask if you can stop by your visitor's office or call when you have a moment. Be direct or you will become a victim of your unwelcome guest.

MISTAKES, RESPONSIBILITY, AND THE ARTFUL *MEA CULPA*

Every great mistake has a halfway moment, a split second when it can be recalled and perhaps remedied. —Pearl S. Buck

Everybody makes mistakes. That is human. We all feel bad when we make a mistake. That too is human. Nobody wants his mistakes revealed. That is embarrassing and human as well. But when your mistake or problem will hurt the business or your manager, it is something that while terribly difficult, should be revealed (unless you are super-duper positive that you can get away with it). *What really brings people down is not the crime but the cover-up.*

Everyone from the mail room to the boardroom knows how hard it is to admit a mistake, and people respect anyone who has the strength of character to admit what is hardest to admit and to accept responsibility when otherwise not required.

When your mistake is caught by others

However, when your mistake is discovered first by others, you have a problem. Before you are told of your mistake, other people often have already become aware of the problem. A sense of impending capture is building. You notice a funny look here and there. Messages are being sent; you are not competent. And if you knew of the mistake you made and elected not to reveal it, then you are more than merely incompetent: you are more aptly described as a liar who has been revealed to be so self-preserving that you are not worthy of association.

Just admit it!

Admitting a mistake by falling on the sword is one of the hardest things anyone can do. If you reveal the problem or mistake, then you can get the message out your way, minimizing any personal embarrassment and limiting the potential problem, all the while allowing the business to quickly address and resolve the problems.

But while hoping mistakes may just vanish may be the proper *strategy* from time to time, albeit the riskiest, the revelation will allow others to forgive you and return focus to solving the problem caused by the mistake.

Strength of character is not easy. It's not supposed to be.

THE ART OF THE PAPER AND PEN

He listens well who takes notes. —Dante Alighieri

Your job, quite literally, is to follow all instructions that are given to you and to never forget anything that is ever told to you. From a perception perspective, your job is to convince people around you that you can be trusted not to forget those things that other people expect you to remember.

Pen and paper as basic equipment

No matter your skill and memory faculties, if you don't have a pen and paper (or the equivalent e-device), you can't take notes; and this indicates to the speaker that you had no intention of taking the conversation seriously in the first place.

It is a good practice to always have a pen and paper (or other form of note-taking device) with you, whether it is a cheap pen and loose pad, or a fancy tablet. This is one area where some managers are fanatical, and those who aren't saying anything are certainly still paying attention.

Personally, I get terribly frustrated when I am giving instructions to a person who is not taking notes, and particularly when that person, as expected, forgets what I asked for or fails to follow explicit directions, I regard it as a personal insult. This is a sign of a person who should be let go.

But don't overdo it (or doodle)

Now, there is such a thing as overdoing it. People who take too many notes are transcribing but not really listening. Being able to transcribe a conversation doesn't mean that you understand it. It is rare for an instruction to be given that does not require questions or clarifications.

If you are writing without using your mind, you will not truly understand the discussion or consider the questions you might want to ask. Further, many people who take voracious notes never consult those notes. Those of us who have been around the block know that too much note-taking is brainless and administrative.

And for goodness sake, do not doodle. That's worse than doing nothing at all.

YOUR OUTGOING VOICEMAIL MESSAGE

I have an answering machine in my car. It says," I'm home now. But leave a message and I'll call when I'm out." — Stephen Wright

Creative messages on your voicemail are *almost* always unprofessional and stupid. Long announcements or instructions on your message are an intrusion.

While there is the occasional entertaining message, it is often entertaining only once (the first time it is heard); no one respects a person with a creative voicemail message any more than if the message were strictly professional.

In general, creative outgoing messages make you look goofy. Callers want to tell you that they called. That's it. Don't reveal to them that you are out there emotionally dancing among the daisies, but that you are the mature, serious, and responsible person for the job.

Although sales people are often taught otherwise (see Jeffrey Gitomer's wonderful book, *Little Red Book of Selling*), most people's messages should strive to draw little attention to themselves but rather provide merely enough information to prove their professionalism and to let callers know that they have the correct number and other important details. Letting people know if you are in the office that day is helpful too.

No one wants to hear your message in the first place, so if you take up the caller's time, what you say should matter to them (for instance, how to skip your message in the future).

THE VOICEMAILS YOU LEAVE

Verbosity leads to unclear, inarticulate things. —Dan Quayle

The Holocaust was an obscene period in our nation's history. I mean in this century's history. But we all lived in this century. I didn't live in this century. —Dan Quayle

Watch others listen to their voicemail messages and you'll see the typical things: the eye-rolling, seat-shifting, and universal wrist-rolling sign for "get on with it."

Some people (myself included) tend to delete messages very quickly, cutting off messages at the moment their meaning appears to have become clear. My speed-deleting is a common habit, motivated not by disrespect but with the belief that the substance of the message has been communicated.

On most occasions, I am right. There is typically a point at which the gist of the message has been delivered. and all that is left is extraneous nonsense clarifying and reiterating the point.

In rare cases, however, the person leaving the message has an "oh, wait a minute" moment, realizing later in the message that something important has not been said. That part is often never heard.

Important: *Leave your name and number and pronounce them clearly.*

No matter how recognizable you think you are, always leave your name. Absent an unmistakable relationship, even if you are known, it is still more professional to leave your last name as well. With very few exceptions, always leave a number, or you may not receive a prompt response (or any response at all).

When you leave your return phone number, pronounce it slowly and clearly, and give the listener warning before you say something that needs to be written down. Perhaps only a second or two will be helpful; absent this courtesy, the listener must review the message two or more times to get the needed information. Many never do (me, for instance).

Messages should be concise. Apart from the occasional throw-away line such as, "It was nice to see you the other day," get right to the point: "I'm calling because…" If something needs to be written down, consider saying it twice. And for goodness' sake, get to the point and wrap it up.

Keep it discreet.

Some people listen to their messages on their speakerphone or have their assistant or some other person check the messages. Being too loose on a friend's voicemail is one easy way to cost your friend or you a job.

Voicemails are not casual. Don't discuss anyone and don't complain; a comment such as, "We're having some problems over here; please call me back so I can explain" should be more than sufficient.

Finally, remember that some people record all of their voicemail messages. This is legal. And some voicemail systems automatically record their messages in computer sound files—saved forever in cyberspace. Remember that anything you say can and (probably) will be used against you.

ALL THINGS WRITTEN

People tend to treat e-mail like conversation. They don't give it the kind of thought that something in writing should have. If you're trying to be funny and you forget to put in the little smiley face, people could take it the wrong way. —Peter Handal

The written word too lives forever, and our letters and communications tend to find their way back to us, even years later when we least expect it— as on those rare occasions when the business might be in litigation or when you or any other employee or person that you emailed may be investigated for a problem. (They don't even need to be focusing on your communications to discover communications that you'd rather not want revealed.)

Many corporate email systems save every single email that is ever sent or received; some track and audit emails; others even track employee keystrokes. And even if your email server doesn't save your email, it is distinctly possible that the person who received it has saved it or has a system that never deletes a single message.

Many companies actively monitor and maintain their employees' email, either secretly or overtly. Some industries–finance, for example—requires active monitoring and years of backup files. During investigations, I personally have had to review tens of thousands of people's personal emails without their knowledge. Trust me: bad things happen from even the most mundane notes, if embarrassing information is revealed.

Assume that every single written document will be copied or forwarded. Use fewer words. Make no accusations or apologies.

It is a challenging, uphill battle for me to convince my clients to stop writing things that incriminate themselves or the business. I see examples every day of people who get themselves in real hot water for words that they may have thought were completely innocent.

The politics and protocols of email

Email and instant messaging are worth special mention, particularly because of their prominence in business and the likelihood that your emails will cause you embarrassment or get you in trouble at some point in your career. Because of the informality of the email process, a person can get in trouble when emails are sent to the wrong address (through inadvertent use of the "reply all" button), are unexpectedly forwarded (accidentally or otherwise), or contain material that can be taken out of context.

Work very hard to not allow anyone to put you in a precarious position with an email. Watch those cc's and bcc's, and read everything you get. Check the recipient list twice. *Expect your emails, texts, IM's, and other writings to become public, and write with the broader audience in mind.*

And it is quite possible that those emails might be someone's attempt to cover his or her hind-quarters with yours. When you sense that an email you received has gone too far, unless you intend to correct the record with your reply, pick up the phone or go have a face-to-face. On more than one occasion in the past, I have even gotten on a plane to fly to see someone instead of replying. It is infinitely more effective.

Even the most shy and mousey people can write very stern emails. When you receive one of these forceful messages, remember that most people cannot back it up orally, and particularly not in person. Don't get mad, get oral. But be sure that in the end, the last email sent does not hurt you. Try to avoid jokes. Humor does not translate through short notes, and that little happy face emoticon is really not all that professional (albeit often required in connection with *any* humor at all). When someone like me finds that email during an investigation, you'd better be sure I get the joke.

TELEPHONE ETIQUETTE

A telephone survey says that 51 percent of college students drink until they pass out at least once a month. The other 49 percent didn't answer the phone. —Craig Kilborn

When you pick up the phone, watch your tone.

Our parents taught us to pick up the phone and say "hello." In some cases, we say our name or the company we work for. Answering with just your last name or the word "yes" might convey that you are being bothered and

---

MORE E-DEVICE STUFF

Smart devices raise more than issues of mere etiquette; they raise legal and security concerns as well. The NASA site includes a very nice plain-language explanation of different security concerns, including cloning, scanning, tracking and monitoring issues. The bottom line is that what you say into a cell phone can be overheard in many ways. One famous situation involved the inadvertent taping of a conversation involving Newt Gingrich, former Speaker of the House of Representatives, concerning his party's strategy regarding matters of ethics. See Jessica Lee, "Focus Shifts from Gingrich to Taped Call," *USA Today*, Jan. 14, 1999.

Legal issues abound. Being overheard on a cell phone can be the basis for termination and/or legal charges if the contents of your message involve private matters. GPS tracks movement. Using an e-device while driving, and particularly texting, is an automatic ticket to liability (and possibly even criminal charges) should you end up in an accident. The text messages you send and receive, while they may seem innocuous and fleeting, can be gathered by law enforcement and your employer (particularly if you are using a company device). The photos you have taken on your cell phone camera have also been known to get folks into rather big trouble.

The one lesson here is that what you do on your cell phone is quite literally everyone else's business. You are forewarned.

---

may suggest an attempt to intimidate. If you are in a rush, speeding up your words or tone doesn't actually save any time.

Telephones, like email, allow people to hide. We can more aggressively confront other people by saying things that would never be said in person (in the same way, cars are conducive to road rage, as otherwise calm people find themselves losing their cool because they feel immune and protected).

Dealing with conflicts by phone

In a call with some degree of conflict, the most powerful tactic you have is to take the opposite tone of the other caller. The faster they speak, the slower you speak. The louder they are, the softer you become.

Silence can hinder any aggressive person; it's your most powerful tool. Even as a lawyer accustomed to hard and harsh conversations, I find that it is very effective to keep the flavor of the discussion on my terms. If the other person crosses a line of my choosing, I am comfortable telling someone that I will not accept being spoken to in a certain way (sometimes the phrase "you don't mean that" can directly, yet not offensively, back the other person off); my most powerful weapon is to end the call and offer to talk again when the other person is calm.

Another powerful technique is to say that you expected more of the other person, shaming them into calmness and a more polite tone. If the tone doesn't change, explain that the call will be resumed later. But while you may hang up the phone, never hang up the phone without warning (this is a sign of emotional weakness and something that will be used against you).

And remember, whether the practice is legal or illegal, lots of people record their conversations, and many courts will listen to these tapes, even if it is just to decide whether or not they will allow those tapes to be listened to.

You're on speaker!

The speakerphone is a powerful communications tool. Along with hands-free convenience, the speakerphone can be used for more sneaky purposes— to tell the world of your importance or to allow others to listen in.

Not only is the conversation on the speakerphone fairly public to begin with, but we end up speaking louder, further broadcasting the conversation to every single person in the vicinity.

If there are other people in earshot of the speakerphone, absent a planned strategic goal, you should never answer a call on a speakerphone if the caller does not know that other people are around you (it is not above-board). You can't predict the caller's first comments, and offensive and revealing problems have been caused by an otherwise innocent caller thinking you were alone. Finally, if there are others within earshot, it is your ethical obligation to immediately let the caller know very quickly that the call is not private.

If you want hands-free operation, the best option is not the speakerphone but a headset, some of which permit a wide range of functions right from the headset itself (such as answering, muting, and hanging up the phone). Also, many are wireless. I use a wireless headset that allows me a 300-foot range to pace. Total cost: $125, and no more cramped neck.

CELL PHONES

Cell phone makes those boundaries between public and private very porous. In the past, if you're having a spat with a significant other in a public place, one of you will argue and say, 'Not here' because it's intrusive. But now, with cell phones, there's no 'Not here' anymore. —Geoffrey Nunberg

I honestly suspect that most of the calls occurring on cell phones in public happen not because they must, but because the person using the cell phone decided that it would be fun if everyone around could hear how important he or she is.

As soon as we are left alone, say in a restaurant, we get on our cell phones. The cell phone has taken over for the cigarette as a thing to do to make a person look and feel comfortable in these otherwise isolated moments, and yet unlike the cig, the cell phone is not an act of solitary comfort, but exactly the opposite, embodying a person's desire to be anywhere else other than where that person is at this time. As a result, most cell phone conversations are unnecessary and end up being used for show, as a baby blanket to provide the impression that you are important and not truly alone.

If you are in a group and decide to take or place a call, excuse yourself. It is never polite to have your conversation in the same vicinity as others who are not involved in the call. In any case, speak softly. Your discretion and professionalism will reflect upon you positively.

Smartphones and "being there"

The advent of smartphones has taken distraction to a whole new level. Now your conversation partner(s) can check Facebook, shop for a new car, play Candy Crush, or do dozens of other things along with making and taking phone calls. It is now possible to be continuously interactive with someone other than the person you're supposedly talking to.

To some people (like your boss), this is a consummate act of discourtesy. Let other people be rude. Let them compromise your valuable attention with their gadgets. Previous advice is worth repeating: keep your own smartphone in your pocket until the conversation or meeting is over.

THE EVILS OF WHISPERING

It isn't what they say about you, it's what they whisper. —Errol Flynn

Whispering is unprofessional and immature and should be left to adolescent schoolgirls. Consider how the whisperer looks: is he or she looking for a job? In trouble? Getting someone else in trouble? Sharing gossip? Sharing secrets? Does he know something about you? Our imaginations run wild. Can the whisperer be trusted? Certainly not by the people who feel left out, because they may be personally exposed by the whisperer.

Keep in mind that whenever someone of sufficient power or authority closes his or her office door to speak on the phone or engage in a meeting, it is a more acceptable, businesslike, adult form of whispering.

That said, there are countless reasons why it is essential to keep something secret. Doing this in a respectful manner, like everything else, is the way of the dignified leader.

THE POWER AND FRAILTY OF APOLOGIES

In politics...never retreat, never retract...never admit a mistake.
—*Napoleon Bonaparte*

There is almost no greater virtue than providing a sincere apology in response to an act for which you feel remorse.

The act of apologizing is built into every major religion, as well as programs such as Alcoholics Anonymous' Twelve Step Program. Sincere apologies are heartfelt and humble. Apologizing helps clear your and your victim's personal slates. In fact, there are a number of medical studies that demonstrate that a sincere apology has health benefits directly related to stress levels and anxiety, including insomnia.

Similarly, receiving an apology as well has been shown to positively impact tension, blood pressure, heart rate and sweat levels. A tremendous number of disputes could have been prevented with simple apologies, allowing both the culprit and the victim to move on.*

In the business world, leaders rarely apologize. Most often, when a leader apologizes, it is person-to-person and behind closed doors.

Public apologies happen only in the most egregious circumstances, as, for example, when an important person is caught doing something undeniably wrong. In politics, the common phrase is "Although my comments have been taken out of context, I apologize to anyone I may have offended"— actually a negative apology which in effect accuses the offended of failing to listen and being oversensitive.

However, just like any forced apology, the apology is often a self-serving tool; apologies need not come from any place of remorse. Demanding an apology is typically done to make a point or to humiliate the person asked

---

* See Lisa Habib, "Saying 'Sorry' Goes a Long Way," *WebMD Medical News,* *http://www.webmd.com/balance/news/20021003/saying-sorry-goes-long-way.* There are also numerous studies concluding that medical doctors who make mistakes and apologize are much less likely to be sued for malpractice than those who do not apologize. However, the simple apology is loaded with potential risk—including that the apology can be easily construed as an admission of guilt.

to apologize, and the person who ends up apologizing often doesn't even believe that an apology is warranted.

On one occasion (I was a lawyer at the time), the business demanded that an employee accused of sexual harassment apologize to the accuser as part of an overall plan to keep him employed. That person appeared to *sincerely* apologize even while continuing to assert his innocence. In most criminal systems, penalties are far harsher for people who do not apologize. Government can come to a halt while politicians require apologies from one another in hopes of seeking political advantage.

The politics of apologizing

Despite all of their virtues, and there are many, apologies are a sign of humility and weakness. In the workplace, the apology, or, more aptly, the demand for an apology, is a tool for the savvy politician. The person on the receiving end feels better because of the humiliation that accompanies the moment of the apology, and political advantage is gained.

While apologizing is important in some circumstances, avoid apologizing as a matter of course. Don't start sentences with the words, "I'm sorry." If you are late or sick or busy, do not apologize as a matter of default. Leaders and respected people do not apologize often.

But when you do have to apologize in the normal course of business, do it directly and without further modification or self-deprecation: "I'm sorry that happened. I made a mistake. *Never follow up with a re-framing word, such as "but"; that shows quite clearly that the apology was not pure.* Then stop offering a defense to your actions. Wait for the reaction. Don't keep talking. Force the next person to take the next step, acknowledge and move on.

Once this is done, usually in the next sentence, you and the apologizee are often ready to change the subject. The listener might want to harp on the apology for a little bit. Let them do this. Pay 'em now or pay 'em later.

Personally, I find the tactic of demanding an apology quite distasteful and disingenuous.* Nonetheless, it continues to be used to great success. Perhaps the spectators enjoy watching the train wreck. My contrary approach is let people off the hook whenever I can. I find that they appreciate it more.

RESTROOM ETIQUETTE (HOW NOT TO MAKE A SOUND)

If you reveal your secrets to the wind, you should not blame the wind for revealing them to the trees. —Kahlil Gibran

It should not come as a surprise that many people have been fired for saying something they shouldn't have said in a bathroom or an elevator. When employees let their guard down in the bathroom and other private/public places, they may gossip, make offensive jokes or statements, or reveal company secrets.

So when you want to speak but know that you shouldn't, squeeze your lips so tightly together that no sound comes out—except, of course, the old favorites, "Hello, how are you?" "Fine," and "If you want to chat, stop by or give me a call." You never know who might be close by and quietly listening.

---

* For child education, however, I do favor demanding an apology since, for all of the reasons mentioned, the humility built into the apology itself is much of the educational lesson/punishment. With adults, I prefer to seek advantage in other ways. Politicians may disagree.

USING TECHNOLOGY TO IMPROVE PERCEPTION

But men labor under a mistake. The better part of the man is soon ploughed into the soil for compost. By a seeming fate, commonly called necessity, they are employed, as it says in the old book, laying up treasures which moth and rust will corrupt and thieves break through and steal. It is a fool's life, as they will find when they get to the end of it, if not before. —Henry David Thoreau

We spoke earlier about the use of technology to make you more efficient. Technology can also help you demonstrate that you are dedicated to your business when you are out of the office. Just a single fast response here and there will suggest to the people around you that your work is your top priority.

Taking your work home may not seem like fun, but that occasional email you send from home or that project you completed over a weekend can tip the balance toward your potential promotion. Cell phones these days are mandatory, so make yourself available to your office.

Leaders can be found. Peons can't.

EXPENSE REPORTS AND SELF-SERVING OPPORTUNITIES

When I was a kid I used to pray every night for a new bicycle. Then I realized that the Lord doesn't work that way so I stole one and asked Him to forgive me. —Emo Philips

Companies vary in their approaches to expense reporting. Some are very conservative, while others encourage their employees to be aggressive in what they spend and what is claimed. More often than not, it is the manager's style that dictates how expense reports are reviewed, submitted, and approved.

Expense reports as a test of character

The expense reimbursement, the classic example of a self-serving opportunity, is often used by managers to test the trustworthiness of an employee.

First, did you spend within reason? Then, don't nickel-and-dime the report. For instance, although snacks in the airport are covered in my company's policy, I don't claim them. I've seen too many people lose the trust of their manager because they requested reimbursement for a silly 99-cent candy bar.

Keep the report easy, clear, and obviously compliant. Take meal and transportation options below the maximum allowable to show that you are not looking to squeeze every possible dollar out of the company. This added trust will go a long way, particularly when you have incurred a more significant yet otherwise questionable expense that you want the company to cover.

This is a game of perception. If your business or manager believes that you are trying to get (or steal) those extra reimbursements, then your manager will consider you dishonest. If you are not sure of an expense, consider asking before you spend the money. If the expense report is submitted and your manager is taken by surprise, that's when the real problems begin.

MULTITASKING AS AN ACT OF PERCEPTION

Is reading in the bathroom considered multitasking? —Unknown

Multitasking pisses people off. While we did cover this in the efficiency section, it is important enough to merit a brief note here..

There is nothing more frustrating than waiting for something important from someone who has multiple windows open on his computer or is attempting to multitask. Obvious multitaskers can easily appear flighty and sporadic.

But confidence is inspired by a person who appears to focus on you, your problem and the solution. When faced with an opportunity to focus, shut everything else down and keep distractions out. If your Internet browser is visible to someone who is waiting for something, you've just been caught. Even something as simple as taking a phone call or displaying an inappropriate browser screen proves that you aren't focused on what needs to be done.

INTERNET USAGE FOR DUMB-ASSES

Getting information off the Internet is like taking a drink from a fire hydrant. —*Mitchell Kapor*

Using the Internet at work for personal reasons—unless permitted and done during your personal time—is stealing. And using web-based email is not only a theft of corporate time, but it may also be a violation of your company's email policy.

It's overwhelmingly common, yes, but it doesn't reflect an unequivocal respect for the business' needs and best interests. Like so many other admonitions in this book, this obvious point should not need to be spelled out, yet violations are so common (by myself included), and the frequency has somewhat watered down the seriousness of the violation. Nevertheless, the caution bears repeating.

There are countless stories of people, even in the most welcoming work environments, crossing the line and finding themselves right out on the street for even the most simple and naive transgressions.

Don't think you can't get bagged

One of the most common lies told in the workplace happens with a simple click of the mouse. Someone walks by or into a position where your computer screen is visible, and you immediately click off the thing you were inappropriately doing—searching the Internet, for instance.

First, the ruse rarely works. People detect the secret click. Second, the click often happens late; the passerby sees the original window vanish. There is now firsthand knowledge of the deceit and your attempted (unprofessional) cover-up. Third, you don't always see the gawker until it's too late—after the screen contents are revealed. Caught again. Instantly revealed for your inefficiency, distraction, lack of dedication during the workday, and, let's just say it, lying.

Note: In a pinch, and for what it's worth, the Alt-Tab keyboard combination (Control-Tab on a Mac) is often a more effective way to click off a window, happening without taking your fingers off the keyboard, and avoiding the obvious click-away.

LIFE BALANCE (A.K.A. BALANCE, SHMALANCE)

Perpetual devotion to what a man calls his business, is only to be sustained by perpetual neglect of many other things.
—Robert Louis Stevenson

Every business hopes, expects, and pays good money for employees who are entirely committed to their work. While it recognizes that people have personal lives as well and supports the ideal of work-life balance, the business and people that count on you are looking more for performance than for you to be satisfied in your free time. Although a satisfying personal life may ultimately make you a better work performer, most businesses do not want your personal life to become an unproductive distraction.

Work/life balance — and separation

Consequently, in most work environments, strive to keep your *balanced life* as far away from the business as you can. This advice is justified mostly by the perception that outside life discussion is not efficient, helpful to others, and demonstrates distraction and a lack of presence.

If you are sharing good news about your life outside of work, your discussion may be viewed as braggadocio, and conveying personal challenges as weakness or frailty. Be cognizant and remember that no one truly cares, so keep these kinds of conversations to a minimum. And when you occasionally do decide to talk about this stuff, remember your audience and consider how the people you are speaking with view you, particularly those who are below you.

TAKING THE BENEFITS THE COMPANY GIVES YOU

It's no longer a question of staying healthy. It's a question of finding a sickness you like. —Jackie Mason

Although businesses offer benefits, if legitimately taking advantage of those benefits (such as vacation/sick time, volunteer leave, flying first class, etc.) hinders, obstructs, or otherwise causes problems for your company, then taking advantage of the benefits may label you as someone who is not a team player.

Considerations in taking/not taking benefits

Since benefits are part of your compensation package and intended to promote a balanced life, leaving benefits on the table is never the smart (or right) thing to do. But what if the company is in financial trouble? What if there is an impending deadline? What if your manager is depending on you?

While no person is essential and everything will survive without you, one thing is for sure: the person who takes advantage of every single benefit and takes every possible day off and sick day is often the same person who leaves the second the work is finished.

This is often the same person who never makes him or herself available to help the business or colleagues—and the first person to disappear when a crisis is at hand. This person will not be perceived as a dedicated or loyal employee, but rather someone who cannot be depended on.

I am not advocating that you leave benefits on the table—to the contrary. But *looking like a selfish brat is not the way to convince your company that you are the best person for the job. Winning the perception game requires a fine balance*; you must constantly find ways to prove that the business' needs are more important than your own.

BEING SICK

> *Employees have come to think of sick time as a vested benefit, but that's not what it was meant for.* —Jack Curley

Do you know how I know that you're probably lying when you take a sick day? Because at companies where sick time is taken against a pool of days off that include vacation time, statistics show that employees take a fraction of the number of unscheduled days off. And the idea of using sick time for mental health days, the exact thing that vacation time was designed for, is transparent as well.

You are forgiven for being sick and unable to work (and you are forgiven for your child's sickness as well). But you won't be liked or respected for it. You won't be trusted for it. And you will inconvenience others for it.

Fake and real illness

We all learned as kids that the only way to get out of going to school was to play sick. Even as adults this technique is still fundamental in our arsenal. Managers, often former illness-feigners and now parents, are on to this.

Managers respect health issues enough to allow you to keep them personal and private, and so while a manager may not ask too many questions when you say that you are sick or have a doctor appointment, that doesn't mean that your manager or anyone else believes you.

Actually, job interviews often happen when people claim to have a doctor appointment; managers notice the days when you have a "doctor appointment" and are dressed particularly well.

We notice people with too many doctor appointments and stop trusting the employee, no matter how legitimate. If you are having a health problem, it is often important to preserve as much of the trust as you can and be forthcoming about your otherwise highly personal issues. Otherwise, regardless of how legitimate your illness, you may find yourself perceived as a liar or short-timer.

In the end, get to work. Let your manager look you in your sick little bloodshot, half-closed eyes and send you home. Otherwise, you might end up suffering in more ways than one.

GETTING PREGNANT

> Doctor says to a man "You're pregnant!" The man says "How does a man get pregnant?" The doctor says, "The usual way, a little wine, a little dinner...." —Henny Youngman

Society and the law demand that the workplace allow time off for maternity leave. Companies offer generous time off and monetary packages, and they permit company time to be used for baby showers and picture-sharing moments.

But make no mistake, for as much as the business likes the stability that comes from people with children, managers fear pregnancy, babies, and maternity leave. The business is required to keep the new mother's (and for paternity leave, the father's) job open and available for their return many months later. Although these are important rights, understand that any person's leave of absence can paralyze a business.

Few businesses can really afford to take all the time, energy, and money that come from hiring a person, only to lose that person for many months. No business wants to hire or promote a person likely to take an extended paid (or partially paid) vacation a few months later. The business hires and pays people to work, and it has a hard time coping with unfilled positions and paying people who are not working.

Worse, after all of these benefits, a significant number of mothers take the money and the paid leave and never return to work (or return for only a minimal amount of time).

Managing pregnancy issues and perceptions

These are legitimate and often backbreaking problems for a business; pregnancy is one example where the business is truly scared of hiring a person at higher risk of taking maternity leave. Like all other perception issues, this is one that you can manage to a certain extent. If you are likely to have a child, whether you even realize it or not, you may not be perceived as a good hire or promotion.

Although a business is not permitted to base a decision on your chances of becoming pregnant, the issue is nevertheless very present in the mind of the business, so consider revealing an intention *not* to have children. Even if you do plan on becoming pregnant, doing whatever you have to do to quell the business' fears may be the best way to get the job or promotion.

SEX AND RELATIONSHIPS IN THE WORKPLACE

Employees make the best dates. You don't have to pick them up and they're always tax-deductible. —Andy Warhol

There are many different reasons why people have relationships in the workplace, including the fact that we truly know each other, spend time together, and find the relationship convenient. For most of us, work is such a large part of our lives that an outside social life becomes difficult. In the office, we have time to flirt, to fall in lust and love, and to sneak away. Despite all of the better advice to the contrary, people will always date, marry, and have affairs within the workplace.

Your company may ban, or require disclosure of, some or all workplace relationships (particularly manager/employee relationships or intra-departmental relationships). Follow the rules if you can. Violations of these rules must be kept absolutely confidential, since they are grounds for termination.

Don't get romantically involved; what to do if you must

In any case, remember that *relationships in the workplace are rarely helpful to your career goals and reputation and they almost always find their way into public viewing.* Your company needs the ability to take precautions with (and establish rules about) office romances; it is deeply afraid of relationships because of the negative repercussions, including office problems, decreased morale, or getting sued when things go awry.

Even those relationships that are outside of work inevitably end up getting in the way. Regardless of whom you are dating or what is going on in your personal life, work very hard to avoid discussing your relationship with people in the office. And people in relationship-spats always look childish. After you have worked so hard to do your work well, this stuff can bring you down in a flash.

Sleeping your way to the top

There is also such a thing as sleeping your way to the top. It can be a very effective tool to induce direct benefits, both from preferential treatment and the resulting fear of a sexual discrimination complaint.

Sleeping with a manager can be a very reliable way to guarantee some future preferential treatment, since the law requires only a *quid pro quo*, and claims related to sexual harassment can be all too easy to prove, particularly once the manager has slept with a subordinate.

While others may offer more principled words of warning (using words such as "self-respecting"), I will offer only two pieces of advice: Only a stupid manager engages in casual social activities with subordinates, and if you decide to sleep your way up the ladder, be discreet. No two people are less respected than the sleazy manager and the person who is known to have received preferential treatment in exchange for a personal relationship or other illicit interaction.

BOOBS, CLEAVAGE AND CROTCHES

Looking at cleavage is like looking at the sun. You can't stare at it long, it's too risky. You get a sense of it then you look away. — *Jerry Seinfield*

You don't need to be dressed in a sexy manner to be noticed sexually.

If you are a woman with exposed cleavage, or if anything is visible through your clothes, you will be noticed with no further effort on your part. These physical attributes have proven to be powerful weapons when used correctly, but if you don't want to be noticed for them, don't show them. Our female business leaders are not walking around flaunting their bodies, and the quick flash is not regarded as a key indicator of success.

If you are a man, keep the shirt buttoned most of the way and keep your chest hair and biceps out of plain sight. While not as overtly sexual, and a far less effective tool than feminine sexuality, the impact can be perceived as unclean, immature, or unprofessional.

Most workplaces don't know what to do with sexuality. Unless sexuality can be helpful to you or is an element of your occupation, your image usually takes a professional hit when your sexuality is introduced in the workplace.

SEX STINKS

If they knew what we were really thinking, they'd never stop slapping us. —*Larry Miller*

We are talking figuratively, of course. Our sense of intuition often tells us when someone else in the office is expressing a sexual interest or making sexual advances toward another. Managers and colleagues observe this, smelling all those pheromonal interactions when people are interested and on the prowl.

We watch those employees who frequently "visit" other employees. We see the people who lean over the desks of assistants, and we see who lingers where. We watch the posturing and giggling and see the glances and the casual touches. We aren't blind or stupid, and we've been there before ourselves and are quite familiar with the little dance.

No matter how you think your interest is hidden, it is not. The business is watching, and the way you answer your phone, glance from the corner of your eye, whom you go to lunch with, and whom you pay special attention to are absolutely noticed. Hormones are a poorly kept secret.

Avoid sexuality—in *all* its guises.

A sexual advance always looks shady to everyone else, no matter how harmless (or invisible) it may appear to the participants. It is unprofessional (and dangerous) when a person's eyes wander to another person's body. Peeks can never be sneaked. We are all far too sensitive when it comes to visual communication, and we pick up tiny shifts in people's eyes and bodies, and the peak-sneaker, while not always confronted, always looks scummy and unprofessional.

It is not enough to merely avoid the bad conduct, but necessary to avoid even the thought. Sex is so aromatic that we can smell each other thinking about it.

You take a big risk when you can't keep this stuff out of the office (even a glance can be sufficient to create a hostile work environment), and even without any further action, these perception issues can be your downfall. Simple office affairs are never forgotten, and even those that start so well can unravel into endless problems for the business and management. Since we in management know that, you should too.

Sex is loud as well. Sex, like conflict and gossip, is like an earthquake that reverberates throughout, permeating walls and floors, with aftershocks that can go on and on. Some of your colleagues and even your closest friends will tell stories of your activities, particularly the juicy stuff, and the words will spread like disease.

If you choose to have a sexual relationship in the workplace, rest assured that everyone will know. If not now, then soon enough.

HUGGING, TOUCHING AND WRESTLING

It is not a crime nor an impeachable offense to engage in inappropriate personal conduct; nor is it a crime to obstruct or conceal an embarrassing relationship. —Asa Hutchinson

In the workplace, hugging and other touching are almost always wrong. Even with good intentions, they are easily misinterpreted.

Even male-to-male bonding, such as throwing elbows and shoulders, should not be done in broad company (particularly between people much different in size or among people of different sexes). People-bonding, even if consensual, will be perceived by others as exclusionary. Rarely has anything truly positive ever come out of such behavior—and it looks immature to the people who are much more senior.

The boundaries of camaraderie

As someone who appreciates bonding and camaraderie, I'm pained to recognize the dangers in these otherwise innocent acts. The problems arise in all aspects of bonding, including clowning around and office games.

In one former workplace where the hours were long, I remember that as time passed into the late evening, tired employees would meet for games of "hallball," similar to street stickball, but played in narrow hallways where, in our version, a rubber ball is hit with a tube of paper and ricochets off of people, walls, and objects at a surprisingly fast speed. As they say, all is fine until someone loses an eye. And eventually, someone always loses an eye.

DRUGS, DRUG TESTING, AND DRUG TALK

If addiction is judged by how long a dumb animal will sit pressing a lever to get a 'fix' of something, to its own detriment, then I would conclude that net news is far more addictive than cocaine. —Rob Stampfli

Drug testing may happen for any number of reasons. Perhaps your company is legally required to do it. Perhaps it has safety standards to uphold. Or perhaps your office believes that employees who use drugs may cause problems for the workplace or themselves and has decided to manage this risk.

Drug testing is the employer's right. Even during a trend in some jurisdictions for legalization (or partial legalization), employers rights even with regard to legal substances remain in some or all cases. Courts have gone both ways regarding employer rights with regard to medical marijuana. On the whole, drug and testing policies must be disclosed as a policy upfront; in other cases, such as with a person who is an employee-at-will, the drug testing can come with little warning at all.

Using drugs, whether illegal or not, may not be suitable to your profession or job site. Nonetheless, no matter the policy, illegal drugs are just that—illegal, and thus grounds for termination. Whether or not you or I agree, the drug user is a criminal—and few businesses can afford to be in the business of employing criminals.

As to legal drugs, there remains a stigma against casual use (this is not merely related to marijuana, but also sleeping pills, anti-depressants and in many cases even alcohol). With that in mind, silence on the subject is typically the best policy.

Just stop

In today's environment, if you are looking for a job, stop using drugs that may impact you're ability to be hired. If you are working in a job that engages in drug testing, random or otherwise, stop using drugs. If you know that you risk not getting a job, or being fired, yet proceed in the face of losing your livelihood, then you meet the definition of an addict.

Regardless of your views about drug use or even your use of drugs, I should not need to remind you once again that you should avoid talking about drugs. Whatever your opinion of the government's drug policies, keep it to yourself.

Talking about drugs reflects poorly upon you and is an implied admission to use and possibly a crime (as well as an act of immaturity). If you want to do drugs, do it in a way that has nothing to do with your workmates or the workplace. Many people still think that anyone who has used drugs at any time in the past is a bad person.

So be an adult, keep quiet, and don't draw attention to the things that some people, including your manager and colleagues, may not respect or want to be associated with.

No way to bond with employees

And if you have employees, it is highly inappropriate to be anything other than a role model. Using or discussing drugs is not how you bond or connect with others; instead, it is one way to get in really big trouble if for no other reason than that others will be able to use your participation against you. If you cross this line, you deserve all of the trouble you get.

However, if you need me to tell you not to do drugs at or around the workplace, not to do drugs with colleagues, not to discuss drugs, or not to risk your job for a little high, then you're probably in too much trouble for this book to be of much help. Nevertheless, it is truly remarkable what happens in this regard even at the highest levels of reputable businesses.

HUMOR AND JOKES

Oh, you hate your job? Why didn't you say so? There's a support group for that. It's called EVERYBODY, and they meet at the bar. —Drew Carey

As funny as the workplace can be, most of the time it's really not very interested in humor. It is a place where we are lulled into a false sense of comfort, and where land mines abound. People pass around jokes and tell funny stories when the hectic moments settle down. And every joke made in front of someone whose sensibilities are not clearly known is a big risk for the jokester.

People are very touchy—strive not to offend!

If someone can be offended by something you say or do, even in the case of an extremely oversensitive victim, your professional life can become horribly difficult. Unfortunately, work is no longer allowed to be too much fun, not only in a literal, but in a practical and legal sense.

An even bigger problem comes from online video sites such as *YouTube. com*, which often include content that may be distasteful to someone. Even when you are watching a mainstream video news story on *cnn.com* or *msnbc.*

com, the content can offend your colleagues. What's funny, entertaining, or interesting to you is rarely going to be the same to someone else.

Funny = dangerous

In truth, almost all of the best jokes are designed to address a stereotype or deficiency in a class of persons. What makes them funny *is* what makes them dangerous, and practically anything can be offensive to someone.

There are subjects and words that are absolutely off limits in the workplace. This is not about your First Amendment rights (note: you have no First Amendment rights in private sector employment). This is about ideas and words that can literally end your career in an instant and destroy your reputation.

No matter the context, politically sensitive subjects that touch morality, religion, or race, as well as any words that refer to a person's sex, appearance, sexual orientation, or political persuasion can result in heightened sensitivities. The word "boy" or "girl" can get you in more trouble than the old-fashioned four letter words. The "n-word" is a ticket to places you'd rather not be.

When it comes to this stuff, the *context* of the things you say is of little or no relevance. There is no defense for certain words and ideas that are destructive by their nature. The standard for crossing the line is far less than being intentionally insulting—and it is confusing, as even the consideration of a person's race to describe his or her physical attributes might be perceived as a racist comment.

Political correctness and political savvy

Even the most innocent compliments have gotten people in as much or more trouble than insults. I once had to deal with a problem caused by a person who complained about a plainly worded compliment that her clothes looked "really great." The offender was sent to a special class.

This is not merely about being politically correct but about being politically savvy, and *it is correct politically to avoid any language that may demean, insult, or draw attention on the basis of anything other than intellect and work quality. Do not take this lightly.* Many people are oversensitive, and it is not possible to push the limits without something at some time coming back to hurt you.

Quality people are fired every day for what would seem the most innocuous comment or minor offense. Don't let yourself be one of them. Everything that comes out of your mouth should be unequivocally G-rated.

OUT-OF-THE-OFFICE EVENTS AND DRINKING TO EXCESS

Always do sober what you said you'd do drunk. That will teach you to keep your mouth shut. —Ernest Hemingway

Something tangible happens when employees, managers, and executives step out of the office and into the "real" world. People become themselves again, informal and loose, and they pay less attention to the subtleties of effective corporate behavior. When drinks are flowing and conduct standards are loosened, people can get themselves into the most trouble.

Now don't get me wrong. I enjoy a cold one as much as the next person. Corporate standards and work relationships, however, travel with you wherever you go, and what you say and do outside of the office is directly relevant when it comes to your success and survival in the workplace.

Perils of inappropriate out-of-office behavior

For example, sexual harassment charges or other preferential treatment allegations are often born outside the office. That out-of-office joke can absolutely form the basis for the hostile work environment claim. All someone has to say is "I can't work with that person," and your employer is put into a position that may result in harm to you.

An older partner in my first law firm became famous for drinking to excess and hitting on the young female associates during the yearly Christmas party. Two years in a row he made passes at multiple women and ended up passed out on the floor. While he (and we) never got sued, many people refused to work with him, and he became a laughingstock.

In a later job I remember an incident in which a woman who liked a nice young new-hire made her move at a local bar after work, only to discover that another of her colleagues had already snatched him up. The evening conflict that ensued ended up costing both women their jobs.

Bad things can happen after work. Having drinks may provide a terrific opportunity to bond, but always keep very much under control. Drunk is never pretty and often is offensive to someone.

It is not an overstatement to say that you should *never* be drunk in front of those people you need to respect you. If you have low tolerance, perhaps a secret non-alcoholic beer or virgin drink is in order. Even if you can hold your liquor, try to force yourself to stop drinking after only a drink or two at the most. Drunk is always bad—and anything stupid you say or do will become associated with who you are when you're sober. The stories will spread like folklore.

And for goodness' sake, no cameras or video.

NEVER TIE YOUR IMAGE TO THE IMAGE OF IDIOTS

> *Never argue with a fool, onlookers may not be able to tell the difference.*
> *—Mark Twain*

Whenever you associate with someone, you become tied to that person. If your business or your manager does not like the person you are associating with, you will be considered guilty of bad judgment—or even disloyalty.

And if you refer someone to another, no matter how fervently you try to disclaim your affiliation with the person you are referring, you ultimately vouch for his or her character. This includes any candidate you refer for a job, or any business referral you make. Even if you make it clear that you don't know the candidate, if the referral goes bad, you will forever be remembered for the inconvenience you caused. And heaven forbid that you make the bad hiring decision—you will be forever blamed.

My point: *We judge people in large part by their associations and recommendations.* When someone tells me what music or movies they recommend, I learn about that person. Their referral enhances my ability to judge them.

The lessons here are twofold. Even though it may seem unjust, be wary of association with the people you are not *supposed* to be friends with. And

IT'S (NOT) JUST BUSINESS

unless you are receiving a great benefit from the referral, never ever recommend a person you aren't willing to vouch for. Every recommendation always brings with it risk. And that idiot that meant nothing to you can end up costing you an awful lot.

CHANGING THE PERSON YOU ARE PERCEIVED TO BE

It takes 20 years to build a reputation and five minutes to ruin it. If you think about that, you'll do things differently. —Warren Buffett

Most people never overcome their flaws. Some never grow out of them.

Furthermore, becoming labeled as something has a tendency to cause the labeled individual(s) to act the part. This is a very effective tool for inspiring behavior—both good and bad.

Nevertheless, once you are perceived to *be* a certain person, it takes a real jolt to change this perception (particularly by your manager and co-workers). When it comes to positive changes, perceptions are much harder to alter.

The people in your world will not change their view of you willingly, especially if they have come to know you over months or years. *Changing perception is very hard and, depending on your past actions and the character of the judges, may be impossible.*

If you are perceived to be a slacker, you must stay much later and give up a weekend or two to show that you have received the advice and have taken it to heart. If you are perceived to be self-centered, then it is important that you make sweeping gestures to prove that you are a new person; for example, start bringing things in and doing favors for your fellow employees.

Making up for your mistakes means needing to overcompensate. We live in a world where extreme actions are noticed and others usually slip away. Force your manager to notice the sweeping change with a sweeping gesture. Without this, your changes may never be noticed.

PERCEPTION & SELF-REFLECTION   169

"*No institution can possibly survive if it needs geniuses or supermen to manage it. It must be organized in such a way as to be able to get along under a leadership composed of average human beings.*
—Peter F. Drucker

MANAGING
& BEING MANAGED

MOST MANAGERS STINK at managing. That's okay. Most employees stink at being managed.

Attorneys, accountants, medical and IT personnel, along with professionals in other finely-tuned occupations, are notoriously bad managers, because what has made them good at their jobs and got them their promotions in the first place is vastly different from the skills that make a good manager.

The essence of management

Managers, unlike skilled craftspeople, are responsible for one basic task: getting others to achieve business objectives. While some managers drive for an objective without regard for anything other than achieving it (*e.g.*, sales performance numbers), most *corporate* managers succeed by actively managing, educating and encouraging their employees.

Employees report that the best managers succeed when they pay attention to employees' hopes and dreams and are sensitive to their needs—teaching, leading, and earning the respect of the people they manage.

And although most managers are required to give employee evaluations and reviews—an opportunity they should cherish as the most important function of their job (and the justification for their higher pay)—most despise this task, waiting until the last minute and rushing through the process. The most common excuse is that the manager was too busy working on other things and ultimately fails to get to the most important job—being a manager.

Why many managers can't manage

Why are so many managers incapable of basic management? Part of the problem is the "every man for himself" nature of business, along with the fact that the common manager views his strength not as a manager but as a person who is capable of, required to and often rather enjoys performing the tasks he is managing. Another factor is the basic truth that most managers are judged primarily on the completion of business objectives other than managing (such as the tasks being performed by subordinates). These factors create a strong temptation to avoid work distribution altogether or micromanage.

Thus, many managers focus on the task, and they end up bypassing the act of managing. Many are willing to sell their people out at the drop of a hat in order to get a task done, to fix blame for failures, or to seize their own personal opportunities, such as stealing credit for achievements. I once had a manager who would actually *allocate to herself* nearly all of the financial bonuses she was supposed to provide to her people!

Most managers ignore management

Management, unlike a specific area of expertise, is a craft based on finesse, interpersonal and communication skills, motivation, and morale building.

And yet, with all of the management seminars out there, we spend our time going back to the seminars that relate to our chosen professions, rather than spend our effort improving at our craft of management, thereby further abandoning our people and the business' needs. *Management, as a craft, is wholly ignored by the majority of managers.*

Demoralized and disengaged

Most businesses leave it up to managers to "make it up" as they go along. Some offer basic management technique seminars from time to time, with their lessons forgotten shortly after the activity concludes.

The statistics prove this. According to recent surveys, most employees do not think that their manager or company cares about them; surveyed employees cite failed promises, stolen credit, and even the silent treatment by managers.

One recent Gallup study shows that only 27 percent of employees are engaged in their jobs, while 59 percent are unengaged (as evident in indifferent behavior resembling sleepwalking) and another 14 percent are actively disengaged and undermining the morale in the workplace and even the goals of the business. Other studies show that at any given time, more than 25-35 percent of employees are looking for work elsewhere, and fully 60 percent are unhappy in their jobs.

Occasionally a business gets lucky if bad managers step down, rejoining the technical or professional fields that they loved in the first place. But in most other circumstances, the bad managers wallow forever, and your greatest skill as an employee may be to navigate the choppy seas in a boat being captained by a disloyal, incompetent fool.

ALL LEADERS FAKE IT

In response to a reporter's question of what kind of governor he would be, "I don't know. I've never played a governor." —Ronald Reagan (1966)

One of the best kept secrets in the workplace is that even managers know that they, as well as most other managers, lack basic management skills.

The quality manager* not only knows how to manage people and find their strengths, but also recognizes those things that his/her people don't understand.

---

* The words "leader" and "manager" are used interchangeably throughout this book. This is more for ease of communication than for accuracy. As explained by so many of our top experts in business and academia, the crafts of leadership and management are entirely different things. In actuality, managers are successful if they manage to get their employees to complete objectives—they manage stuff—an achievement which may or may not accompany characteristics of leadership. For our purposes, managers are defined as successful if their employees want to follow them. While this is more a characteristic of leadership rather than management, this book is really a discussion more of earning respect and perception, things common among inspirational leaders and somewhat fewer successful managers.

The great manager also knows how to address his/her own weaknesses, by fostering improvement (through tutoring and mentoring), as well as by hiring better people, asking the right questions, writing and speaking articulately, espousing confidence, and earning the trust of colleagues and underlings. On the other hand, one of the greatest strengths of many outstanding managers is knowing when and how to fire people.

A peek behind the curtain

If you take a sneak peek behind the curtain, however, you will find that if you can get managers to speak openly, many/most will tell you that they don't know how they got where they are, and they believe they are not necessarily any better or smarter than the people who work for them. And many regard management as a burden and imposition rather than a blessing.

DARWIN'S RISE OF THE UNFIT LEADER

A funny thing happened on the way to evolution. When the strongest survived, they brought their flaws along as well.

Business is saturated with unfit leaders—people who ended up as leaders for any number of reasons. Ironically, the leadership resources tend to focus on good leadership when far more can be learned from bad. Barbara Kellerman takes on these same questions in her book: *Bad Leadership: What It Is, How It Happens, Why It Matters (Leadership for the Common Good)* identifying the seven most common categories of *bad* leaders, including incompetent, rigid, intemperate, callous, corrupt, insular and evil. The book contains case studies of some of our most popular bad leaders and worst leadership scandals.

Is it possible that the unfit leader is actually the most prepared leader? Could it be that the best leaders are incompetent, rigid, intemperate, etc.? Perhaps these characteristics, while seemingly undesirable, actually make the leader best able to survive in his particular environment. In any event if you are incompetent, abuse dangerous substances, lose your temper, give bad advice, lie, cheat and exhibit no compassion, then take solace in the fact that you too can make it straight to the top. It's the survival of the fittest with all his/her flaws.

The fact that we perceive our managers to be a step above is the real secret; their expertise is in managing perception. No person, no matter how brilliant they seem, is brilliant at everything, and most are not really brilliant at all.

Every person is "reporting to" and seeking support and comfort from someone else in this world. Even our CEOs need the support of their shareholders, spouses, children, parents, and mentors. We are all human and fallible. Even managers.

Welcome to Oz.

LEADERS ARE TALL, THIN, AND FIT

You've got to do your own growing, no matter how tall your grandfather was. —Irish Saying

Economists have long known that tall people on average make more money and hold higher-level jobs than smaller people. Some studies imply that it is the height that matters most (intimidating and dominating); others show that it is actually a question of self-esteem, and tall, fit people (particularly those who were tall and fit in high school, when self-esteem is formed) have more self-esteem than short, fat people (particularly people who were short and/or fat in high school—regardless of how they look today).

In this regard, some people try to make up for their lack of height with the volume of their voices and size of their presences, revealing an inferiority complex that actually amplifies self-esteem issues.

Comfort in your own skin

It is hard not to notice an institutionalized discrimination against people who are overweight. But it is not too far a leap of logic to presume that people who don't take care of themselves are not able to take care of others or that people who don't believe in themselves or lack self-esteem may have a harder time believing in, leading, and managing others.*

---

* These attributes of physical appearance and self-esteem are also thought to trigger a subconscious belief that a person may make a good lover, spouse, bearer of children, or protector of family. While I am a mere reader of these studies, the conclusions do follow basic rules of logic and raise interesting questions.

Self-esteem and comfort in one's own skin are vital to a person's chance for promotion. Those with self-esteem are viewed as capable of being leaders. We look to the people who seem to have command and control over themselves to find some indication that they are capable of looking after others.

Is this fair? No. And yes. We evaluate our leaders based only on what we know about them, and how they look is the one thing we know for sure. Being yourself is good enough only if people can feel confident and comfortable with you. If they can't, then you are not the right person for the job. If the problem is weight, looks, style, tone, or whatever, then that is *your* hurdle to overcome.

We look like a leader before we become one. That's just how it works.

LEADERS DON'T FART

All of the great leaders have had one characteristic in common: it was the willingness to confront unequivocally the major anxiety of their people in their time. This, and not much else, is the essence of leadership. —John Kenneth Galbraith

Most of our best leaders are never seen cursing or insulting other people; nor do they complain, get stressed, or feel depressed—and they don't fart.

Now, we all know that leaders *do* fart, because the human digestive system makes this a part of our overall anatomical makeup. And at home, our leaders do resume a normal anatomical form and they complain, feel stress, get depressed, yell at the kids, fight with the spouse, clean up dog poop, and so forth.

But this "real" stuff is kept very far away from the public eye. If we saw it, we would realize that the leader was just like us, and we don't want to follow someone who is just like us. We want to follow people who are a little bit superhuman. Worthy or not, these are the people we trust with our lives and livelihoods.

This is not to say that a *normal* person cannot rise to the level of the superhuman leader. Sam Walton, the founder of Wal-Mart and *Forbes'* rich-

> ## SMARTER PEOPLE ACTUALLY ARE HARDER TO WORK WITH
>
> Intelligence does not bring happiness. Happiness is closely tied to acceptance—including the acceptance of one's limitations. However, research studies have shown that intelligent individuals tend to be less accepting, more ornery, and generally frustrated at their less intelligent colleagues and at the decision making process in general. It's nothing personal.

est man in America from 1985 to 1988, still drove to work in his pickup truck and wore clothes from his discount store. He is a classic example of a *regular* guy who was viewed as a highly respected and loyal father figure. His humanity gave him character. But despite his humanity, Sam was more than a fair bit superhuman. And superhuman beings don't fart.*

THE SHOES OF PAST LEGENDS NEVER FIT

Stop following me, are you following me? That'll get you twelve years at Leavenworth, or eleven years at twelveworth, or five and ten at Woolworth's. —W. C. Fields

We can *never* fill the shoes of people that are beloved. The more beloved the person whose shoes you are trying to fill, the more different from that person you will need to be. And once our great leaders depart, they assume an even higher stature; they become legends remembered without flaws. Trying to follow and surpass them is like kicking the company's beloved mascot.

---

* While obviously an overly broad simplification, there are two kinds of leaders in this world: those who are leaders by occupation or appointment and those who inspire others to follow. Those who inspire others tend to eventually find themselves in a position of leadership. Leadership expert Warren Bennis (in *On Becoming a Leader*) elaborates on characteristics of the leader who inspires others. Highly recommended.

Pay homage—but be yourself.

This dynamic means that any new generation of leaders must tread gingerly. Pay homage; share in praising your predecessors. We sit in the shadows of our legends, with gratitude and humility, and only then can we stand on the platform they have given us, taking what they have left us to build upon and give to the next generation. We don't do that by being them. We do that by following them, being ourselves, accomplishing great things, and earning respect on our own terms.

SURROUNDING YOURSELF WITH BETTER PEOPLE

First-rate people hire first-rate people; second-rate people hire third-rate people. —Leo Rosten

Perhaps the most common trait of great leaders is that they surround themselves with great people, and then, with humility, depend on those great people to help them live up to their potential.

Great leaders are also adept at knowing whom not to surround themselves with and are capable, with compassion and humility, of separating themselves from those people who are not the right fit. Great people are loyal, hard-working, dependable, and dedicated, not just to the work but to the success of the manager. Not-great people are not.

Deathly loyal

Great leaders motivate those people not only to live up to and collectively exceed their potential, but to remain deathly loyal—not to the business, but directly to the leader him/herself.

THE POWER TO CAUSE INSOMNIA

We are, perhaps, uniquely among the earth's creatures, the worrying animal. We worry our lives, fearing the future, discontent with the present, unable to take in the idea of dying, unable to sit still. —*Lewis Thomas*

Managers, common as they are and barely a step or two above their minions, often fail to realize their tremendous power. ***The mere power to hire, pay, promote and fire is the power to control people's lives.*** With the simplest of off-hand comments, these people, who are otherwise common, can send their employees home in tears.

The manager's awesome power

Managers have the power to ruin their employees' sanity, families, health, and even lives. Simple statements can have great effect. The manager's power is truly godlike.

If you are a manager, bear this power in mind. We all know that you are not the Almighty, and it is as much accidental as purposeful for you to find yourself with this power. While you have earned the right to be a manager, you never earned the right to assume this powerful control over other people's lives.

The managers' God-complex

Nonetheless, acting the part of God seems like a pastime for many managers. If you are the person on the receiving end, remember that the manager, no matter how respected and intelligent, is highly flawed. This God-complex thing is the manager's flaw, not yours. This, however, can be very hard to navigate.

In any event, don't give another person the power over your emotions and life. This is just too much to sell in exchange for a salary.

YOU ARE NEVER AS GOOD OR SMART AS YOUR BOSS

If the king says at noonday, "It is night," the wise man says, "Behold the stars!" —Persian Saying

With that said, when you work for someone else, you are a supporting cast member. Whatever your relationship is one-on-one, you are, in front of other people, a loyal soldier and a cheerleader, and it is in that role that you are of the greatest value.

Being a soldier means fighting the battles that soldiers are assigned. When it comes to getting things done, smart followers, even when smarter than their leader, are still followers. We support the people whom we follow, and the people who work for us must support and follow us.

BE A MANAGER, GO TO JAIL

Managers get fired every day over the failures of employees. An obvious example is the football coach who gets fired when the team loses, no matter the quality of the coaching. The successes and failures of employees determine a manager's career and reputation— and can even lead to civil and criminal liability, as with incidents of sexual harassment and hostile circumstances. These are examples of the way managers must supervise and act quickly in the event of a claim. If the manager doesn't, the company (and the manager) may be liable, even if there was no knowledge of the events.

Employers have also always been held *vicariously* liable for the negligent acts of employees if the negligence happened *within the scope* of the employee's job (even if the employer had no knowledge of the offense).

There are even more facets of a manager's responsibility. Some jurisdictions are criminally pursuing corporate officers and managers if their employees break the law, even if the manager had no knowledge of the violation, and even if the offense was as simple as the accidental mislabeling of a product or filling out a legal form incorrectly.

The California Corporate Criminal Liability Act (dubbed the "Be a Manager, Go to Jail" law) imposes liability on managers (including people put "in charge" for the day) when all of the risks of an activity are not disclosed (such as reminding a paint crew that paint fumes may be harmful). No one said that it was easy to be in charge.

Here's a thought: try not to outshine your manager. Part of being subordinate means following another person's lead. Shut up in meetings with your manager's until you are asked or expected to speak. Never surprise your manager publicly with something you should have brought up privately. Speak at your manager's pace and tone. Follow your manager's lead when it comes to posture. Publicly you are a team, and individually you are owed no credit. When it comes to the corporate hierarchy, managers have already earned their stripes. You haven't.

A single leader, even when flawed, means improved efficiency. Oh, and you're never as funny as your bosses, either. Yes, that means that you should laugh out loud at their jokes. It's silly and artificial, but they'll like you more.

THE MANAGER GETS THE CREDIT

Soldiers generally win battles; generals get credit for them.
—Napoleon Bonaparte

Credit works its way up. The manager gets the credit for his team's successes. That doesn't mean that the employee shouldn't get any credit, but we follow our leaders, and our leaders get our victories. This is a fair allocation of credit, not only because we take instructions from our leaders, but also because our leader is responsible for our inspiration, and moreover, the leader takes responsibility for our defeats. Our leaders present ideas and projects and are responsible for giving them life and legs. Give your manager more victories, whether or not you are credited, and you might even get to share in some spoils.

ROLE PLAYING: TEACHERS/STUDENTS, PARENTS/ CHILDREN, ATHLETES/CHEERLEADERS

First organize the inner, then organize the outer... First organize the great, then organize the small. First organize yourself, then organize others. —Zhuge Liang

All managers believe that they have a role to play. Some are teachers, parents, peers, cheerleaders, drill sergeants, or saviors. Based on your manager's role, you must assume a persona that complements that role, or, in some cases, manages its impact. If your manager wants to be a teacher, then it helps if you become a quiet, attentive and responsive student, whether you like it or not. If your manager wants to be a parent, then you must be the good child. If your manager wants to be the athlete, then you must be either a training partner or a cheerleader. If your manager wants to be a drinking buddy, then it helps if you are a drinking buddy.

In short, if your manager needs your support or is otherwise self-conscious or critical, you are a far better employee if you give your boss the tools he/she needs in order to be successful.

Unsavory manager roles

The most common examples of less acceptable roles that managers might choose include the drill sergeant and the savior. If you are sensitive to being yelled at, or if you feel humiliated or embarrassed, you might consider constructively explaining to your manager that there must be a different manner of communication—but the drill sergeant personality will rarely be deterred.

The savior is a different beast altogether. The savior considers himself to be your personal angel and lifeline, and anything you are permitted, such as a day off or other benefit, to be a personal gift from him or her. If you allow this kind of dynamic, eventually you become subject to the personal discretion of your manager. The savior manager will even try to suggest that your bonus or raise is a personal gift. This, of course, is not accurate.

Roles you'd rather not play

It is not easy to take on a role that you'd rather not play. Personally, I usually hate it when a senior executive decides to take on the role of teacher (particularly if I don't respect the more senior person). I learn more and perform better when I talk to someone not as a student but as a colleague. After all these years, I've earned that.

But in some cases, they have earned the right to act as a teacher, and I respect that. When someone wants to take the time to *teach* me, even in a condescending manner, I tend to let them. I take on the complementary role of student. This allows everybody, often except for me, to be happier in their roles and therefore happier to work with me.

And of course the higher we go, the more often we can dictate the role we wish to play. That right is earned as well.

YOU ARE MOST VALUABLE WHEN YOU ARE EASY TO MANAGE

Accomplishing the impossible means only that the boss will add it to your regular duties —Doug Larson

The more you do well and the less you ask for, the easier you are to manage and the more valuable you are. And the more valuable you are, the more money you will get and the more likely you will be promoted to higher and higher ranks.

Solutions, not problems

When it comes to communicating with your superiors, as well as your subordinates, try to be a source of solutions, rather than of problems. If you have bad news to deliver, try to do it in a manner that does not inspire panic but conveys that you are engaged in the solution.

Being easy to manage also means showing up every day, doing the job diligently, and displaying a willingness to learn and yield to others when appropriate.

Accept criticism graciously and subordinately. Allow the manager to feel good about his or her role. Never let the boss look bad. Be a loyal soldier.

Meet deadlines. Demonstrate that you are willing to make a real personal sacrifice from time to time.*

Be calm. Talk less and listen more. Take special measures to make sure that you don't interrupt your superiors. And anything else you can do to make yourself more easily managed will make you all the more appreciated.

DICTATING THE AGENDA AND TONE (MANAGING THE MANAGER)

> *For the hand that rocks the cradle—is the hand that rules the world. —*
> *William Ross Wallace*

Most managers already have too much to think about. They will gladly relinquish a portion of their management obligations, particularly when an employee comes along who is able to demonstrate real competence.

Managers are flawed, and many forget the instructions they give or the priority of the work that is assigned. If you have this kind of forgetful or fickle manager, be sure to do a superb job of documenting and communicating. Find a way to take charge of this process.

It is never enough to document with, say, nothing more than an email in your file (you might wind up proving your manager wrong, and you don't want that). Consider keeping a whiteboard of projects in order of their priority and visit that list regularly with your manager.

Trust and role reversal

When you are trusted, a bit of role reversal takes place. The trusted employee assumes the role of the teacher. This is often called *managing the manager*. When you do this well, you can set the agenda, the tone, and the priority of projects.

The key is honest communication in which you become your manager's most trusted resource on the things you are working on. In this way, it is important that

---

*   There are exceptions to this. See the section on *The Ways of Politics*, below.

you are not only honest about the good, but that you communicate the bad before the manager finds out the rest of the story from some other person.

Manage your meeting agenda, too.

This is not some casual process. Have an agenda for every meeting, and, if possible, share it in advance, along with a note explaining what you want to discuss. Of course your manager may change the subjects, but you are making it easy for your manager to defer to you.

The endeavor of working toward managing your manager and your meeting agenda helps keep the conversations predictable and therefore puts you in a much better position to prepare for your conversations. Additionally, if you set the agenda, you can frame the issue and present your views in the way that offers you your best opportunity to be heard and to accomplish your goals.

How to win the right to manage your manager

Lastly, your manager will permit you the right to manage part or all of your relationship only if you are able to demonstrate competence, performance, thoughtfulness and an even keel. In my occupation, where million-dollar crises come up out of the blue, your manager's complete confidence and trust are necessary to avoid agonizing micro-management; and even then, with so much at stake, freedom to act autonomously can be quite limited.

I try to never have a mere problem to report. I always bring a proposed solution or a plan of action. I work hard, regardless of my inner concerns, to communicate calmly and clearly.

I frame the issue in a way designed to best control my manager's reaction. Then I am quiet and listen to thoughts, responses, reactions, and suggestions. In this way, I build trust and am permitted great latitude in managing my own affairs.

My clients, colleagues, executives, and managers never see me panic or look helpless, and while they see someone who knows that he is fallible and far from an expert on everything, they see a person who is doing the best he can to manage all of those very difficult issues that surround all of us every day. Of course, sometimes I am pretty panicked on the inside. No manager should ever see that.

Whatever helps them, helps you.

HEARING WHAT THE BOSS IS TRYING TO SAY

Wisdom is the reward you get for a lifetime of listening when you'd have preferred to talk. —Doug Larson

When it comes to receiving feedback, most employees rarely hear what their managers are *really* trying to say. The average employee dismisses negative feedback as unfounded. Dismissing feedback is as easy as saying, "My manager just doesn't understand," or "No, I'm not like that."

Denial is a natural response. We know that while some criticism may be pure and constructive, other criticism may be unfair, coming from the other person's insecurity. That is why it is so hard to figure out the real from the fake. But I promise one thing: everyone, including me—and even you—can improve.

One reason people don't recognize their own faults—apart from viewing themselves through their own subjective mirrors and being expert at lying to themselves—is that *a person's biggest faults may also be his greatest strengths, just misapplied, exaggerated or hidden a little bit.*

Strengths and flaws

For instance, a person who is persistent may come across as inflexible. A person who is honest may come across as brutal and hurtful. A confident person may come across as bullheaded.

The difference between a brilliant strength and a self-destructive flaw may be ever so slight. But this subtle distinction may be the reason employees feel misunderstood, particularly when receiving feedback or running into obstacles. If they could only see the subtleties...

Workplace advice, however, is offered like an auction item. It is going once, and then going twice, and eventually it will be gone, as managers get fed up when they are ignored. Eventually, the possibility of utilizing the good advice disappears.

Truth is very hard to find.

Friends and people who report to us are rarely able to provide us with genuine feedback. If you need to, find a trusted colleague or coach/mentor, and create a way to solicit some honest advice. And stop, listen between the lines, and take it to heart.

GET A MENTOR. THEN AGAIN... MAYBE GET TWO.

Mentorship is a support program in which one person shares education, experience and wisdom with another. It is one of the most important relationships for anyone at any level. To seek a mentor is to accept the fact that you can continue to develop and improve. While humbling, it is generally pretty accurate.

Almost every successful business person can cite one or more individuals who were of great influence along the way. Looking for guidance and advice you trust is invaluable and itself an important reason to find a mentor.

But there is more. Mentors are like found loyalty. Since those who would mentor you are senior to you, the mentor relationship is a direct connection, perhaps otherwise unattainable, to senior people who have an impact on your career. And mentors tend to look out for their own.

TAKING THE INITIATIVE: KEY PROJECTS AND BRILLIANT IDEAS

You have to know one big thing and stick with it. The leaders who had one very big idea and one very big commitment, this permitted them to create something. Those are the ones who leave a legacy. —Irving Kristol

One path to garnering great reviews and promotions is not merely to perform your tasks brilliantly, but to find a way to be assigned to those few special projects that will be most remembered (or just elbow your way in).

There are always those projects that receive extra attention and often provide special recognition for the people involved. Those people who work on the business' most desired initiatives will always be regarded as higher-level employees than those who perform their day-to-day work perfectly.

Come up with one or two things every year that will help your business do something better. This isn't really that hard. A new filing system, a computer program proposal, or a volunteer/publicity opportunity can really make you stand out as a *special* person. Great day-to-day performance will make you a good employee, but an initiative or two will make you a leader.

CONSTANTLY PREPARING FOR YOUR REVIEW

Even a stopped clock is right twice a day. After some years it can boast of a long series of successes. —Marie von Ebner Eschenbach

If you're like most people, you might not remember the things you did just last month. We remember the big stuff, but the small victories disappear into the morass that is the corporate existence. If *you* forget what you did, then you should know for sure that on matters that relate to you, your manager has an even shorter memory.

You are judged by only one thing: *what is remembered.* And typically what is remembered is often only *what is most recent.* Someone who is performing poorly in a recent week, even if that same person had a terrific year, could be rated worse than a person who had an average year but a superb week. *Your job is to make sure that the good stuff is remembered and that as the review approaches, your performance excels.*

Exceeding expectations

Keep a running list of successes, and consider providing that list to your manager on a periodic basis. This list becomes living proof that you are performing well. Be careful not to be petty or include things of little value. The purpose of your list is to be a healthy reminder of why you are *exceeding* expectations.

If your manager doesn't want to see this list, keep it for yourself and attach it to your review or use it when you submit your documents or otherwise communicate with your manager about your performance. (Of course, this must be done before your manager completes his or her paperwork.)

Pay attention to corporate and developmental goals.

It is worth remembering that you are also judged against often silly review criteria based on your developmental goals and corporate initiatives. Don't forget these, because as useless and fleeting as they seem at the time, they come back to life when your manager is completing your review and looking to see if you satisfied your last year's goals. If something like "greater communication with your manager" is a stated goal, excel at this goal until both you and your manager agree that you have performed (or outperformed) in that area.

Lastly, in most corporate environments and economic times, there is a fixed bonus and salary pool to draw from. Since the business does not have an unlimited amount of cash to spend, it will spend it on the people it feels are more valuable.

A zero-sum game

This is a zero-sum game—the *Prisoner's Dilemma*. Life is graded on a curve and, as with dream opportunities, there are only so many passing grades. No matter what you are told, you are competing for your money and recognition against your peers and colleagues at all levels and throughout all departments.

If a corporation needs to, it will ask its managers to grade on a curve to assist in helping identify its most (and least) valuable people. Your manager may have no choice but to find a way to provide lower ratings, either in general or relative to other people. In this dynamic; *your job is to do whatever possible to be perceived as better than your colleagues. This is what the business wants you to be doing.* Game on, and watch your back.

Later on, we will talk at greater length about making your colleagues look bad.

A FEW (MORE) WORDS ON LOYALTY

> *We credit scarcely any persons with good sense except those who are of our opinion. —François de la Rochefoucauld*

Loyalty can be a person's most powerful tool. We help the people we like and who are loyal to us. People who like us and who believe in our loyalty are going to help us. *True loyalty means true commitment, never bad-mouthing or backstabbing, and always being willing to give up some personal liberties in favor of the person you are loyal to.*

The rewards of loyalty

We love people who are loyal to us and hate the people who aren't. The disloyal are inherently untrustworthy. As a result, corporations seek to promote the people who are loyal to it, and managers tend to aggressively help the loyal, in effect being willing to hurt everyone else, regardless of talent.

It's not enough to merely be loyal; finding ways to prove your loyalty is the key to having loyalty work for you. This doesn't happen automatically.

In almost every case, ensuring that your manager is successful will set a foundation that can offer you enhanced opportunities. Being anything other than absolutely aligned with your manager will cause perpetual doubt. Sacrifices—including being willing to give up personal time—prove loyalty. Take on more work and go over and above.

When it comes to winning a manager's love, loyalty often matters more than competence.

When you give your loyalty to someone, however, *you should expect loyalty in return.* Letting your loyalties lie with people who are not able to share in this relationship is wasteful, unproductive, and damaging. This is a mistake made by people who will never truly own their own destiny.

NEGOTIATING AND DEMANDING EXTRA CREDIT

My grandfather once told me that there are two kinds of people: those who work and those who take the credit. He told me to try to be in the first group; there was less competition there. —Indira Gandhi

In my youth, I used to mow the lawn of my neighbor in exchange for $10. One month I mowed the lawn once a week for four weeks when it turned out that my neighbor was on an extended vacation. That forty dollars was important to me. But I never got my money.

Later, when I worked as a valet for tips at a casino in Atlantic City, a car got a flat tire. I changed the tire in hopes of a big tip (giving up an hour of otherwise steady tips, but didn't get anything at all for my effort). I made assumptions that shouldn't have been made.

Although some things must be done to prove your competence and loyalty, acknowledgement and credit must ultimately be part of the deal. Staying late, giving up vacations and personal time, and other examples of great sacrifice will rarely be considered as going over and above, particularly if no one knows the sacrifices you are making or if the work you are doing is part of your job.

What they really care about

Although someone may lose credit for not getting his job done, there is no credit for merely finishing your work, no matter the sacrifice. Many managers, particularly seasoned ones, do not care how late their people stay if the job gets done—only how early people leave.

I used to be surprised at the people who regularly spoke with their managers about money and job titles, or even their job description. I thought they were ungrateful and disrespectful.

I couldn't have been more wrong. Discussing money and promotions with your manager is just fine; it is done by the people who end up with the promotions, the most money, and the best benefit package. It sets the playing field and conveys your expectations, although it does ask for a response that may not be the one you expect.* Keep this in mind not only for when you're hired but throughout your employment.

If you want extra credit, or anything else for that matter, it should be understood up front as part of the deal.

WHEN THE CAT'S AWAY...

No man goes before his time / unless the boss leaves early.
—*Groucho Marx*

Being the stand-up employee when the manager isn't looking makes the best impression, while a single indiscretion when you are left on your own can damage you forever.

You're just the mouse, and take my word for it—the cat is pretty smart.

WHEN THE CORPORATION LIES TO YOU

One of the saddest lessons of history is this: If we've been bamboozled long enough, we tend to reject any evidence of the bamboozle. The bamboozle has captured us. Once you give a charlatan power over you, you almost never get it back. —*Carl Sagan*

People lie all the time. We've covered that.

But when a person in management lies, the business is really doing the lying. When the lie is something that hurts you, it becomes incumbent upon you to decide how you might want to take that up with the business and if it is time to leave or adjust your priorities. If you stay, you are no longer a victim but a knowing participant.

---

* Since managers are great at doing things behind your back and not to your face, this may also place you at an advantage. Provided that the manager does not feel bullied or annoyed, this approach may also succeed by capitalizing on your manager's general reluctance to directly turn you down.

Be smart and cynical, and remember that *the more the business looks out for itself, the more you need to look out for yourself.*

PRAYING TO CORPORATE INITIATIVES, WORKING FROM THE INSIDE, AND TOEING THE PARTY LINE

I'll take fifty percent efficiency to get one hundred percent loyalty.
—*Samuel Goldwyn*

Regardless of how stupid or ineffective a corporate practice, policy, or initiative is, you must believe (or pretend to believe) that it is the best thing since sliced bread. You are being paid, often quite well, to be a cheerleader.

When it comes to influencing company policy, start the dialogue in the capacity of a believer. Outside critics or nonbelievers are rarely given the right or credibility to offer a dissenting voice. Changing policy starts from the inside, and from people who are loyal. It is only with that credibility and shared values that we are given a voice.

Most big initiatives fail, however, as companies either use techniques that are not good fits, do not get enough lower-level employees to buy in, or do not allocate sufficient resources or time. In the end, many initiatives turn out to be gigantic wastes of money, and most of us see that coming from miles away. Granted, however, that the few that work can save millions of dollars.

You must buy in.

In senior management, once your company decides to allocate tons of dollars and thousands of man-hours to an initiative, you must buy in.

There can be no dissenting voices; insubordinate employees are a risk to these massive resource-demanding expenditures. Unless you are in senior management, you are absolutely required—at substantial personal risk if you do not—to buy into these initiatives, no matter how stupid. It is a good idea to be sure that you are protected if/when the initiative is completed and/or abandoned.

Changing things starts with being in the room when decisions are made. If you do not appear to be a part of the team, you will not be in that room.

KNOWING WHERE YOU WANT TO GO

I'm extremely ambitious. I don't know why people are afraid to say that. I won't sell my soul to the devil, but I do want success and I don't think that's bad. —Jada Pinkett Smith

Although every person seems, on the surface, to be interested in a promotion, many people aren't, hoping instead to change jobs or careers, or even preferring to stay right where they are. Our business aspirations comprise not just money and titles, but also our values, interests, dreams and circumstances.

Imprint this on your mental whiteboard: *It is not okay to be honest with your manager if you're considering other job options.*

You will find yourself disadvantaged when it comes to compensation and available internal opportunities. And if your manager knows of your intentions in advance—and unless the business decides to fight to keep you—you will likely not receive the highest rating, promotion, raise or bonus you would have otherwise been entitled to. And if you are perceived to have been dishonest or disloyal, you are less likely to receive a counteroffer for you to stay.

But be honest with yourself. Where do you want to go and what do you want? It is only when you are armed with those answers that you can be certain you are on the right path toward achieving your goals.

BEING THE PERSON THEY WANT TO PROMOTE

Asking 'who ought to be the boss?' is like asking 'who ought to be the tenor in the quartet?'. Obviously, the man who can sing tenor. —Henry Ford

When you decide what you want to achieve, assume that role. Become the next role and you will be seen in that capacity. Even adopt the dress code of the aspired position, and develop and reinforce the traits necessary to define you in that position. Prove that you can and they'll let you. Note, for instance, how important it is for our presidential candidates to be viewed as "presidential" before they are elected.

The better a fit you seem for your next role, the more likely the business is to take a chance on you.

ASKING FOR RAISES AND OPPORTUNITIES

Well, last year my performance review started with Michael asking me what my hopes and dreams were, and ended with him telling me he could bench press 190 pounds. So I'm not really sure what to expect. —Pam Beesly (fictional character, The Office)

There is the adage that says, "Ask and you shall receive." It is true that you must ask for the things that you want, or learn never to expect anything at all. The business worries about the business, and each person in it worries mostly about him- or herself. While there may be some "extra" money to throw around, people would usually prefer to merely *take* that money for themselves.

The real reason why they pay you

With these motivations in mind, remember why you are paid the amount that you are: *because the business thinks that they have to pay that amount or you will leave.* What you *deserve* is not really a factor. It is the threat of your leaving versus the cost to the business that causes the business to pay you what they do and inspires the business to consider and reconsider your pay rate.

Some positions have lots of competent candidates waiting in the wings, and those positions are paid less. There is no generosity in business. The cleaning staff is usually paid very little, and the business simply does not feel guilty about that, no matter how important their role is. Cleaning people can be replaced. When they can't, they are paid more.

In the entertainment world, where unknown candidates are lined up for miles just to have a chance to work with the top actors and studios, they are paid nothing (or next to nothing)—so merely taking the job turns them into a 24-hour servant.

Supply and demand

It is all about the business' need—and supply and demand. If you are the best option for a business and they are unsure if there is another person who is as competent as you, knowing that it might take years of training to replace you, then you can be paid well. If not, then you won't.

With this framework in mind, know where your leverage is. In what way do they need you? In what way is it difficult to replace you? In what way do you satisfy management's own personal selfishness? (You might help them get better reviews and opportunities, make more money for the business, or simply go home, to bed, or to the golf course, trusting that everything is in good hands.) *If they know this, then asking is the key to receiving. If they don't, no amount of asking will make very much of a difference.*

Also, having to *tell* them that they should love and/or need you can be a desperate act. *Showing* them that they love and need you is the key. Then when you ask for something, you will have already made your case (and the risks of your departure will already be well known).

Management love

That's why when all else fails, some employees take dramatic measures to prove how much the business should love them, including such actions as going on strike. When the management says things such as "Pay whatever they want," they have really learned to love.

However, sometimes they realize how much they *don't* love or need you; they may realize how disloyal you are and how replaceable you thereby become. In these situations your value goes down.

It's all just basic negotiation.

PERCEIVED EXPERTISE: THE ONLY GUARANTEED KEY TO SUCCESS

I read somewhere, that the more a man knows, the more [that] he knows he doesn't know. So I suppose one definition of an expert would be someone who doesn't admit out loud that he knows enough about a subject to know he doesn't really know how much. —Malcolm Forbes

There is one way to virtually guarantee respect, employment, trust, promotions, big salaries, and love. Be an expert.

As I've mentioned before, if you are recognized by your industry, your company not only wants you to stay but will look like a fool if they don't recognize and promote you. Become an expert by writing articles or a book, participating in forums, becoming an accomplished speaker or advocate, or doing something that sets you apart from the field.

This stuff is easier than you think. Often all it takes is just deciding to put yourself out there. It might only take a little bit of extra research for you to know more than most of your industry. It's not that hard.

The difference between the person regarded as an expert and the thousands who aren't is often quite subtle.

WHEN OTHER PEOPLE AREN'T DOING THEIR PART...

If you treat the people around you with love and respect, they will never guess that you're trying to get them sacked.
—David Brent, The Office (Ricky Gervais)

Poor performers are every manager's greatest challenge, and we all react in different ways.

Some managers fire first and think later. Most others yell first and rarely ever act, unless they are engaging in the more passive acts of limiting pay raises and bonuses.

It is very difficult to tell someone that he or she is not doing well, particularly if that person is trying as hard as possible. Some managers try to communicate openly, and end up either with someone who improves or with a disgruntled employee. There is rarely any in-between.

Working with sub-par employees

If you are the manager, follow the bad-employee guidelines of your company. One of the best ways to work with someone who is not living up to expectations (particularly if you are thinking about letting your employee go) is to provide work that can be judged objectively, with fixed time periods and/or requirements. The objectivity provides instant and easy criteria for judging.

I tend to advise managers to place poor-performing employees on probation and development plans very quickly, so that when all else fails, the manager is in a better position to terminate the relationship.

People who aren't getting work done often use the defense that they were distracted by other, higher-priority work. If you want to use objective criteria, and if you really intend for the person to face a true and honest test, give your project the highest priority on that person's plate—and document everything.

This is one of the areas where people of character rise up. It takes real guts to deal with this bad stuff. And act fast. Fix the problem, especially if a person is the problem. You have a job to do, and anyone who hinders the work, or the efficiency or integrity of the work, or reflects upon you or the work, must be addressed very quickly.

TO MICROMANAGE OR NOT TO MICROMANAGE?

If you want children to keep their feet on the ground, put some responsibility on their shoulders. —Abigail Van Buren

Micromanaging has negative connotations. Dictionary.com defines it as "to manage, especially with *excessive* control or attention to details." Merriam-Webster's also uses the word *excessive*, which says it all.

How much attention is too much?

Most people like autonomy and need to believe that they can do, on their own, what is asked of them. People like to be trusted and respected and when trusted are more likely to successfully complete their assigned tasks. Employees like to rise and fall on their own merits.

Vicious circle of micromanagement

Micromanaging tends to weaken the employee and suggests that he/she is not trusted or respected; the employee begins to withdraw from the project or become submissive to and dependent upon the manager, leaving the real meat of the project to the manager, who never really let it go in the first place—only to make the manager feel as though the employee is not capable.

Micromanaging is typically quite unproductive. But on the other hand, some things matter more to managers than others, and managers might want to assert extra control for those special things.

This is a difficult balance in any organization, best accomplished with restraint and communication. For those moments, explain why you, as a manager, are paying extra attention. If you can find a way to let your workers share collectively in the reward for great work, you will overcome many of the negatives. But don't make it a habit.

And if you are the one being micromanaged, live with it. This is your job, and you are being paid to show up and do what you're told. Still, communicate with your manager. If you're good, you'll get your chance.

THE CARROT AND THE SHTICK

The act of policing is, in order to punish less often, to punish more severely. —Napoleon Bonaparte

Some people manage with lots of sugar or by dangling a carrot, offering sweet incentives to persuade people to do good work. Others manage with sticks and cattle prods, scaring and intimidating people along the way. Some are bulldozers, clearing a path wherever they go. Get in their way and you will be crushed.

And as any good football coach knows, what motivates one person might not motivate others. Sometimes it is respect that motivates; other times, loyalty. Sometimes, all it takes is a little shtick (defined as a gimmick or comic element—although also used negatively to mean an over-used act).

Scientific studies have shown that people are not generally motivated to do well while under threat. Stress results in unpredictable behavior and should be expected to produce a flight-or-fight instinct. Unless a person has no other options, from a probability standpoint, the stick is usually not very effective. And yet, a good proverbial smack from time to time might be enough to help people appreciate the sugar a bit more.

Your managerial toolkit

There are many tools available. As a manager, lose the emotion and address the matter at hand.

If you are in the role of leader, or if you want to be the leader, a very powerful tactic is to treat people engaging in childish acts like children. Shame works. Phrases such as "this is not helpful to me," "you disappointed me," and "this has let me down" can often be more powerful than any lecture, explanation, or emotional outburst.

Notice that these are direct and rhetorical. No response is expected or, in most cases, appropriate. Limit the ability for a response, since any response greatly lessens the impact.

Unless you have decided to finish in a collegial and feel-good manner, simply end the conversation and dismiss the child (I mean, the employee) immediately after you have said what you needed to say. A simple "thank you, we can talk about this more later" is often sufficient.

Great leaders do not drone on. They say only what needs to be said.

DEPARTING YOUR EMPLOYMENT

It's not that I'm afraid to die, I just don't want to be there when it happens. —Woody Allen

It is a sad show when a person who dislikes the company, or who is disliked, departs employment, whether quietly or angrily. This is a sad demonstration, not only of a beaten person, but also, often, of lost opportunities.

If you are the departing employee, your greatest opportunities occur during those moments when you are departing. In these circumstances you are no longer a slave to the hierarchy, and for the first and last moment in your employment, you have the opportunity to look your manager and other executives and higher-ups in the eye and talk to them person-to-person.

You are in the position of building relationships, even with people you've never even met. This is your chance to turn something negative into something brilliantly positive; get business cards and begin to transform your work relationships into professional networking relationships. Offer to take them out to lunch. Tell them not about the mistakes they've made, but why you value them.

Departure behavior tips

Complaining on your way out the door is meaningless and reflects poorly. Shake every person's hand firmly, while being sure to maintain a confident and comfortable eye contact, whether you are fond of this person or not. This simple gesture could be remembered forever.

And do not linger. Do not come back to the office except on the most special of special occasions. Be invited. You are not a dog that has been cast aside. Get up on your feet and walk away.

Then, when the dust has settled, drop a personalized email to senior people, with specific issues to discuss. Asking advice is often a reason to send a note. If you're in the area, buy a lunch or two, or send cards to stay in people's memories; use all of these people to continue building a network. This is how you create your legacy. As your career progresses, this stuff pays off.

Always: a better opportunity

Also, whether you are leaving on your own terms or theirs, publicly you are always leaving for a better opportunity. This is still true even if everyone knows that you are not. It's just one of those classy things to say, and you will be respected for it.

Even if you are expecting to sleep late, drink until you become sick, and eat yourself obese on pizza and chips, make sure you have a better story to tell. This is about respect, image, and lifelong relationships. If you do anything to damage these relationships, no matter how good it makes you feel at the time, you will have lost more than you may ever know.

AND AFTER YOU ARE GONE...

*To withdraw is not to run away, and to stay is no wise action, when
there's more reason to fear than to hope.*
—*Miguel de Cervantes Saavedra*

Managers are always placed at a disadvantage when an employee leaves,
and they like to be able to pick up the phone from time to time to get information from the departed employee.

Even after your departure, there may be opportunities for you. It's nice
to be a tiny bit helpful, but if the business still requires your ongoing expertise (any more than for just a few minutes of your time), let them pay
you on a contract or consulting basis for your time and knowledge. They
should continue to pay you for your time whenever they need your services.

If they need more of your time, offer to give them a few hours per week
for a few weeks of consulting time and have them set a price (perhaps higher
than your former per-day rate). If you don't put your foot down, your past
employer will get whatever it can out of you for as long as possible.

Your leverage here can be quite good. Business pays for its help. If they
need you, they'll come up with the cash. It's only fair.

I formed a corporation this year, and I'm the president, my mother is vice president and my father is secretary and my grandmother is treasurer and my uncle is on the board of directors - and they got together the first week, and they tried to squeeze me out. I formed a power block with my uncle and we sent my grandmother to jail. —Woody Allen

THE ART OF
POLITICS

ALL POLITICS, even the most innocent kind, can end up leaving somebody on the short end. More aggressive tactics can leave others scarred and tattered. And while it is impossible to be *successful* while avoiding politics, it is nearly impossible to play politics defensively; waiting until you are under attack means being put in the awkward position of looking wrong or guilty. Your best defense is participation—and typically a planned offense (a.k.a., a strategy for actually getting something accomplished, ideas adopted and your voice heard). This generally requires that you intuitively know how others are likely to react and behave in different situations and that you carefully consider your path to success. Savvy business people do this. Most others do not.

The value of politics; offensive and defensive

Most savvy politicians participate in business assertively, setting boundaries, engaging in meetings, and establishing working relationships. The cleanest, value-driven politics can provide a terrific basis for the adoption of good ideas, and it permits others to save face so that relationships are not damaged and problems are not inadvertently escalated.

Politics on offense (assertive politics) can be genteel and humane, and it can be practiced in a manner suitable to personality and values. Perhaps you might choose to play inclusive politics, getting other people to join you, or play exclusionary politics, leaving certain people out.

As we get into a discussion of power politics we find collections of more aggressive and at times mean-spirited behaviors. For instance, a form of subtle offense power politics is to look helpful as you set another person up for failure by assigning tasks that can't be successful. When you are on the offense, you hold the cards and you dictate the tone.

Defensive politics is much more challenging. Once you or your ideas are under attack, or when you have already been blamed for something, any blanket response or counter-move can be seen as petty, predictable, and untruthful. Disproving the negative or responding to no-win inquiries such as "Did you make a mistake in this draft or in that one?" complicate the field of play. Playing effective defense often requires greater subtlety as well as the use of truly political tactics, something that the common employee might not want to engage in.

Politicians reluctant and great

The reluctant politician's greatest weakness is his tendency to become offended at others' methods or tactics. In business it is difficult but important to keep emotions under control so that objectivity and perspective can be maintained. Any negative reaction—including poor morale, imprudent behavior or a childish response—exacerbates the problems that are already present.

Great politicians tend to appear to take the workplace as it is (note: one exception may be the ruthless politician who obscures dangerous retaliatory tactics and the anger that prompts them, under the guise of loyalty to the business).

It helps if you are familiar with all of the characters playing the game and with the tools and tactics they are likely to use. As I mentioned in my discussion of negotiating, it is often enough to reveal the politician's tactic in front of other people, if necessary, to cause the attacker to back off and deny the approach. In other cases, recognizing the tactic tells you what you need to do to protect your ideas or yourself.

Politics is hard stuff. It takes time, patience, and practice. <u>And actual consideration and planning.</u> It requires knowing and considering how people think and make decisions. And the more savvy the players or the place, the more complicated, and methodical, the game.

SSSSSSHHHHHH. WE DON'T TALK ABOUT THIS STUFF

With Foxes we must play the Fox. —Thomas Fuller

We all know that politics are everywhere, yet we all pretend to not be political. Outside of your strategic group, you should never talk about political strategy. Many of the best politicians are all pretending that they are clean, that playing politics is beneath them, and that they are only acting for the best interests of the business.

SCHMOOZING UNDER THE GUISE OF WANTING NOTHING

If you're a gifted flirt, talking about the price of eggs will do as well as any other subject. —Mignon McLaughlin

Politics starts with whom you know: your friends, your loyal team, and those people you can count on because your interests are aligned (or because they like you or owe you a favor or two—although these last factors are less reliable).

Building relationships is not easy. Businesspeople are smart and don't like to be sold—our default reaction is to immediately reject salespeople, sales calls, and visits. We make it hard on people who want something from us. And as a general rule we do not help people out of sympathy. We help people and get to know them because we believe that they will eventually help us.

The advantages of wanting nothing

On the other hand, we have none of these same barriers when it comes to building relationships with people who want nothing from us. We appreciate the idea of networking and welcome opportunities to shake hands and spend time with people we might one day want something from but who want nothing from us today. Inroads are best made before you want or need anything.

Keys to building business relationships

Remember the basic keys to building a business relationship:

1. Be known, liked, fun and funny.

2. Have some special thing, perhaps company information or market connections that can one day make another's life better and easier.

3. Offer ideas, events or *secrets* that prove your value or create a bond.

4. Become a friend. Stay in touch!

In short, people already have too many contacts. The best in any field already know everyone of importance. So *in order for them to want to know you, you must offer the idea of something that can be of interest to them down the road.*

While you are acting in your self-interest, they are acting in theirs, and neither of you really cares very much about the other's. Come to the networking game from a position of value.

Get into the conversation. And then follow up immediately. Get that lunch or drink meeting scheduled right away. Get on the golf course.

Do something! If you don't, you might as well have stayed home and watched television.

MONEY BUYS FRIENDS, LOVE, HAPPINESS, AND SUCCESS

> *Money is power, freedom, a cushion, the root of all evil, the sum of all blessings. —Carl Sandburg*

Do not underestimate the power of money. It most certainly is capable of buying happiness, friends, and love. For that matter, money buys success and even more money (money is one of the leading causes of fights among friends and in divorces). Friendships based on money are often the most productive relationships in all of business. Money also buys talented employees and everything else that can be purchased to enrich and pamper those people and their businesses, thus magnifying the spender's power all the more.

How money buys opportunities

Relationships are a major key to success in business, and money buys relationships and opportunities, mostly through planned events and shared benefits. Successful people like to hang out with people who have box seats to major league sporting games, memberships at prestigious golf clubs, and other perks that we would never otherwise enjoy. The more you spend, the more you get.

Also, money brings with it the perception that you are a worthy person to associate and do business with. Spend wisely, however, or you will be taken advantage of. Pay for the things that will be remembered, and you are in a great position to have your calls answered and to pull all kinds of strings. With the right friends, no matter how you get them, you can do pretty much anything.

FRIENDSHIPS DO NOT LAST FOREVER

Have no friends not equal to yourself. —Confucius

Regardless of how loyal a person is, everything can and does change. The cold, hard fact is that many friendships should not last—or pretend to last beyond their actual expiration date. Some break down, only to rebuild later. Others collapse, causing each former friend to declare himself an archenemy of the other. People's interests and opinions change over time as we grow in separate directions and perhaps tire of one another.

When a friendship fails, there is an emotional component—hurt and regret. This is normal. There can be great longing and a time-consuming desire to achieve a fresh start.

But without burning any bridges—since even a basic contact (such as an old friend) can be important—do not cling to the idea of loyalty where it no longer exists. When someone is no longer a friend or his or her interests no longer align with yours, you should bear in mind that most friendships do not last forever and consider what this might mean to your business dealings.

KNOW THE PEOPLE WHO KNOW STUFF

Position yourself as a center of influence - the one who knows the movers and shakers. People will respond to that... —Bob Burg

Without looking obvious or sleazy, get to know the people who have information that would be helpful to you. Mostly these are the assistants to the bigwigs, but they can also be the people that just have a knack for hearing things and getting things done.

When it comes to corporate politics, these people are worth more than their weight in gold.

IF YOU ARE NOT NOTICED, YOU DO NOT EXIST

If you don't get noticed, you don't have anything. You just have to be noticed, but the art is in getting noticed naturally, without screaming or without tricks. —Leo Burnett

Regardless of whether a person is doing well or poorly, we tend to offer the most glory and promotions to people who have let us know their expectations and aspirations. We respond to the squeaky wheels, sometimes just wanting them off our back or to keep the status quo. And we often promote not the best people but those who have indicated to us their undying desire for career enhancement.

Promote yourself (tactfully)!

The quiet, brilliant worker who is not asking for recognition or promotion has a far worse chance of receiving even the simplest gratitude than the less competent person who is doing a great job hustling or letting his or her aspirations be known (tactfully, of course). The diligent employee is seen as the stable employee, best left alone for fear of upsetting whatever delicate balance he/she has.

If you want more than you have, you must be active in your manager's and the company's consciousness—in a good way, of course.

In the entertainment world, great publicists keep their clients in the public eye, whether it is for the good, bad, or controversial stuff. Being a household name (and face) matters.

If you are *present*, if you are sending email updates, attending meetings, taking/making calls, taking the initiative, voicing educated opinions, and in the end expressing your interest in money and promotions, then you will be the first one on others' minds when these issues are considered. Throw your hat in the ring for whatever you want. And make your case. If you don't, you might as well not exist.

GIFTS, GOLF, CIGARS, SHOOTING POOL, AND BONDING

The American businessman is somebody who talks about golf all morning long in the office, then for the rest of the day discusses business on the golf course. —Jerry Lewis

Send gifts, early and often. We remember those few people who send us gifts.

Playing golf or smoking cigars with the executives, or doing anything else (such as playing poker, skiing, attending conferences, or shooting pool) that gets you in the room with the key people on a friendly basis is tremendously important, but continue to work on how you are perceived, because your interpersonal mistakes may be magnified in this context.

In addition to name recognition, the advantages from person-to-person contact can provide nearly instant payback. It is no exaggeration to suggest that many of the biggest business decisions are made away from the workplace in lower stress, fun environments. The games are non-threatening, and the shared activities place you in close and friendly proximity with business leaders who will, in turn, notice you and hear your ideas, comments, and concerns.

This is why aspiring business people pay for membership at the country clubs where the rich people hang out.

And when you are engaging in a competitive game, be sure to remember to lose a round from time to time.

PEOPLE WITH WHOM YOU MUST NOT BE FRIENDS (AND THE IMPORTANCE OF AVOIDING THEM)

If you wish to be held in esteem, you must associate only with those who are esteemable. —Jean de la Bruyere

Loyalty to the wrong person will hurt you. This is a bit of a different twist on tying your image to idiots (covered previously), but here we are talking about the politics of the matter.

Outcast acquaintances make you an outcast. If your boss doesn't like one of your work colleagues, and you are friends with this person, your boss will not only not respect your decision, but will justifiably question your loyalty and your judgment—and you are not as likely to be confided in.

Avoid the lepers

There are lepers in the office. Some people are lazy. Others are bad news. Others aren't trusted or respected. Others gossip. Many are just not liked. People who are miserable or complainers are known and despised by management. And while you need to protect your perception and not be connected to this negative baggage, your best approach is to identify these outcasts and keep your distance. You undermine your credibility and your connection to your manager and to the business when you associate with these hooligans. If you are going to socialize with them, do it far away from the spying eyes of the workplace.

This is one of those harsh rules (we have a few). It tells you not to help the weak. But in business there might be no other way. Known interactions, including talking to people of disrepute or seeing them after work, can hurt you. It may not be decent or charitable, particularly when these people start out as your friend, but when management clues you in to its feelings about certain people, you are being asked to choose between the business and the bad crowd.*

DEAD EMPLOYEES MAKE FOR THE BEST EXCUSES

I never blame myself when I'm not hitting. I just blame the bat, and if it keeps up, I change bats. —Yogi Berra

The key to mastering the blame game is to blame people who can't or don't defend themselves. Examples of terrific people to blame are employees who are on the outs with their managers, are otherwise not trusted, or have departed the business.

Although this tactic can be unethical and distasteful (no surprise there), it is tremendously common and effective—so effective that even if people recognize it as a weak attempt at passing responsibility, they will allow the blame to go on for years.

It's easier (and accepted) to blame people who have no voice or who allow themselves to be blamed. If you want to see this process in action, just look at how our national leaders blame past presidential administrations, Congress, the other party, the weather, other countries, and elected officials not limited to those just recently out of office, but people dead and gone for decades.

When you are the one who is gone or suffering, expect to get blamed. But if you are not gone, defend yourself aggressively or the blame will continue *ad infinitum*. It is the cycle of life.

---

* We find examples of the tremendous power of association, sometimes just from a monetary contribution or even an appearance in the same photo, in campaign politics, in which the negative aspects of all known acquaintances are attributed directly to the candidate. Here, even the loosest connection between two people may be enough.

POWER *SHOULD* ALWAYS WIN

> *You can get much farther with a kind word and a gun than you can with a kind word alone. —Al Capone*

When it comes to a head-to-head dispute, the person with the most power or leverage in a given situation *should* always be able to get his way and to control the outcome of a situation.

And yet, they often don't, commonly losing out to people who are more politically savvy. Instead, compassion, the acceptance of lesser power as something greater than it is, bad decision making, poor negotiating skills, and an overarching sense of fairness get in the way, undermining the powerful person and allowing the less powerful to end up in control.

Pay attention to your sources of power and to the other person's perceived power. Maximize your position; diminish theirs.

Being truly powerful…

… means wielding power (not subjugating yourself to lesser power), winning negotiations by being *unwilling to concede*, making decisions, dismissing opponents and critics, and doing all of this in a manner that does not ultimately damage your credibility, likability, and the power that allowed you to do all of this stuff in the first place.

POWER IS *FOUND* IN WEIRD PLACES

> *If you owe the bank $100 that's your problem. If you owe the bank $100 million, that's the bank's problem. —J. Paul Getty*

In almost any dynamic, power can be *found* and *created* by the person who is most aware. It is more a matter of perception than a reality.

Toddlers in grocery stores understand this power-play better than most adults. In hoping that Mom will buy him a candy bar, and with no money or bargaining power apart from the volume of his voice, the child shrieks until the mother gives in, unable to handle the embarrassment. The child simply invents his own source of power.

We see customers use this technique every day when they threaten to notify the newspapers or Better Business Bureau (or threaten to leave negative feedback on the Internet).

If the business feels threatened, then the disgruntled customer finds a source of power. We see examples of this same power shift in people who are victims of a hostile work environment or sexual harassment. Other power grabs include questioning subtle legal issues that the other person might not be familiar with, or finding discrepancies in facts.

If the child can get a candy bar out of a parent by simply screaming—and the child is entirely dependent on parents for everything—than you can find *real* power *anywhere* if you look hard enough.*

IGNORE THE THINGS OTHER PEOPLE WANT YOU TO CARE ABOUT

Necessity never made a good bargain. —Benjamin Franklin

You realize one of the greatest sources of power when you simply decide not to recognize another person's power. When the mother ignores the screaming child, the child's power is eliminated. When the child ignores the mother's instructions, the mother's power is eliminated. When you don't care whether or not you go to jail, then the government's power is eliminated.

In the business world, when a person doesn't panic over deadlines, then the other person's delaying tactic becomes irrelevant. When you don't care about being fired, then the looming power of the company and your manager vanishes.

Oftentimes we have to work very hard, and may become highly emotional, when we are pretending to dismiss another person's power. This bluff is life's poker game (and one reason why people use agents and intermediaries

---

* It is understood in negotiating theory that the weakest party in any given situation is to be most feared. A person (or group) with nothing to lose can find substantial power in simple acts of disruption, accusations or other activities to cause major nuisance or casualty.

who really don't care about the outcome). Someone might call your bluff, in which case being revealed can end up costing you.

But *if you can succeed in not becoming emotional and not caring (or appearing to not care), you can have more power than anyone else in the world (or at least in your department/business unit).*

WHEN THEY CAN SEE YOU COMING...

You have to be 100% behind someone before you can stab them in the back. —David Brent, The Office *(Ricky Gervais)*

The study of war tells us that our best weapon is surprise. If others cannot see our strategy, then they cannot prepare for us. Keep your competition on edge and don't let them see you coming.

This is the strategy embodied by Sun Tzu's quote: "Keep your friends close, and your enemies closer." The more you know about the people you are dealing with (and against), the better you can address the tendencies of that person. In times of conflict, this also means that you should stay agile, changing tactics as necessary, to keep the balance of power in your hands.

THE FUNDAMENTAL TACTIC: THE *EX PARTE* AND LOBBYING

The first duty of a wise advocate is to convince his opponents that he understands their arguments, and sympathizes with their just feelings. —Samuel Taylor Coleridge

A game learned in our infancy is the *ex parte* tactic (meaning "without a party").

This tactic involves simply leaving people out—you take your case directly to individuals without anyone present to interfere with your argument, offer counter-opinions or other ideas to get in your way.

Children are expert in this, asking each parent separately and then playing one parent against the other ("Dad said we could get some ice cream")

or by going from parent to parent to babysitter until they are awarded the thing that they sought.

So get your opponent out of the conversation, or amass other people against the dissenter, and you can control everything that happens in the dialogue. Each person you speak to will get your undivided attention and you will get theirs; you can thus convince them of your thought, request or idea without opposition.

The downsides of the *ex parte* strategy

This brings us to two of the biggest problems with the strategy.

First, because there is no one to refute your statements and opinions, the person you are speaking with expects that you are speaking accurately and completely, representing all sides of the issue (including your opponent). If that person later finds out that you lied or didn't tell a complete story, you will lose far more than you gained. Second, in any *ex parte* communication, each person you speak with wants to feel as if he is the most important, worthy of your bringing the issue to him directly; such a person could feel insulted when it becomes apparent that you have brought the issue to others. If this is a concern, consider revealing that you are building consensus.

In the end, splitting people up and lobbying is effective (often required) as you build the consensus on an individual-by-individual basis until eventually you have sold your ideas to the group.

If, on the other hand, a person approaches you in an *ex parte* manner, recognize the potentially manipulative nature of the discussion and feel free to put an end to it by bringing all the other people and opinions involved into the conversation.

PLAYING THE INFORMATION GAME

To find out a girl's faults, praise her to her girlfriends.
—*Benjamin Franklin*

We don't know what we're not told. And we don't know what questions to ask if we don't have sufficient knowledge.

If you are the only person with information related to a particular subject, then only you can decide how to use the information. In fact, the more information you have, the better you are able to spin the facts and statistics to suit your needs. Since it is difficult to ask questions when you don't know what you are hoping to learn, the person with the information is in a far better position than any person without it.

For instance, I understand technology to a degree that allows me to work constructively with my technology department. When they tell me something can't be done, I know enough to know when they're wrong or not thinking something through (or lazy). When IT tells me something is complicated, I can help offer ideas and solutions.

Other business colleagues who lack any IT expertise would have to take whatever information provided at face value. Because in my case *they* don't have all of the information, I can get us to a much more favorable outcome than if I were ignorant on the subject. If I were less familiar with this stuff, I'd have to trust everything they told me as absolute truth.

Of course, this is a fairly innocuous example. What if you wanted me to fire someone and only brought me (as the company lawyer) the bad information—but not any of the good information? Then you are controlling all of the information that goes into my decision. You are almost certain to get your result unless I take some more drastic measures, such as interviewing the people involved, including other people that have some information—all things I might not want to do.

Other tactics for using information in order to make someone else appear incompetent: giving incomplete, incorrect, or confusing information, or providing information to people so late (such as right before a meeting) that they don't have time to prepare or ask questions.

The defensive tactic is to explain to the group (a public reveal) that the information has only just been provided rather than risking any discussion in the moment, "Unfortunately, I haven't had a chance to thoroughly read the information that I just received ten minutes ago, so I may have to discuss this matter at a later date."

The rule here is to know *everything* about *everything*. If you don't have the information, you are in no position to be able to make any competent decision (including the management of people higher and lower than you).

Develop a sense for when you need to learn more or talk to other people. Remember that everyone who speaks to you has a bias for how they want things decided. Talk to everyone and build relationships, make small talk, and learn stuff.

Mastering the information game means learning your job and everyone else's to the point at which no one can get away with telling you only part of the story. It means being smarter.

CREATING CRUSHING FAILURES FOR OTHER PEOPLE

Never interrupt your enemy when he is making a mistake.
—*Napoleon Bonaparte*

Setting other people up for failure or not coming to the aid of people who are failing is another of the most effective tactics. It allows you to achieve your goals, often with very little personal exposure.

The tactics here are simple; get someone to fail (or don't help them as they fail) so that you can achieve an objective, or so that their damage can provide you or your project with some business or personal advantage.

The most common way that a more senior person might utilize this approach (often carried out to give people a lower rating, hurt their credibility, or get them fired) is to assign work that they know can't be completed or achieved. The employee who then fails is viewed to have failed in the eyes of the business and his colleagues, and the manager escapes untarnished. Other variations of this tactic include giving the target employee too much work, then watching passively as the employee misses deadlines. Then, of course, the devious manager or person requesting the assistance holds the person accountable for the failure.

Or you can simply watch a person who is making mistakes without assisting (or actively encourage ongoing mistakes by sending the person down the wrong path). Peers might do this to one another in order to gain a personal advantage, such as a larger bonus, a raise, a promotion, or credit for saving the day.

There is very little risk to a person who is passively engaging in this tactic. As a manager, the worst that can happen is that the target might actually accomplish the assignment, in which case you can offer little praise and hit the target employee with another impossible-to-complete task.

Now if you are the victim of this tactic, being set up or allowed to fail or being placed on a limb that is sure to crack, you cannot wait for failure to become imminent before acting. Report your progress, defaulting to over-communication. If you are on a limb, get other people on the limb with you. The more people who are vested in seeing a project succeed, the less likely that the business will allow the project to fail.

The power in this tactic lies in the idea that the politician does not appear to be doing anything wrong, that success is made impossible or fruitless, and that imminent failure can result in anything from not being awarded a promotion to being demoted or terminated. The victim is sure to be branded as incompetent or insubordinate.

Surviving this tactic is not a victory. If a manager has it in for you, your victories will not be rewarded, and along will come another failure project. If this is the dynamic, become engaged in the game, change your loyalties, find secret angels, develop shared interests, set up your manager for failure, and, if all else fails, plan your departure.

THE LAND GRAB AND EMPIRE BUILDING

Bureaucracies... cannot be relied upon to defend existing regimes once they suspect that the victory of a new regime is probable. —E.J. Hobsbawm

Although neither you nor any other person is truly essential, it is possible to make the business sufficiently dependent upon you that it becomes thoroughly inconvenient to replace you or terminate your position. This "essential-*ish*" role also makes it hard for the business not to value or promote you, particularly when you are otherwise at risk for departure. One way to do this is to build an empire (known in the pejorative as being *territorial* or engaging in the act of *empire building*).

How to build your empire

Expand your territory of power and control. Build *institutional* knowledge (be the one who knows stuff). Go get the people. Fight for open positions and reorganizations that center power with and around you. Under the guise of full disclosure, stop disclosing information. Be the only person responsible for knowing how things work and get done, and then keep this stuff a secret so that people have to come to you in order to get those things done. Be the only one who knows the filing system. Be the only one who knows certain people or those can do certain things, and then the business will be more inclined to foster its relationship with you.

The most powerful (or at least the most entrenched) people tend to have the most information and control. If it would be inconvenient for people within the company to lose you, everyone will be much more reluctant to do anything that hinders you.

PLAYING THE "SLOW THINGS DOWN" GAME

> *Delay always breeds danger and to protract a great design is often to ruin it. —Miguel De Cervantes*

While we spoke earlier about meeting deadlines, there are a number of reasons, some legitimate and others political, why you might want to slow a project down.

You might think that people aren't considering all of the facts or the risks of a particular course of action. Or perhaps you believe that a project is not good for the business or for you, or that their idea will kill yours or otherwise inconvenience you in some way. In fact, studies reveal that simply slowing a project down is the best way to kill it.

Ways to slow down

There are many ways in which you can slow or kill a project. Although contrary to prior advice on deadlines (from an efficiency and perception standpoint), it can be a tremendously powerful political technique to delay, miss deadlines and drag out a project's phases.

In other cases, assign work that is related to the project but not necessarily required (such as special research projects). In other cases start asking questions and refuse to proceed until the questions are answered satisfactorily (a tactic used most often by more senior people).

Other ways to slow or kill a project include identifying problems and asking that the problems, no matter how unreasonable, be resolved right away; or identifying risks and asking that they be entirely eliminated (this tactic is effective because almost no business risk can be entirely eliminated).

The risk here is that you will be seen as a frustrating person to work with or, more aptly, as an obstructionist. These are undesirable perceptions, so be sure to balance your approach with your need to be perceived as a collaborator who is looking out for the best interests of the business.

If *you* are being slowed down

When a project you care about is seemingly being slowed down, try to figure out the different players' motives and address each directly (perhaps with individual communication). If you can get everyone's buy-in, or at least figure out where problems may lie, you are in a far better position to get your work through. Shifting corporate priorities and resources is the most common way to achieve this.

Defending against the slowdown tactic starts by recognizing this tactic before the project has entirely stalled. Then find a way to induce your adversary to get out of the way.

You might put everyone together in a room, headed by a person more senior than the person who is trying to kill the project. Set firm deadlines and take a project management approach that highlights individual people's failures. Align powerful people's interests with the project's completion. Require that all known issues be put on the table and discussed, that certain risks be accepted. When the obstructionist runs out of tools to use, he will become either a supporter, a reluctant participant, or irrelevant—but if that happens, you should avoid implementing a system that will allow the obstructionist the time or opportunity to come up with more obstacles.

CALLING ALL CRITICS

Had we not faults of our own, we should take less pleasure in complaining of others. —Francois Fenelon

A large portion of some people's individual politics involves sitting in meetings and attacking other people's ideas, often throughout their whole careers, without ever offering ideas of their own. This can be highly effective. Victims of this tactic can suffer greatly, rarely if ever escaping the shadow of the criticism.

Critics exist to be critical (obviously)—to announce what is wrong and why ideas stink. This is often a politically effective tactic with little or no personal risk at all, hurting others without repercussions. Dish it out as necessary—if done well, it will make you look like an expert and protector of the business' bottom line.

On the receiving end, appear to take what is legitimate, but call the critic on the critique. It can be very dangerous (*i.e.,* weakening) to allow you or your ideas to be attacked without a swift defense. *Require* your critics to offer real ideas. Politely find a way to get any critic, no matter how senior or junior, vested in the solution. Sometimes it is as simple as publicly saying, "I hear your concerns and I don't really see the risks. But I think you and I should get together to come up with something we can propose together." *

---

*   Provided, however, that while this may help to eliminate a critic, it may end up rewarding the adversary with a portion of the credit. Balance this defense with other possible alternatives such as those for defending against delay (see *Playing the "Slow Things Down" Game* above).

THE MOST EVIL TACTIC: PUBLIC HUMILIATION

The one sure way to conciliate a tiger is to allow oneself to be devoured.
—*Konrad Adenauer*

People who say things in front of other people are often the dirtiest of politicians, often because most people don't respond or react well to attack and criticism in front of others. The publicly attacked end up looking helpless and exposed. Any natural defense other than flair and skill risks looking fabricated and defensive.

If the attacker does not have a legitimate criticism, he might assert managerial authority in assigning criticism, tasks, and instructions, and if you have done everything right in the first place, he will change the criteria.

Even when this tactic is anticipated, bystanders tend to *enjoy* these events just as spectators enjoy traffic accidents and train wrecks—with a twisted curiosity. There are a few effective responses. Know your enemy and anticipate this public attack, prepare for the surprise, and, while this is all quite personal, avoid any indication that it's anything other than pure business. *Information is key.* If you can, withhold a tidbit or two to show that the other person is out of the loop. Communicate with others privately beforehand to build consensus.

Keep a calm head—but you must respond. Even when a confrontation is not appropriate, failure to respond is a glaring sign of weakness. Take a huge breath and slow down, and demand time as appropriate. Do not be hasty or emotional. Try to place the attacker into a position of having to offer up solutions. Or ask the attacker for something that you have expected from him all along but not yet delivered.

The Darwinian aspect of public business humiliation is that we all sit in the meetings and watch a person be skewered in slow motion. And we rarely if ever come to the victim's aid.

This is the business version of survival of the fittest. Politics for each of us is about *our own* ability to stand up on our own feet, and when we encounter these situations, standing up means being capable of firing back (while appearing constructive).

And the last key to dealing with public criticism: if you don't know something, don't pretend you do. Saying stupid things is a gift to any person who wants to make you look the fool.

USING OTHER PEOPLE'S MONEY

There are more important things than money—the only trouble is they all cost money. —Louis A. Safian

Anyone who is successful in business knows that no one ever has enough money to do everything he wants. Success means finding other people to buy us what we want and letting them finance our dreams. This is the way it's done.

For instance, when it comes to buying a house, banks pay for our house by letting us take their money in exchange for some interest on their loan. Then we get to live there, enjoy the tax benefits, fix it and sell it, and we get to take whatever capital appreciation occurs over that time without ever sharing any of that with the bank.

Using the bank's money, we get the opportunity to make lots of money (hopefully—or lose only the much smaller amount of money that we put up), and in some cases, people can buy and resell a piece of property at a profit without ever even taking ownership or making a single payment!

Many of the richest people in the world have mastered the art of using other people's money. These tactics are highly relevant in the workplace as well. If you can get other people and departments to invest in your projects, you not only have extra monetary resources, but you have other people vouching for you and your project, and taking a vested interest in your success. And here's the best part: you get to take the credit.

Let's think about this as an investment—monetary, reputational, etc. The fewer strings that are placed on your use of other people's investment in you, the better. But be ready to take this investment. Good ideas, fancy plans, a strong outlook on returns and sharing credit are all common ways to persuade a person to invest in you. And with their reputations at stake, you might end up with a whole lot of people in your corner cheering you on.

When it comes to being able to succeed at anything, you need the money and the people to get the job done. Having even a person or a penny less than you need to accomplish your tasks can mean failure. If your heart and soul is wrapped up in a project that you do not wish to fail, do whatever you must to get the investments you need to allow you to be successful.

HOME FIELD ADVANTAGE (BEATING UP YOUR GUESTS)

The first thing that strikes a visitor to Paris is a taxi. —Fred Allen

You have more power and leverage in a conversation that is held on your home field. You have the power to stand, sit, move, access information, and so forth. The president has his Oval Office, and while your office may not be nearly as special, it can be a surprisingly powerful space.

Dynamics of being on your own turf

You feel more powerful on your turf. Perhaps you have summoned the other person, who then has to present himself to you. You get to sit behind the desk, with access to whatever resources you need, while the other person is forced to work off his lap with only the tools that he/she has brought along.

If power is truly in play, you can set up the office in such a manner as to convey even greater power, including raising your chair and lowering others, perhaps opening shades behind you (let the light shine into their eyes), and employing other tactics that can induce discomfort.

In your office, you decide where to position your guests and whether to require someone else to have a seat or stand. You decide if there is stuff on the chair or a place for your visitor to put his papers or coffee.

Instruments and strategies of power

In those moments when you need to connect with your guest and diminish any adversarial tone, move out from behind your desk and sit next to him or her. When you want to connect, you need to get the desk and other barriers out of the way. Psychologically, the desk makes you more adversarial. In those intense moments, take your commander seat back behind the desk.

In the compassionate moments, offer a drink and tell a joke. In those more difficult moments, take a drink yourself without offering hospitality.

As childish as it seems, it is not uncommon for power plays to involve two players who each become unwilling to meet in each other's offices, ultimately settling on neutral conference rooms.

When it comes to gaining power by the arrangement of a setting, I am reminded of the scene in the movie *Men In Black*, in which the potential candidates were asked to complete a test with pencils and flimsy packets of paper on their laps, but with no flat surfaces to write on. All the candidates suddenly had something to cope with that put them at a disadvantage.

Time can be an instrument of power, such as when a more powerful person awakens a subordinate at home in the wee hours (see the movie *Wall Street*).

TAKE ON THE KING/CRUSH THE PAWNS

When you argue with your inferiors, you convince them of only one thing: they are as clever as you. —Irving Layton

Like drug dealers who send kids out onto the street to deal the merchandise, great leaders seldom fight battles themselves, preferring to sit immunized in their offices where they pull strings in substantial comfort.

When you are at war, do not tussle with the pawns. Pawns are expendable and, like the Energizer Bunny, fight on and on with essentially nothing to gain or lose. Pawns are infinite in number, like enemies in a computer game.

There is no virtue in winning against a lower level employee. Your stature is lowered, and the fight will just be fought again by more senior personnel. When you want to earn respect, or at least a meaningful victory, you must escape the pawns and find a way to approach and engage the king. If the pawns give you problems, surpass them. The leader learns to dismiss the pawn when the conversation is finished.

Do whatever is necessary in order to avoid trying to get things done with pawns. Find a way to get meetings with decision-makers, and directly provide those leaders with your message, not some watered-down version delivered by a person who does not share your interest, viewpoint, or intellect or is likely to steal your credit.

If the decision-makers won't work with you, take a step back, disengage, and behave like a leader among children. Otherwise, the decision-makers won't even be invested in your low-level battles.

And when you take on the real issues, when you confront the king, your accomplishments become the stuff of legends. We respect the people who stand up and fight the real fight, win or lose, and even in defeat become better situated, if for no other reason than having risen above the rest of the pawns.

STEALING CREDIT

Ability is the art of getting credit for all the home runs somebody else hits.
—Casey Stengel

Credit stealing is overwhelmingly common. In the workplace, the more credit a person has for the business' successes, the more valuable he/she is to the business, and the more likely to get bonuses, pay raises, and promotions.

Good politicians keep a running list of their victories and want that list to be as long as possible, no matter what, and it is unbelievably easy to steal part or all of the credit in any given task. Still, people steal credit more from their own employees and peers than from anyone else.

Stealing some or all of the credit happens almost too easily, by simply showing up at a single meeting, helping format a document, or drafting a paragraph or two of a report.

If you are in a position where you are hoping for a victory but are concerned that you may have others hopping onto the victory bandwagon, it is worth taking measures to ensure that people who do not deserve credit are not able to claim it.

One of the best ways to do this is to form (and announce) an official working group, task force, or committee. Make this group meaningful and keep credit claimers off. The benefit of this dedicated team approach is that it makes it very hard for people not on the team to claim credit. If people are hopping aboard your project, consider publicly thanking them for their limited role.

On the other hand, if you are the one seeking credit, do not let a task force be formed without your name being associated with it, or you might kiss any real credit goodbye. If you find that communications are occurring around you, make as big a stink as you need to in order to announce your involvement and take your credit—even prematurely, if necessary.

Be fast and stealthy

And given the value in receiving credit, you will be at a disadvantage if you don't become engaged in the credit game. Be fast and stealthy. Get your name out there and attached to the things that your business cares about.

Be the first to email your manager when the victory is achieved, and remind your manager of your involvement. Be sure to congratulate others when big successes are achieved, perhaps highlighting your involvement in a couple of words. If you do this, you'll find that most people will never know the difference, and the victory will be awarded, at least in part, to you.

THE ART OF SPIN

> *Ever negotiate with lawyers at a huge company? If they saw you drowning 100 feet from the shore, they'd throw you a 51-foot rope and say they went more than halfway.* —Paul Somerson

Nothing, no matter how good or bad, tells its own story. When it comes to finding out what happened, or learning whether something is good or bad, we depend on the storytellers and assume that the stories are accurate. Adept spinmeisters are so powerful that they can even change our interpretation of things that we witnessed firsthand.

Make the facts work for you.

The idea of "spinning" facts is another way of saying that you should make the facts work for you and your interests. No facts are perfect, and while spin is perceived as dishonest, making facts work to your greatest benefit can be entirely ethical, effective, and powerful.

One of the reasons why there are so many average executives is that so many of them are merely adept at making themselves and their companies look good with whatever cards they are dealt at the time. Otherwise, they're just like everyone else.

To make facts work, it's helpful to know and consider all of the facts (especially if you know more facts than everyone else) and to be prepared to use or dismiss these facts when you are engaged in any kind of debate. Appear knowledgeable and calm. Use statistics, because with a little bit of thought, they can be used to demonstrate pretty much anything.

For instance, one argument that politicians use against the legalization of marijuana (found in a former Administration's white papers) is that marijuana use is a key factor found in people who eventually commit murder. The papers explain that the statistics show that more than 80 percent of the murderers have used the drug at some point prior to their criminal act.

Available statistics, however, show conservatively that between 40 and 60 percent of the population has at one time smoked marijuana (between 45 and 50 percent of the population of 12th-graders have used marijuana), a percentage that increases substantially as we look into lower socioeconomic classes. Another study indicates a much higher percentage of use, at some point in their lives, for people attending college or Grateful Dead concerts. Does this mean to suggest that the average member of the population, and particularly hippies, surfers, and those who attend Grateful Dead concerts, is predisposed to commit murder?

Speaking of spin, it turns out that 100 percent of the murderers have at some point breathed air and worn shoes. Could air and shoes be the real culprit?

Spin techniques

Other highly effective spin techniques include the simple use of language—including the use of jargon to confuse, euphemisms (words that make offensive things seem less offensive) such as "climate change" in place of "global warming," and reverse euphemisms (to make things seem more offensive) such as "death tax" in place of "estate tax." Some words make people happy and others make them sad or scared. For some illustrative humor on this point, see George Carlin's monologue on "Euphemisms."

Some people can successfully employ spin throughout their entire careers and lives, even if other people think that the spin is not accurate. If you or your opinions are being spun in a way that is not favorable to you, spin back (note that simply revealing someone's spin is surprisingly ineffective).

The defense against spin should be counter-spin or another broad attack, including revealing motives and bias and other ways of undermining credibility. Absent a good counter, no one will ever even question the story that is laid out by the spinner.

Why spin works

Spin works partly because it allows other people to draw logical conclusions without thinking. And beyond convincing people of something, it gives them the justification they need to simply side with your position.

In the workplace, people rely on other people's conclusions and repeat what they are told. When I brief the board on something, they often take those talking points that I offer. Whether or not I am wrong (and I can get in trouble if I am), my spin becomes theirs and is passed along. Once we lay out the facts and couple them with our conclusions, our story takes on legs of its own.

GET IN THEIR FACE

No matter how much cats fight, there always seem to be plenty of kittens.
—*Abraham Lincoln*

Most people are very comfortable being tough when hidden behind a shield, such as email, telephone, or their automobile. Most people aren't all that tough in person (except in airports, however, where some people will yell at anyone—even security personnel).

When you are having a difficult interaction, sit down with that person face-to-face. The trip to see them will not only show that you care, particularly if you have gotten on a plane to do so, but the face-to-face dialog will reveal the other person without the usual protective shield.

Consider showing the other person some photos of your significant other, child or your pet. Ask about his. Offer a secret. Bring some donuts. Learn what he does and whether he likes his job; get him talking. Barriers may come down, and many people will even begin to volunteer a tremendous amount, much more than they should, to their new face-to-face friend.

THE NAME DROP

Bragging is not an attractive trait, but let's be honest, a man who catches a big fish doesn't go home through an alley. —Ann Landers

Most name-drops are lies, and situations in which the person whose name is being dropped wouldn't even know the person doing the dropping.

Occasionally, however, some are true.

We all like to know important people and perhaps may even derive a portion of our personal value from the people we know or who surround us. Many people, however, invest so much of their self-worth, value, and esteem in the people they know that the drop itself is riddled with self-interest and deception. In some cases, the dropper may even be deceiving himself.

Name-dropping, while potentially effective, can backfire.

For one thing, it is puffery and is often seen skeptically. Often enough, the name-drop is nonsense, and the average successful businessperson may be turned off at the unnecessary mention of another person's name. Also, the more important the person you are speaking to, the more likely he or she may personally know the person whose name you are dropping; trust me when I tell you that if successful people to whom you name-drop are curious, they will either ignore the drop, assuming its falsehood, or they will verify your assertions and find humor in your failed attempts.

Yet, ironically, it is when we talk to powerful people that we want to do the most name-dropping to prove our worth.

When I listen to dropped names, and in my business that happens all the time, I tend to first doubt the name-dropper's credibility. My experience tells me that most of us respect our real friends too much to run around dropping their names; and so it is our loosest acquaintances that sell their limited interactions in hopes of proving that they themselves are credible and competent.

The three lessons here are:

First, be careful of dropping names. In most circumstances, you immediately put your credibility in doubt

Second, when you are the recipient of a name-drop, remember it is likely meaningless and dismissing the reference will typically let the other person off the hook, and

Finally, when necessary, as the recipient of a name-drop, consider asking on the spot (or when offered, agreeing) to take advantage of the drop.

How do you do that?

For a number of reasons, and for the best of business reasons, you might force the credibility issue and/or attempt to take advantage of the other person's stated relationship. Sometimes just a simple follow-up question will reveal the puffery—but that follow-up might provide a true benefit if the drop is real.

If the person whose name was dropped would be helpful to you (that is why it was mentioned, wasn't it?), then I might ask if the three of us could do lunch. I might even ask if I can call the person and let them know that I was referred by the name-dropper.

In truth, I'm not giving the dropper a hard time as much as I want to benefit from the relationship. This, after all, is simple networking. While usually I might hear some hemming and hawing as the person tries to back out of the affiliation, perhaps explaining that they only met the person once or the person might not even know their name, I have on some occasions ended up making contact with some very fascinating people.

THERE ARE NO SECRETS, ONLY THINGS THAT CAN HURT YOU

Gossip needn't be false to be evil—there's a lot of truth that shouldn't be passed around. —Frank A. Clark

No one can keep a secret. Therefore, no one should be trusted to. If you have a real secret, keep it to yourself. Otherwise, you are bound to be disappointed.

People reveal secrets not only because they feel the urge, but because revealing the secret indicates that they are important and, ironically, worthy of this non-public information. Many people, as with some of the "anonymous sources" who leak to the press or tip off the police, will even spread a secret just because they have the power to do so—and not for personal benefit or the benefit of others. In many ways, it is the same as name-dropping, and most can't refrain.

So drop information that you want spread (perhaps leak an idea if you are curious about how it would be received). But never be upset if anything you said in confidence gets out. That's how it works. You knew better before you opened your mouth.

A GOOD ASS-COVERING

Blame someone else and get on with your life. —Alan Woods

The workplace is consumed with people skillfully creating a paper trail to prove that they have notified other people of problems and issues and demonstrating that they have moved work off their desk and onto others'. In many environments, a person's primary job is quite simply to cover his or her patootie.

Don't sit back and passively receive communication (it is all intended to cover other people's backsides). Read everything that comes in and respond.

And never let someone accuse you of something bad without dealing with it quickly and directly. In a court of law, you might simply deny the accusation. In the real world, you have two choices: admit, so that you can move on and get the subject changed, or counter. Denial is often a form of weakness.

Finally, as I said at the very beginning, never let others cover their backsides with yours unless you are fully comfortable in the defeated punching-bag role.

DEFLECTING AND AVOIDING BLAME

If at first you don't succeed, blame your parents.—Marcelene Cox

When something looks like a lost cause, people will try to separate themselves from the problem and try to lay the blame on someone else.

For instance, if a sale does not go through, it is easy to blame the salesperson, the product, or the shipping department. The first one to blame the other is on the offense, and the scapegoat immediately must defend himself. Some people start covering their butt to avoid blame upfront, with emails and memos waiting to show that they were aware of a problem with the person/group that is being blamed and that they even tried to warn others about that risk.

Although the blame game is unproductive, it is extremely common and one of the primary means in which a business determines who is valuable and who is not. Blame is a form of spin and people who are at risk are more likely to blame others, and many will prepare documentation to support their concerns.

RAZZLE 'EM UP AND HIDE

In cross-examination, as in fishing, nothing is more ungainly than a fisherman pulled into the water by his catch. —Louis Nizer

This "razzle 'em up" ploy involves getting other people all worked up so that they look immature or behave erratically. After employing this tactic, you, on the other hand, can sit back and watch the havoc you've created.

You might have learned this tactic when playing with your pet cat or dog (that's the *razzle 'em up and laugh game*). Or perhaps you learned this in your youth if you had siblings—when one sibling would instigate a situation to cause the other to get caught retaliating and acting inappropriately while the *bad* child watched with apparent dismay and innocence. There is often a set-up and a retreat.

It is the retaliation or reaction you want noticed, just as on any football field, where the referee calls the foul on the one who hits *second*. In the corporate world, this tactic is committed under veiled innocence. Common examples include anything that works someone up to the point of panic or causes another person to lose his cool. The instigator is bringing the worst out in people, and then sits, watching and enjoying the fallout.

This tactic can be hard to defend against. If you lose your cool, no matter what the reason, you have a problem. The only real defense is to not act as expected—and overcome any hurdles placed in your path.

In short, don't let 'em get to you, or you are an easy mark.

PLAUSIBLE DENIABILITY AND THE DOCTRINE OF CLEAN HANDS

I never deny. I never contradict. I sometimes forget.
—Benjamin Disraeli

Remember the phrase: "plausible deniability." It is the most fundamental method for surviving political, immoral, unethical, and even criminal behavior. And, ironically, it is found extensively—and is fundamental—in the business world.

In essence, *plausible deniability* is the *capability* to deny involvement in something, perhaps a decision or an act in which you were (or may have been) otherwise involved.

It includes alibis (*e.g.*, "I couldn't have given that instruction," "I never talked to that person," or "But I was in Antarctica without electricity or a cell phone"), creating a fake record (*e.g.*, sending an email or memo that is actually contrary to what has happened or been decided), and disassociating yourself from the issue (*e.g.*, having provided no written communications or left any voicemails on the subject).

Sometimes, *plausible deniability* is asserted even more directly, such as when people say, "If asked, I'll deny that we ever discussed this."

Plausible deniability is commonly seen in the movies, in lines like "This tape will be destroyed in five seconds...", "if you say anything, I'll deny it." We see it in *The Godfather, Part II*, in which a hit man is explaining to Congress that he never received orders from the top: "Right, yeah, a buffer, the family had a lot of buffers."

We also find it in real-life crime, when people are hired to kill other people or sell drugs without ever knowing who is really paying for the hit or supplying the drugs.

In the business and political world, the ability to deny involvement is what has allowed countless business and political leaders to avoid jail by delegating responsibility to their minions (some of whom have ended up in jail).

What to do if you see it coming

If you feel people are positioning themselves to deny their involvement, the defense tactics are to build that paper trail that they so much want to avoid and gather evidence that will later prevent the other person from denying his or her involvement.

Get the other person on the record. Since people who engage in this tactic are often highly skilled, it might be pretty difficult (people might say that they don't read every email and that sorting emails is their assistant's responsibility), but be persistent. You'll get 'em.

One sure-fire technique is to halt work until you receive an on-the-record instruction from the top. However, this is an ultimatum, possibly resulting in your being perceived as insubordinate. Unless you can get people on the record, you may find yourself entirely on your own.

ASS-KISSING

People can be induced to swallow anything, provide it is sufficiently seasoned with praise. —Moliere

Most people want to be respected. Some need to be worshipped. Everyone wants to feel valued and appreciated.

Kissing someone's ass might be anything from an honest "you-da-best" to an artificial and transparent act of feigning true worship.

Mostly, people are regarded as ass-kissers not by virtue of their own actions *per* se, but by the jealousy of others who fear that one person's connection with management may be to their disadvantage. Even if the act is done with genuine admiration, it is often seen as disingenuous and artificial behavior designed to offer the ass-kisser some personal advantage. Sometimes it is.

In some cases, however, this connection is not only not disingenuous, but rather quite honest and real. The tactic might work from time to time to endear the kisser to a higher-level person because of that person's particular needs. If that is what is needed and that is what the kisser is doing, then the kisser seems to have things figured out.

As a word of caution: many people know full well when their ass is being kissed, particularly if they are in a position of power or in a dominant position to the ass-kisser. While some might like it, others despise it.

I, for instance, am very much bothered by it. Although I certainly want to be respected and appreciated and sometimes will look for a bit of reassurance among friends and colleagues that something was handled in an acceptable manner, I never want someone to tell me that I'm super-human, especially a lower level person who might be more inclined to kiss up. And I do not like or respect any person who does that.

However, entire industries have been built upon the ass-kissing of others — much of the entertainment industry, for instance. Entertainers surround themselves with courtiers (I mean "interns") who exist for the sole purpose of kissing ass. For the power-hungry, this sure can be fun.

NEVER BREAKING PROMISES BY NEVER MAKING PROMISES

If you wish to be a success in the world, promise everything, deliver nothing. —Napoleon Bonaparte

It is impossible to lie or be wrong if you never represented anything as a fact. Some people are never wrong because they never put their opinions on the record, and others are quite skilled at saying an awful lot without ever saying anything at all.

But that won't stop the person who never says anything from stepping up to accept the credit if things go well. Yet these people will be nowhere to be found if things do not.

IF you promise—deliver

It can be a big mistake to promise anything—except, of course, if the outcome is based on promises rather than on successes, as with political elections.

If you promise something, even something as simple as setting a time by which you will call someone back, *make sure that you deliver. If you aren't sure, don't promise.*

And by making promises that you are absolutely certain you can fulfill, you earn a perfect track record. For instance, take note of all of those criminal prosecutors who have a perfect record in court—most are perfect only because they have refused to go to trial, or bring cases to a jury, unless the case was a slam-dunk.

Pin them down

If you see this tactic being used against you, perhaps with people who always leave the final decision up to you, or won't tell you what they think without modifying or nullifying their opinions (such as "But what do I know?" or "If my understanding is correct..." or "Based on what I have been told..."), then consider doing what is necessary to pin them down. People can be pretty evasive. Otherwise, you'll be sharing the credit, but bearing the losses, entirely on your own.

SEX, DRUGS, AND LEVERAGE

I wouldn't recommend sex, drugs or insanity for everyone, but they've always worked for me. —Hunter S. Thompson

Drinking, doing drugs or participating in lewd events can be common in business circles. While these experiences can create a bonding experience, they inspire more-senior people to offer preferential treatment, particularly for those events that cause fear for their own well-being after the fact.

Although I've already covered this subject, it bears revisiting because it's particularly apropos to this discussion of politics and power.

Sex and drugs can be synonymous with *leverage*. There is tremendous power over people who want things kept secret or are vulnerable to embarrassment or shame. And since workplace sex and drugs are naturally risky and reputation-tarnishing activities that can get people fired, divorced or ruined, they are natural tools of extortion.

And you rarely need to mention a word about it. Participants will remember that you have this information. Of course, you will too.*

USING CONFLICT AND MAKING PEOPLE SUSPICIOUS OF ONE ANOTHER

During times of war, hatred becomes quite respectable, even though it has to masquerade often under the guise of patriotism. —Howard Thurman

The business world is filled with planted seeds and floated rumors. And whether the seed ever fully takes root, or the rumor flight, there is always some doubt left behind. People remember the signs they see along the way.

When it comes to being considered for promotions, instill doubt in the ability and competence of others. Plant the seed in a subtle fashion.

---

*   Participants will maintain mementos, including emails, voicemails, text messages and so forth. While psychologists might value openness, a cognizant politician will suggest the opposite—no recorded or memorialized statements (or emotions) which can be embarrassing if shared or, particularly in heated discussions, threatening or illegal.

Here's a true story. One day at about 11:00 a.m., I was looking for a particular person whose colleague told me that the person probably wasn't in the office yet and often arrives a bit late. I immediately doubted that the person I was looking for was the right person to do the job. Later I found out that the original news was not correct, that the person was in the office and always arrived first thing in the morning but had been in meetings. Sabotage, and by a trusted associate nonetheless!

A little bit of doubt may be enough.

BEING THE LESSER PERSON MAKES YOU THE DOMINANT ONE

First they ignore you, then they laugh at you, then they fight you, then you win. —*Mahatma Gandhi*

Many people have a strange tendency to be competitive, not only when talking about life achievements, but even with simple, personal details.

One person tells of his vacation, and the other feels he needs to talk about his bigger, longer, more exotic vacation. You went canoeing? I went white water rafting. This works in the negative as well. Your kid's got ADD? Mine is sickly and insane.

Communication experts call this "topping," something many conversationalists will often even want to incite in order to create a good conversational dynamic. Jokes and stories are other common examples; when one person tells a joke or story, and before the dialog is even finished, others come in to top it.

Have you ever noticed a conversation when people are just spouting out their favorite restaurants without ever really listening or expecting anyone else to take their recommendations, or expecting that they would take ours? The entire conversation is built on topping one another, and the participants feel a bond. Yet nothing beyond the conversational bond was accomplished, and no information will ever be remembered.

A competitive conversation can be bonding, but the words are lost to the wind. *Instead of always one-upping the others, take a step back and ask for a story or advice. This places the other person into a position of teacher/mentor and gives him the power in this conversation.*

Don't fight over who is smarter; the other person is. Don't go back and forth over who had the better vacation; the other person did. Don't fight about your opinions with respect to a piece of news; the other person is right. Bend, don't break. Give them your humility and respect and then, magically, they will begin to listen to you offer your ideas in a non-threatening way. Give them the title of master and you slip into the dominant role.

MARTYRDOM, PICKING YOUR BATTLES AND NEVER REALLY LOSING

Pick battles big enough to matter, small enough to win.
—Jonathan Kozol

Not all battles are worth fighting, and many cost you more than you'd have gotten in victory. And, like a Pyrrhic victory (a victory in which the triumph is overshadowed by its cost) many victories are so costly that they were not worth winning in the first place.

In business, every time you engage in a battle, whether it is to have your opinion or ideas heard or adopted, or if you are fighting for resources or a promotion or any other thing you can imagine, you place at stake your reputation and your credibility, not to mention your relationships with others.

Victory is never free

Getting your way always comes at a cost.

Many of the most successful people will tell you that they have suffered far more losses than wins. If we bet everything we have in every battle, we will eventually lose everything.

Smart people don't do that. We pay attention to our overall plan and try to avoid becoming preoccupied or overly invested in the meaningless little battles along the way. Sometimes we let other people win, whether it is a goodwill tactic or a temporary retreat and opportunity to regroup.

As Kenny says, you gotta know when to hold 'em and know when to fold 'em. The key to survival, throughout all of the ups and downs, is to live to fight another day.

Don't bet the farm on things not worthy of such a big bet. "Live to fight another day" is a philosophy that does get you to the big-time fights.

Don't be a martyr!

In the business world there are countless opportunities for you to make yourself a martyr and to throw yourself on the sword.

Sometimes our chosen battle to the death will involve a fight for the rights of a minority, a battle against the glass ceiling, standing up for the weak, or some other situation in which our values tell us that we have come to the fight we have always been waiting for, the fight that needs to be fought to the death.

Martyrdom happens when we are coming to the defense of values. Unfortunately, too many martyrs could have won if they were still there the next day.

Nevertheless, the business martyr often fails to realize one most essential truth—that *martyrdom has no value when it is over nothing of any real significance.* The boss gets the right to make final business decisions, and sometimes decisions are wrong—and all you can do is to express your opinion without emotion or insult. When you don't know how to give in and lose, ask, "Ok, so what do you want me to do?"

There are very few fights, particularly few in the workplace, that need to be won in one round at all cost. Figuring out which of these battles is necessary can be quite difficult. It often is the battle that places you at its crossroads, with few other options other than engagement or total defeat. But remember that martyrdom is most often only a source of self-pride, is of little value to others, and rarely accomplishes anything beyond putting you in your grave.

In the end, these magical causes that suggest that your life is worth less than the cause are very rare. In general, if you get fired or professionally crippled over an opinion, no matter how right, you're usually the idiot.

Power in losing

With this defeatist suggestion in mind, there can be great power in losing, particularly if you allow another person to falter or use up too much political capital in the process. And there can be tremendous power in stepping aside to allow someone else to win. Not only do you earn favors, but it is only the other person's competence that is put at stake, so in most cases your loss can cost you nothing.

So win when you need to win. But you rarely need to win without compromise, so pick your battles wisely. And most of the time, just live to fight another day.

ULTIMATUMS AND EMPTY THREATS

I eat death threats for breakfast. —Miriam Defensor Santiago

A person who does not follow through with a threat or an ultimatum is a weak person, a substantially diminished and often irrelevant person. Never make a threat that you don't intend to carry out, and if you decide to bluff, you have to know how to play the hand. If you are not prepared to engage in this type of game, don't play it.

CRUSHING YOUR ENEMIES

Whoever has his foe at his mercy, and does not kill him, is his own enemy.
—Muslih-uddin Sadi

Playing hardball can mean many things in the workplace; it may involve a power-negotiating tactic or your willingness to actually hurt another person. There is enough hardball in any modern-day business to suggest that you either play the game or be prepared to duck.

We've talked about the individual battles, as well as figuring out when you need to win and recognizing when you don't. But when you decide to engage in the hard-core battle, you not only must win, but you must truly crush your opponent.

Now, this must seem a bit harsh, and it certainly doesn't mean the same thing every time. But whatever it means, it suggests that *the people and projects you defeat must be so utterly defeated that they cannot come back again*, as things tend to do in the workplace (similar to those monsters in horror flicks). If you are trying to wipe out a competitor, make sure he or she is dead before abandoning the body. Defeated competitors turn into enemies. We're talking here about a commitment to the battle, as well as showing no mercy.

Mercy is what eventually gets us killed

If your idea is in competition with another's, and if this is a fight you decide to win, it is not enough to lob a few strikes and see what happens. *Go kill it.*

Lobby, wrangle, pull favors, bash the merits, suggest greater risks and potential damages, and do whatever must be done to finish this thing once and for all. If this is personal, find a way to get the other people off the idea, reassigned or fired, and attack credibility with whatever tools you feel comfortable with. In these interactions, win by winning. No other debates. No other battles.

AVOID CROSSING THE WRONG PERSON

You moon the wrong person at an office party and suddenly you're not "professional" any more. —Jeff Foxworthy

Don't offend or be disloyal to the wrong person. You should already know this. If you don't, you will find yourself forever dealing with a ferocious enemy, eternally set back, or without a job.

It is sometimes hard to figure out who should not be crossed. Obviously, it is usually good not to cross the boss. But sometimes it is a person who has the boss' total trust and attention, so look for that. In most cases, however, we are talking about some very ambitious and/or ruthless person along the way. Or perhaps a person who oversees the business or likes to point blame. Figure out the people to be wary of, and if you decide to go to battle with these people, you'd better win big.

PERSPECTIVE, PLEASE

In any great organization it is far, far safer to be wrong with the majority than to be right alone. —*John Kenneth Galbraith*

Almost all political and social maneuvers leave someone hurting on the other end. I don't defend these tactics as right, or just, or decent, but I recognize their commonness and effectiveness. And I defend them only insofar as to suggest that they must be learned and perfected, because they can and will be used against you.

A final word: we are political animals.

I hope that this section on the tools and techniques of politics is particularly useful, not just for the people who want to hurt others, but for everyone else to use in accomplishing the real goal of politics: to get the best ideas implemented, to get the promotions they deserve, and most important, to recognize the tactics that surround them so that they can defend themselves and participate more effectively in the world. If all of this offers any value, I hope that it actually makes political maneuvering less effective.

But I doubt that it will. It can't. Politics is just too much a part of who we are.

The heights by great men reached and kept
Were not attained by sudden flight,
But they, while their companions slept,
Were toiling upward in the night.

—Henry Wadsworth Longfellow:

SURVIVING DAY-TO-DAY CHALLENGES

KEEP PERSPECTIVE.

When it comes to keeping a cool head, it helps to remember that there is nothing your business can do to really hurt you. Yes, they can choose to not promote you, not offer you the position you want; they can even demote or fire you. But in no instance can they make you subservient or a victim. That is something we do to ourselves.

The (ir)relevance of fight-or-flight

Somewhere buried deep in our subconscious is our instinctual reaction to dealing with threats—either by squaring up for the fight or by running away—known as "fight or flight." This defensive reaction brings every aspect of our physical body into the fray. When you want to fight, every emotion and muscle is tied up in the process of preparing for battle. The same is true when you want to flee.

These instincts, however, are likely left over from very long ago, at a time when everything wanted to eat us. Nowadays, these instincts have a tendency to change otherwise logical problems and the problem-solving process, as well as office conflict, into emotional and instinctual battles.

We are filled with adrenaline and sometimes panic, *regardless* of whether we are fighters or fleers. This physical embodiment of the fight-or-flight process contributes to stress, weight issues, cardiovascular problems, skin and other diseases, and hair loss. People cry, shake, get sick, and suffer from insomnia. Physically, we see the strain—tense belly, hunched shoulders, stiff neck—and psychologically, in an over-active mind and self-defeating, aggressive decision making.

Develop stress-fighting tactics

Find out what works for you to alleviate this stress. Most importantly, learn when you are being overtaken by your stresses so that you can work to re-ground yourself.

When I feel the symptoms, I tend to make lists of tasks that need to be attended to, and I usually feel better. Be sure to step back and remind yourself that there's no longer anything out there that wants to eat you.

If you know that the reaction you feel is natural, perhaps you can better achieve a sense of control and make some of those inevitable challenges just a little bit easier to survive. I know... easier said than done.

Other people's stresses are yours to manage too

While this chapter is largely about personal workplace balance and survival, let's start with the reminder that no matter how calm and controlled you are, others in the workplace are suffering through these same challenges, and how they deal with them will affect your workplace environment, situation, productivity, efficiency—and career path.

Our job is not merely to manage ourselves and to adapt to the surrounding environment, but also to control, induce and at times inspire the emotions of others.

LIFE IS EXCEEDINGLY FAIR

Life is never fair, and perhaps it is a good thing for most of us it is not!
—*Oscar Wilde*

We tell our children that life is not fair. And we need to remind ourselves as adults—not that life is not fair, but rather that success at anything demands certain pre-requisites. It is the ones who don't achieve those objectives that believe most strongly in life's unfairness.

Apart from those things that are really unfair—such as physical attributes we cannot change, illness, etc.—life in the workplace seems particularly unfair to people who do not take advantage of their opportunities.

On the nature of "fairness"

But life is not singling you out. Life offers chance after chance. Sometimes it leans a bit in your favor to see what you'll do—and sometimes life hits you a bit harder than everyone else. *That's actually the definition of fair.* No one is immune.

If you want cards dealt to you that are a little more in your favor, you have to sit at the table and play the game. Set yourself up to get the breaks. Someone always wins for every time someone else loses. But when the cards are good, you have to play 'em.

Remember that different people will perceive the same set of facts differently. Some will perceive that something is fair that others feel is unfair. With fairness as relative, both are always right—and wrong. In the end, with this mushy standard, the concept of fairness is largely irrelevant.

Listen to the advice you pass along to your own children. You're a grown-up now. Now act like one.

GOOD DAYS AND BAD DAYS

*"You're fired!" No other words can so easily and succinctly reduce a
confident, self-assured executive to an insecure, groveling shred of his
former self. —Frank P. Louchheim*

Everybody, no matter how powerful or wealthy, lives a life filled with good
days and bad. People with the best jobs and most money still have bad days.
People with what can easily be perceived as nothing going for them often
have lives filled with wonderful things. Studies related to suicide, as well
as statistical rates related to contentment and depression, have shown that
people with stable jobs but who earn less money (meaning lower-middle to
middle class) have more laughs and days which they believe to be "good days".

I believe that. I've worked in construction. I've delivered pizzas. I've
been a grill chef and a bartender. I've loaded boxes as a roadie on tour with
bands. I've been a lawyer, musician, photographer and family guy. And
my conclusion is that I laugh far less as an entrepreneur and lawyer than
I did at any of those former low-paying occupations. To quote the great
songwriter Jimmy Buffett, when describing a banker's explanation of his
job to a carefree songwriter:

*"...because in my contract there's this clause
that says, 'it's my job, to be worried half to death,
and that's the thing people respect in me.
It's my job, and without it I'd be less
than what I expect from me.'"*

Good day or bad? It's all in your head.

Interestingly enough, absent a dramatic, unexpected event, *people seem to
intuitively know whether a day will be good or bad from the moment they wake
up.* The outcome often rests entirely within our own heads.

When we decide that we are going to have a bad day, we bring bad stuff
with us *into* our interactions, via the tone of our voice, the way we give instructions, and the demands that we make. When we decide to have a good
day, we bring a lighter and more comfortable aura.

And when external circumstances actually do cause us to have a good
or bad day at work, they most commonly have nothing to do with work.

More likely they involve something from our personal lives, such as health issues, problems with the car or house, personal relationships, the weather, kids, and so forth.

In this way, our work becomes a victim of our individual lives—rather than the opposite.

A sense of perspective should tell you, in those moments of clear thought, that somebody is always having a worse day than you are. Just watch the news. Keep an even keel, and keep the complaints to yourself, particularly if you are a person with some degree of authority. Have you ever heard someone who made more money than you complain about money? Have you ever despised anyone more than you did at that moment?

Remember that you impact other people's days. Your can easily make another person's day very bad. And your good day can be contagious.

THE "MIDDLE OF THE DAY" VACATION

Rest when you're weary. Refresh and renew yourself, your body, your mind, your spirit. Then get back to work. —Ralph Marston

When you are being pushed to the line, step off the line. If you need to take a break, take one.

I take an hour and a half to two-hour vacation in a movie theater right in the middle of the day from time to time. It is just a long lunch. Other people go to the driving range, others to the gym, and others to the arcade. Some people walk around the block. Anything you can do to separate your mind from the work environment is worth more than the longest office break that you could ever take.

If you need to, take this little vacation. It requires no time off and may do more for your professional success than you could imagine possible.

BREATHING

Sometimes the most important thing in a whole day is the rest we take between two deep breaths. —Etty Hillesum

People forget to breathe. Really they do. All the time. I don't mean to suggest that they are not filling their lungs with enough air to keep talking (it takes very little air to keep talking), but they are not really breathing, particularly when they're feeling stressed.

Breathing gets oxygen to the body and has the capability of adding instant energy and relaxation. Taking deep breaths has been shown not only to relieve stress, but also to help the digestive system and the heart; during exercise, it also it provides terrific fitness benefits. Additionally, relaxed breaths can instantly reduce stress and even help to reduce pain, including common headaches.

Breathing is as much a mental as a physical exercise. My personal trick is to take deep breath in and hold it, imagining all of the stress, problems, or anything else that I want to rid myself of gathering in my lungs, and when I release the breath all of this negative stuff is released as well. This works for me—often in just one single breath (there are also anatomical reasons why the deep exhale assists in relaxation).*

Some people make it a practice to focus on their breathing, perhaps by allocating time every day to meditate. Apart from my little breathing exercise, I don't meditate, but find time throughout the day to stop and take a couple of nice, relaxing, deep breaths.

---

* If you want a systematic and very effective variation on this, Google Dr. Andrew Weil's "4-7-8" breathing technique.

WATER, EXERCISE, AND A GOOD SWEAT

There must be quite a few things that a hot bath won't cure, but I don't know many of them. —Sylvia Plath, The Bell Jar

Just like breathing, water washes toxins away, and exercise not only keeps the blood clean and flowing, but is an instant little vacation from the stresses of life. Being fit also helps you feel better and improves the way others perceive you. I've read enough to know that I don't know whether vitamins actually work, but I take a multi-vitamin because I believe that it probably offers some possible benefit that might do me good, and it seems to make me feel better.

Unfortunately, on many days I may not even stand up from my desk for the entire day (lunch is often brought right to my mouth so that I don't have to stop working); for much of my career it has been too easy for me to forget to drink water or use the restroom.

But now, I sit on a big bouncy ball for a bit each day, I stand up when I'm on the phone, and when I arrive at the office, I take a very big glass pitcher and fill it with water and some no-calorie flavorings. By the time I go home, I make sure that the water is gone.

And now I no longer forget to use the restroom.

Enough said.

RUTS, TIREDNESS, FEAR, AND DEPRESSION

People become attached to their burdens sometimes more than the burdens are attached to them. —George Bernard Shaw

We must all must bear the burden of our own lives. Many businesses offer wonderful benefits to help out in this regard, including helping employees deal with problems such as alcohol and drug abuse.

The advice is cold but clear; deal with what you need to, and come back and join us. If you need medical or psychological care, go get it. It can be rather self-destructive to wait until you have actually damaged your reputation and career. There is nothing that the business can do to help you until you decide to deal with your issues actively.

No matter what you think caused it, the business did not. It is paying money for your time, and it needs (and deserves) your participation. You always have the right to leave and change your life. Neither the business, nor a single person within the business, changes that.

RUMINATING AND BROODING

Fill your mind with the meaningless stimuli of a world preoccupied with meaningless things, and it will not be easy to feel peace in your heart. — Marianne Williamson

In many ways, the human creature decides to remain stressed. It seems that many people are more comfortable in a state of discomfort, hanging on to their insomnia and physical ailments like trusted companions.

BEING WRONG, MAKING MISTAKES AND MOVING ON

To make mistakes is human, but to profit by them is divine.
—Elbert Hubbard

We've already discussed being effective and the perception issues that accompany mistakes and apologies. From a survival perspective, keep a few things in mind.

First, everybody makes mistakes.

I've made some doozies. For instance, when I delayed in writing up a deal in order to prevent someone from going public with a legal settlement, the person went public and my client went ballistic. In a negotiation I've underestimated the power of the other side, who ended up becoming a far more adversarial opponent than I thought possible. I have missed deadlines. I have lost files. And I have made countless political errors through the years.

And I will continue to make errors throughout the remainder of my time on earth (hopefully that means quite a few more blunders are to come).

I have known brilliant lawyers too who have made some stunning mistakes, many of which make mine appear quite minor. One lawyer colleague of mine missed a deadline that ended up costing his client (and later the malpractice insurance policy) more than $24 million; another's CEO friend made a foolish decision which resulted in a lawsuit that cost his company more than $10 million...and on and on.

Just watch the news and read the papers, and you'll see some stunning mistakes connected to practically every single story. And don't get me started on politicians and their sex scandals.

Second, the higher you are in a business or the greater your responsibility, the bigger the ramifications of your mistake.

So when the CEO makes a mistake, millions of dollars can be lost, as well as the welfare of the entire business—and peoples' hopes and dreams. When a person in the mail room makes a mistake, it is rarely more than an instantly forgotten hiccup.

Third, people torture themselves unnecessarily for their own mistakes. Remember that *no one is as preoccupied with your mistake as you are. Most people forget it as not relevant to their jobs or lives.*

Fourth, and fortunately, most people quickly forgive the person who has made a mistake; they are inclined to put themselves in the wrongdoer's shoes—provided, of course, that there are no subsequent lies or cover-ups.

And finally, *find a way to forgive yourself (even if others don't).*

Keep perspective. Acknowledge what needs to be acknowledged in a manner that allows you to stand up and be a person of respect, regardless of the mistakes.

And take a deep breath.

BEING SECOND-GUESSED

If a man isn't willing to take some risk for his opinions, either his opinions are no good, or he's no good. —*Ezra Pound*

Being second-guessed can be a miserable experience. It tells you that you are not good enough. It is a smack in the face. It indicates that you are not trusted or respected. And it can be highly humiliating.

The positive role of second-guessing

And yet, it may not mean any of this. Get out of your own head. Your emotions are getting in your way as you decide whether to engage in fight or flight, and you are no longer thinking logically.

Logically, there is a decision-making process going on, and ultimately decisions are made by people who do their best. Second-guessing is what helps us figure out what is right.

As a lawyer, I am second-guessed constantly, as the advice I offer is either taken or not. In the medical world, they call this "getting a second opinion." If someone is not comfortable with his legal options, he may keep asking around until the original answer is confirmed or the "right" answer is given.

Quite often people will ask questions that they know the answers to in order to confirm their point of view or to *inspire* a particular answer.

Given that you want to be important and relevant to the decision-making process, it is easy to take this process personally. One reason some people are "know-it-alls" is that, right or wrong, they are trying to teach something. Managers often feel the need to come across as smarter than their employees. That often means *correcting* other people.

The journey to truth

Finding truth, whether in the spiritual sense or when just searching for a simple answer to a simple question, is always a journey. Scientists test theories, and new theories routinely replace old ones. Even Einstein was tested and in some cases proven wrong. We each come to terms with the decision-making process by accepting our role and the process. While there may be a desire to fight each of these battles, recognize that very smart people lose a lot of the time.

BEING WRONGED

To be wronged is nothing unless you continue to remember it.
—*Confucius*

When you are wronged, you can either stand up or stand down; each is absolutely appropriate at times. We trade losses for victories every day, and as long as we get the victories that matter, it is usually good enough.

Sometimes we let other people take our credit, or we deal with public things in private ways. Other times we hurt people who have gotten out of line by proving them to be manipulators, liars, or otherwise less than competent individuals.

But when we overreact or behave aggressively, we are hurting ourselves far more than anyone else.

Being wronged always hurts. My fight-or-flight gives me an upset stomach as I prepare for warfare. I stop sleeping and play out different scenarios in my head.

The right response to being wronged

Then I calm down and remember that it's only business, and that my response must always be calculated and carefully executed. And then I remember that none of this really matters anyway and that everything always ends up fine.

Some battles (like rounds of golf) are worth losing, some are deservedly lost, and some are stolen away. Yet in order to come out smelling like a rose, *it is important to find ways to deal with problems without looking overly passive or overly aggressive.*

When a colleague steps out of line, I often chat privately. Let the documents do the talking if you can. Work around the person, change priorities, and take whatever other measures will address your problem.

Then go get some sleep and save your energy. There must be something good on television. Life will offer you another round, and another chance, tomorrow.

GETTING CAUGHT

In a closed society where everybody's guilty, the only crime is getting caught. In a world of thieves, the only final sin is stupidity.
—Hunter S. Thompson

No matter the severity of the offense, people who get caught look far worse and get in far more trouble if they cover up facts, while the person who has the fiber to stand up and accept responsibility without further excuse is often ultimately forgiven and/or offered a lesser penalty.

Standing up and admitting when we have made a mistake allows the solution to the problem to be largely within our own control. You can frame the problem and offer a solution. There is a time to fight and a time to concede, and figuring out when it is time to do the latter can be the difference between staying and getting fired—even between freedom and jail.

The truest test of a person is how one acts before and after being caught. If you pass the test, regardless of the outcome, you will have truly earned your place in this world.

NOTHING GOOD HAPPENS WHEN YOU PANIC

Do you remember the things you were worrying about a year ago? How did they work out? Didn't you waste a lot of fruitless energy on account of most of them? Didn't most of them turn out all right after all?
—Dale Carnegie

One thing is absolutely certain: *nothing good happens when you panic.* Perhaps we should just say that over and over again—or write a book filled with only that phrase.

Although people do lose their cool in the workplace, no matter how stressful the situation, it is, for most people, rarely effective or appropriate (recognizing that if properly used, extreme emotions can be a very effective negotiating, persuasion or control tactic).

CAREER SUICIDE SURVIVORS

When popular punditry was discussing Britney Spears' actions as career suicide, there were many who knew otherwise. Not only is career suicide nearly impossible for the average person, but we love to watch Britney—and the public was enjoying the show more than ever.

Mark Fuhrman, the Los Angeles officer made infamous for his use of the N-word and audiotapes of how he would beat up gang members, became a conservative talk show host and a New York Times best selling author. Marv Albert, fired in 1997 by NBC after sexual assault charges were levied (including biting and women's underwear), was later reinstated. Down–and-out football coaches are re-hired. Humbled CEOs still end up somewhere else on top (Nardelli survived Home Depot only to end up at the helm of Chrysler). CEO Carly Fiorina of Hewlett-Packard, once named one of the 30 most powerful women in America by Forbes Magazine, prior to her dismissal, was presented with a four page list of problems that the Board had with her. She is a business and political commentator and author and a viable political candidate).

These are high profile career-enders that do not end careers. I have personally been involved in firing people whom I believed incompetent but who later surprised me with their successes elsewhere. A bad day is just a snapshot that—no matter how bad—starts fading the moment it is taken. The key is not in claiming one's innocence—but ultimately in ignoring the bad. Politicians prove this time and time again.

Career suicide is a personal choice—not one that is made for you. I know it's hard, but overcoming the bad is a combination of getting over it, renewing self-confidence and shutting up so that everyone else forgets about your bad days as well.

Panic causes a difficult situation to become impossible. You can't think straight; you might be rude or yell, throw up, or abandon altogether the work that needs to be done.

In my high-stress environment, I see people lose it almost every day. And it is almost always grounds for instant termination.

Why people panic

People panic because they stop worrying about the work and start worrying about themselves. As a manager and project leader, when I watch someone panic, the first thing I do, no matter how busy we are, is try to separate the person from the thing that is causing the stress and try to sit him or her down for a few minutes of quiet time.

I try to offer alternatives that provide different solutions to any given problem. And I speak with a calmness and confidence that reflects a position that all is under control, that I am confident that everything will get done, and that no one is personally responsible for failure (I might let people know that completing what needs to be done rests on my shoulders and that *they* are helping *me*—although I might seek to adjust their employment after the fact).

Then I try to offer calm, simple, distinct, and easy-to-follow instructions.

One thing that panic tells me is that a person is probably not suited for a position. The skills I just mentioned are skills that must be internalized. If soldiers do not panic when they are getting shot at, and astronauts do not panic when something goes wrong in space flight, and firefighters do not panic when saving people from burning buildings, then neither should you panic over some deadline that no life depends upon.

I recognize that it takes a fair bit of growth to understand this, particularly given the emotional and illogical triggers that bring on panic, but at some point it is essential that every person in the workplace either gets it or gets out.

LIFE CAN COME DOWN TO ONE SINGLE MISTAKE

"One 'oh shit' can erase a thousand 'attaboys.'" —*Scott Adams*

Although I'm sure we all recognize that everyone makes mistakes, people do not remember the good as much as the bad. While most mistakes just vanish into a forgotten mist, a single fight can destroy a relationship that has lasted decades. A single affair in a moment of weakness can destroy a marriage. A single statement can destroy your reputation. And a single slip-up can destroy your career. We're talking about those things that are usually within your control but that end up growing their own legs to run themselves out of control.

Life comes down to preparing for that one inevitable screw-up. That one word too many. That one email or memo. That one bad joke. That one drink you shouldn't have had. That one moment when you take your eyes off the road. That one stupid thing that can somehow undo a life otherwise filled only with honor and respect.

While you are allowed to have a bad day, you must be aware of the fact that *it is in these moments of weakness and inattention when career-enders and reputation-destroyers are more likely to happen.*

The case for caution: no do-overs

Recognizing the importance of what can happen in any situation should tell you how careful and considered you should be, particularly within the workplace. There are no do-overs or "Mulligans" in life, and if you play close to the line or do things that would not be well-regarded if revealed, you will eventually experience that one thing that can really hurt you. It's a statistical certainty.

Recognize when you are approaching issues with too casual or callous a manner. If you're having a horrible day or are losing control, stop answering the phone and writing emails if you must. When you do, be extra careful. If you can't remember the risk inherent in every single word you utter, then put a little sign up in your office to remind you that *catastrophic failure can be only one stupid word away.*

CAREER SUICIDE RARELY CAUSES DEATH

You kill me and I'll see that you never work in this town again. —Steve Martin in The Man with Two Brains

And yet, with few exceptions, people have a tendency to survive even many of the stupidest things anyone can do. Memories fade. Other companies and people won't know or care what you've done and will opt instead to give you a second (or a third or fourth) chance, just to get a position filled. When an arrogant boss exclaims, "You'll never work in this city again!" what that boss doesn't realize is that no one else really cares what he thinks.

If you don't think this is right, just ask Elliot Spitzer or Mike Tyson. Ask all those people fired after the economic downturn in 2008. Ask my cousin, who lost a leg in an automobile accident— and so many others who thought they were finished in this world, only to become reinvigorated and successful once the moment of despair was squarely behind them.

WE REMEMBER OUR WOUNDS

The folks you help won't remember it and the folks you hurt won't ever forget it. —Bill Clayton

People hold on to their pain with an illogical intensity. We each have a tremendous reluctance to speak to people with whom we are angry. We even become unwilling to speak to—and even get angry with—people who are angry with us.

We get angry at people with different opinions, regardless of how valid their opinions might be. We get angry at people who catch us in our mistakes or doing things that we shouldn't have been doing in the first place. We even get angry at people who date our former lovers (even many years later) and people who might be friends with our enemies.

Mental-health professionals talk about repressed feelings, memories, and the hurt that we are still holding onto. They've built an entire sub-specialty around forgiveness. We put up walls for pretty much any reason we can think of, and lots of reasons we can't.

Decide for yourself which hurt is real, and work to manage it in a way that is not self-destructive. It's only business.

Start picking up the phone or visiting other people's offices; start talking to the people causing you the problems. It is hard at first, especially with people that are legitimate problems, but keep at it. You will find much of the hurt evaporating. Find closure where you need to, and whatever you do, don't hold on to the pain that is interfering with your functioning on the job and your enjoyment of life.

STRIKING BACK

Never be bullied into silence. Never allow yourself to be made a victim.
Accept no one's definition of your life, but define yourself.
—Harvey S. Firestone

Much of this book regards relationships as our most treasured asset. As Sun Tzu explains, "The supreme art of war is to subdue the enemy without fighting." Yet it is important to recognize that living an honorable life sometimes means standing up for yourself and your values and hitting back, even when the fight or result might be detrimental to your career.

Rarely does direct engagement get you where you want to go. And rarely does it help for other people to know about your personal life, outside interests, artistic tendencies, political interests, and the like. Still, sometimes we must be the person we *need* to be, not the person we should be to promote our occupational ambitions.

Deciding which battles to fight

Many of us face a constant dilemma figuring out which are the battles that we *need* to fight and which of our values cannot be compromised. It can be a tremendous struggle to faithfully adhere to those values, particularly when other ambitions are at stake.

But we need to go to sleep at the end of every day knowing that we stood up for ourselves and the things that matter most to us. *While the workplace martyr very rarely accomplishes his intended goal, there is great virtue in standing up for those things we believe in.*

Recognize that the bully is never liked—but is respected, if for nothing else than for being a bully. The advocate, too, is often most respected not for his position, regardless of what it might be, but for his strength of character.

The bullied, however, are never respected. Apart from peaceful activism, there is little (or nothing) earned by allowing someone else to beat you up.

As Sun Tzu says (yes, two quotes in one section; the similarities between business and war are quite numerous), "Being a friend to your enemy means being an enemy to yourself." Sometimes we fight back, just because we must.

NEVER EVER TURN AWAY

I am a greedy, selfish bastard. I want the fact that I existed to mean something. —Harry Chapin

So let us conclude not only with one of my favorite quotes from Harry Chapin, one of my personal heroes, but with the suggestion that no matter how difficult, you never turn away.

We all, from the most junior to the most senior person in society, want to hide when we are embarrassed, frustrated, or angry. Politics can stink, and stinky politics can really stink. Human interaction can be trying and unpredictable. We make mistakes, and sometimes our jobs, bosses, coworkers, and friends aren't happy with us.

When we don't like work, we want nothing to do with the people we work with. When we are slighted, we want to fight back and/or find ourselves as far away from those people as possible.

That's when it's most important to remember that *emotion and isolation are our real problems.* Turning and hiding exacerbates all of our most difficult situations by allowing the problems to continue, permitting our emotions to overwhelm us; eventually we become perceived as ill-prepared for the business world.

This can all be terribly challenging, but *when we are most alone is when we must force ourselves to stay a part of the crowd.* We all must pick up the phone when we least want to. We all must have the conversations we most dread. And we must get out of bed on those days we most want to just curl up and whine.

And then we can recognize ourselves as the person we have sought to become.

Now bring on the world!

Stop thinking now

Quit second-guessing all your failed relations

With your would've, could've, should've, maybe might-
have-been

I'll show you how

Send your feelings out for lubrication

Lose these blues and screw your head on tight again

//

Your loss is measured in illusions

And your gain is all in bittersweet intelligence

And your winsome smile will lose some of its innocence

Your winsome smile

Your winsome smile will lose some of its innocence

Words and Lyrics by Chris Smither
Winsome Smile

Lyrics © BUG MUSIC

AND ON THAT
NOTE...

I HOPE THAT THIS BOOK has offered you a platform for greater success on your own terms. Hopefully, with an improved understanding of the manner in which people make decisions, react to different circumstances and engage in politics, you will be better able to remain focused, less frustrated, more efficient and better able to deal with issues that arise. In the end, with a greater sensitivity to the decision process, you will be better armed to choose your battles, fighting the ones that need to be fought and winning the ones that need to be won.

Remember that most of society is fighting the same fight right there with you; some are just playing the game better than others. We're all frustrated from time to time; we're all dreaming of somehow getting a little bit closer to achieving our own personal dreams. We're all flawed, victims of our own humanity.

But unlike some (very few) professions where time alone dictates seniority (typically by law or rule), true leaders and performers often assume their roles long before they are hired as such. There are, of course, many bad leaders who do not deserve their position; some of them have gotten where they are in large part by knowing the right people, and others just by hanging on and staying in the game.

But even great performers must be liked, or at least not disliked, to remain in the game. Brilliant performers who are disruptive, controversial or worse are often dismissed, even in fields like professional sports where it would be easy to assume that performance is all that matters. When coaches need to make player decisions, it would be naïve to think that they don't suffer from bias, both with regard to players they like, trust, and wish to reward, and those they don't. Nothing is "just business".

While I wish we could compare success in business to a marathon, we can't. In business, while tenacity and endurance matter, all the effort and time in the world may not bring you across a finish line. Nothing is inevitable or automatic. And yet, just as in the final mile of a marathon, little strides can require a tremendous effort.

In the end, there is no such thing as a formula for succeeding in business. There are certainly techniques that work better than others, as well as commonalities between people that can be successfully exploited. We've covered a bunch of them, though there are countless exceptions.

Don't just take my word for it. Go read the books and watch the movies that illustrate the real-life tactics that people employ every day.

Lessons from *The Godfather*

Watch *The Godfather* movies, not just to hear the characters' words that harsh decisions are "just business," but to understand the wants, needs, aspirations, fears, personalities and other bits of humanity that factor into the decision making. Then watch the people in your workplace, and you'll see much the same dynamic (albeit with much less physical injury).

Understanding the commonness of the human story can be a tremendous education in itself. The one thing that is true is that the people who are often most successful are often the ones who got off their butt and put themselves in the game—and then repeatedly demand their spot on the field.

They asked the coach for playing time. They insisted on a seat at the table. And many persevered through some very difficult struggles. Giving it your best shot can be as rewarding as any other accomplishment. Ultimately you have to live with only yourself as your biggest critic (unless you are married to a person like my lovely spouse).

To quote Ray Bradbury, "This life thing, it's a lark. It's a thing we are lucky to get to do."* And to paraphrase from a Neil Diamond song, "we all sweat beneath the same sun, and we look up in wonder at the same moon."**

Be sure to visit: *http://www.thebusinesspersona.com* to offer your opinions, ideas for future editions, or a war story (I mean a work story) or two. And be sure to drop me a note to let me know what's on your mind. I'm around and would love to hear from you.

Best of luck on your journey.

---

* From a speech to the writers at the Santa Barbara Writers Conference, June 2007.

** *Done Too Soon*, lyrics by Neil Diamond, Taproot Manuscript, 1970.

Look... these Big League hitters are gonna light you up like a pin ball machine for awhile—don't worry about it. Be cocky and arrogant even when you're getting beat. That's the secret.

You gotta play this game with fear and arrogance.

—Bull Durham

Hi Daddy. Hi Daddy. Sit down Daddy. Milk Peas. Mo TV?
—*Gabrielle*

Enough... stop writing and come to bed already!
—*Kahla Nicholas*

ABOUT THE AUTHOR

MARK H. NICHOLAS IS the founder and CEO of Family
Archival Solutions, Inc. Prior to his work with FAS, Mr. Nicholas
practiced law in Boston, Philadelphia, Silicone Valley (CA) and Los
Angeles for nearly two decades largely in in-house departments in
major corporations exposed to the full range of corporate cultural
issues. His practice included a focus on securities regulation, technology, employment, intellectual property and privacy law issues,
regularly negotiating multi-million dollar deals and handling a wide
range of legal matters.

Originally from the New Jersey shore, Nicholas is a graduate of
Susquehanna University and Syracuse University College of Law (*magna
cum laude*). He worked as an intern/clerk for the State of New York, pros-
ecuting child abuse and neglect and later interned in the representation of
prominent collegiate athletes in a series of newsworthy matters. Following

law school, he embarked on a diverse career that has included the practice of law in capacities such as Chief Legal Officer, Chief Privacy Officer and Chief Compliance Officer. He continues to practice law in Los Angeles and works as the founder and president of a technology company.

With his extensive involvement as a negotiator and mediator, Nicholas has embraced the study of human behavior and those human interactions that together create allegiances and animosities and result in business decisions large and small (and, ultimately, business success or failure). He teaches classes in business and negotiation and speaks regularly at national conferences on social marketing, human perception, privacy and regulatory matters.

Working with artists and creative individuals is a true passion, and Nicholas has helped hundreds of clients launch and succeed in their businesses and has consulted in every aspect of the business relationship.

When not doing any of the above, Nicholas has traveled much of the globe, and he has spent time traveling in Europe, the Middle East, Antarctica and Africa. Stateside, Nicholas has lived on his sailboat and sailed in trans-ocean races. As a photographer, Nicholas has become an accomplished nature and commercial/astro-photographer and leads a photography organization with several hundred members.

He lives in Los Angeles with his wife and daughter. For fun he spends time with his family, travels, sails, teaches and takes wildlife and nature photographs.

INDEX

A
Advice, 129-131
Age *vs.* maturity, 120
Albert, Marv, 261
Ambition, 57
Anger, 132
Apologies, 150-152
Apple Computer, 43
Appreciation, 85-89
The Apprentice (television), 86
Archives of General Psychiatry, 74
Arguments, arguing, 93-94
Art of sale, 20
Art of spin, 229-231
Ask, don't accuse, 94
Ass-covering, 234
Ass-kissing, 238
Attitude, spin, 118
At-will-employment, 46-47
Authority, 115

B
Bad Leadership: What It Is, How It Happens, Why It Matters (Kellerman), 174
Balance, 30-31
Balance, schmalance, 156
Basic management, 171-173
Because It's My Job (Song: J. Buffett), 252
Benefits, 156-157
Body dysmorphic disorder, 74

Body language, 60-63
Boredom, 106
Bribes, bribery, 87-88
Buffett, Jimmy, 252
Bull Durham (movie), 118, 272
Business failures, 219-220
Business relationships, 207-208
Buzzwords, corp. speak, code, 73

C
Carducci, Bernard, 134
Care for others, 133
Career
   job *vs.*, 33
   personal identity and, 10
Carlin, George, 25
Carrot and shtick, 199-200
Cat's Cradle (Vonnegut), 87
Cell phones, 148-149
Census Bureau, 9n
Cognitive dissonance, 106
Colleagues, networks, 86-87
Common lies in business, 108-110
Communicating with leaders, managers, 183
Company benefits, 156-157
Competitive conversation, 241-242
Complaining, 119, 130-131
Conference Board jobs survey, 42n
Confident humility, 128
Conflict, suspicion, 240-241
Conflict resolution, 95

QUOTATIONS

Eschenbach, Marie von Ebner, 188

F
Fenelon, Francois, 223
Fields, W. C., 52
Firestone, Harvey S., 265
Flynn, Errol, 149
Forbes, Malcom, 37 197
Ford, Henry, 195
Foxworthy, Jeff, 245
Franklin, Benjamin, 139, 215, 217
Frost, Robert, 32
Fuller, Thomas, 123, 207

G
Galbraith, John Kenneth, 126, 246
Gandhi, Indira, 191
Gandhi, Mahatma, 241
George, David Lloyd, 75
Getty, J. Paul, 214
Gibran, Kahlil, 152
Goldwyn, Samuel, 193
Guiterman, Arthur, 133

H
Hakala, T. I., 34
Handal, Peter, 144
Handy, Jack, 94, 127
Hathaway, Katherine Butler, 66
Hemingway, Ernest, 167
Hillesum, Etty, 254
Hobsbawm, E. J., 220
Holmes à Court, Robert, 80
Hubbar, Kin, 129
Hubbard, Elbert, 256
Hutchison, Asa, 163

J
James, William, 118
Jefferson, Thomas, 94

Johnson, Samuel, 83, 128

K
Kapor, Mitchell, 155
Keller, Helen, 157
Kenny, Elizabeth, 106
Kilborn, Craig, 146
Kozol, Jonathan, 242
Kristol, Irving, 188

L
Landers, Ann, 232
Larson, Doug, 183, 186
Layton, Irving, 227
Lewis, Jerry, 211
Liang, Zhuge, 182
Lincoln, Abraham, 120, 231
Longfellow, Henry Wadsworth, 248
Louchheim, Frank, 252
Louis XIV, 124

M
Mao Tse-Tung, 136
Marston, Ralph, 253
Martin, Steve, 263
Marx, Groucho, 192
Mason, Jackie, 156
Masson, Thomas, 117
McLauglin, Mignon, 207
Miller, Henry, 72
Miller, Larry, 161
Moliere, 238
Montapert, Alfred, 103
Mother Teresa, 132

N
Nicholas, Gabrielle, 273
Nicholas, Kahla, 273
Nizer, Louis, 235
Nunberg, Geoffrey, 148